SUFFOLK FEAST

ONE COUNTY, TWENTY CHEFS

cookbook & food lovers' guide

Glyn Williams and Tessa Allingham

Foreword by Emma Freud

Published by Feast Publishing
E: office@feastpublishing.co.uk
W: www.feastpublishing.co.uk

First published in paperback in 2015
ISBN (paperback): 978 0 9933601 0 7

Editorial: Glyn Williams and Tessa Allingham
Design: Mark Shreeve
Photography: Phil Morley *(except where detailed above)*

Recipes listed in this book have been tested and provided to the publishers in good faith. Feast Publishing cannot be held responsible for any loss or damage, caused by any omissions or errors therein.

Contents

Sunrise Coast at Southwold: A midsummer Suffolk dawn breaks over fishing boats on the Blyth Estuary.

Foreword

Emma Freud

There are four crucial things that make this beautiful book so worth exploring ....

The county... there's something about Suffolk – it defies category, punches way above its weight artistically and culturally, is a brilliant mass of contradictions, and has become a brilliant environment for creativity and spirit to thrive. The corner of Suffolk in which my family have spent their time since 1932 is geographically between Benjamin Britten, Ed Sheeran and The Darkness. That's one hell of an artistic triangle.

The produce... opening The Suffolk Show, Prince Harry (how is that man still single?) said that he was looking at "all that is best about rural England, the strength of community, the sense of a great, long tradition of farming and country endeavour".

He's right. Suffolk producers have a centuries-old tradition of growing fantastic produce, rearing amazing meat and finding the treasures of the sea. These traditions are now being kept alive by growing numbers of clever and passionate artisan producers, who are selling their produce to ever more talented chefs. Blythburgh pork, Orford smoked fish, Southwold bread, Stowupland beef, Deben mussels, Ampton duck, Walpole yoghurt, Peasenhall fudge, Mendlesham ice cream – the raw ingredients are mighty and there is a lack of arrogance in the skilled workers, who harvest and nurture them. Suffolk produce now sells nationally but nowhere is it cooked with more commitment than by....

The Suffolk chefs... we are blessed with some astonishing cooking talent in this county – contemporary chefs who explode with enthusiasm, dedication and a genuine understanding of the land in which they are working. This book puts 20 of our local food heroes centre stage in the context of the wonderful local ingredients they most enjoy cooking in their hard-working, delicious Suffolk kitchens. Whether or not you follow a single recipe inside, the life-enhancing nature of the skill and passion of these chefs is a joy to behold.

The hot butchers... Southwold. Mills and Sons. Just saying.

I'm delighted to declare this cookbook open.

Welcome

Fourteen years in the thinking, one year in the planning, six months in the writing, three months in the filming, several days in the cooking, a few hours in the eating...

From some early scribbles back in 2001 to seeing these pages in print has been a culinary odyssey through Suffolk. Over the past months we have been - in the company of 20 wonderful chefs – through the rich pastures around Stowmarket grazed by Red Poll cattle, to the windswept North Sea shore at Orford where fishermen land their catch daily, and back to fruit farms near Bury St Edmunds. We have met feisty lobsters, inquisitive pigs, nibbling sheep, visited a smallholding, a private allotment, and spent time with the Somerleyton Estate's deerstalker.

Suffolk Feast weaves many foodie strands but there are three common threads that run through the book: a love of good food, a fascination with the concept of farm-to-fork, and an affection for this beautiful, rich county of ours.

Way back when this book was that original scribble, we thought "why not bring these producers together with the chefs that buy the produce, get them talking about their relationship and shared passion...why not try and discover what it really means to source locally and carefully, see why the ingredients on our doorstep are so wonderful, and hear first-hand how much care and expertise goes into bringing fabulous food to our restaurant table..?"

Keeping food miles low, buying from local and sustainable sources, and healthy eating are, rightly, topics endlessly debated in the media. Suffolk Feast reinforces these messages through interviews with the 20 talented chefs and dedicated suppliers featured in this book.

We are hugely grateful to every one of them for opening their kitchen doors and farm gates to us and we hope you enjoy reading their stories. Do try the recipes and, of course, go and eat at the restaurants, all of which are heartily recommended!

Cheers

The Suffolk Feast team
Glyn Williams, co-author; Tessa Allingham, co-author;
Mark Shreeve, designer; Phil Morley, photographer

ASPALL

Cooking notes

We want you to enjoy the exciting, original recipes from some of our favourite Suffolk chefs, that are included in this book. To ensure you get the best out of the dishes, please take time to read the following tips and a few words of caution. Much of it will be second nature to many home cooks, but if in doubt, do refer to these notes.

WELFARE IN THE KITCHEN

Sharp tools, high temperatures and close proximity to humans and pets make the kitchen a potentially dangerous place. Accidents can happen when cooking, so please minimise the risk by applying appropriate caution, care and common sense.

COOKING TEMPERATURES AND TIMINGS

Cookers, and especially ovens, can be fickle pieces of equipment. Please treat all temperatures and times as a general guide and adjust to suit your own cooker.

Temperatures and timings are based on the use of a domestic, electric, non-fan oven so please adjust to the appropriate equivalent level, if you have a different cooker type.

MEASUREMENTS

- General cookery rules and common sense apply
- Spoonfuls are measured level
- Handfuls and pinches are based on an 'average' woman's hand and fingers (apologies if that's non-PC!)
- Bunches for herbs are standard retail sizes
- Eggs are large size
- Milk used is full fat unless otherwise stated

SEASONING

Recipe seasoning instructions refer to adding salt and pepper to taste. We choose to use local Maldon sea salt flakes, crushed between clean fingers or milled for fineness, and black peppercorns, freshly-ground to order. Some dishes may taste or look better on the plate with the alternative use of white peppercorns, eg fish dishes and cream sauces.

FOOD SAFETY

It goes without saying that ensuring the health and well-being of the people eating your food is vital! Use your common sense backed up with a bit of research and advice from reputable books and online sources.

Please do pay particular attention to:

- Quality and freshness of ingredients – check expiry and best-before dates
- Storage of produce and ingredients in the kitchen
- Use of raw and partly-cooked eggs
- Allergen risks
- Cooling and refrigeration where dishes are stored mid-preparation before finishing
- Fridge temperature – are they low enough for safe storage?
- Oven temperatures – is it hot enough before you start cooking?
- Core temperature of cooked dishes – has the food reached the right temperature before consumption?
- Finished dishes, not consumed immediately after preparation – are they stored at appropriate temperatures and consumed within safe time limits?

Well-written, straightforward cookery books such as those by Suffolk's own domestic goddess, Delia Smith, are invaluable. If in doubt, consult the Government's own online health and nutrition website for food safety advice at www.nhs.uk/livewell

JUSTIN SHARP
PEA PORRIDGE

TYLER TORRANCE
THE BRUDENELL HOTEL

REGIS CREPY
THE GREAT HOUSE

RORY WHELAN
THE CROWN HOTEL, SOUTHWOLD

Meet the chefs

Here they are, 20 of Suffolk's finest! Between them they offer some of the most enjoyable meals to be had in our county, representing a thrilling testament to the skill, dedication and flair that it takes to be a good chef.

They are a diverse bunch. Some push the boundaries of invention with artistic wit, others offer straightforward, satisfying food – the sort you'd happily eat every day – at affordable prices. Some fly the elegant flag of classic French cooking, others champion the robust flavours of the Italian table or so-called modern British or European food. All of them draw on the bounty of Suffolk.

We celebrate every one of our 20 chefs in this book. If the words, pictures and recipes have whetted your appetite, go try their food. You will not be disappointed!

JONATHAN NICHOLSON
THE BELL AT SAX'

LEE BYE
TUDDENHAM MILL

PHIL SKINNER
THE PACKHORSE INN

PAUL YAXLEY
THE FOX & GOOSE

STUART PEGG
THE DUKE'S HEAD

SIMON WOODROW
THE LEAPING HARE

SOPHIE DORBER
THE ANCHOR AT WALBERSWICK

ARRON JACKSON
THE ANGEL HOTEL

HONOR TOWNSEND
BUXHALL COACH HOUSE

JUSTIN KETT
THE SWAN HOTEL

JIM SLOMAN
BEN'S RESTAURANT

ROBERT MACE
THE SAIL LOFT

ZACK DEAKINS
1921

LOLA DEMILLE
DARSHAM NURSERIES

LUKE BAILEY
THE CROWN AT WOODBRIDGE

NICK ATTFIELD
THE BELL INN

Refining rustic: Ingredient-led innovation at town centre favourite

Wriggle through Bury St Edmunds' maze of streets to enjoy the robust flavours on Justin Sharp's inventive Pea Porridge menu

L - R: Justin Sharp, Tilly the spaniel, Michael Stone.

Michael Stone tells a lovely story. Some seventy years ago, when he was a shrimp of a lad in rural Bedfordshire, he would bunk off school on a sunny lunchtime, slip home, pocket his precious catapult and head off into the woods.

His mother would turn a blind eye to her son's feigned illness. "She'd give me something to eat, go and do the laundry or something and I'd be off like a shot," Mick remembers, laughing. "More often than not I'd come back with rabbit for dinner or maybe a fish. She was happy with that; I never got into trouble, as one of nine kids, there were always lots of mouths to feed!"

Mick – everyone seems to call him Mick – is days shy of his 80th birthday when we meet in a field in Rougham. He is a true countryman, still happiest with his cocker spaniel Tilly at his feet, out in the fields, airgun at the ready.

"Do you need any rabbits or pigeons?" Mick asks, turning to Justin Sharp as we walk across the farmland where he controls the population of these creatures for the landowner. He sells his catch directly to chefs like Justin, sometimes to local butchers, and keeps a bit back for himself. "I gut them straight away – you have to with rabbit – then either Justin will ring up and buy some or I might give him a call and say what I've got."

Back in the kitchen at his Bury restaurant, Pea Porridge, Justin skins one of Mick's rabbits deftly. He loves the ad hoc relationship with Mick, the fact – it's fundamental for a chef of Justin's integrity – that he can connect so closely with an ingredient. "People think my food is complex but it really isn't. I am all about the ingredient, making that shine, not showing off clever cheffy skills or fiddling with presentation. My cooking is instinctive and simple and I put on dishes that I like and that I hope my customers like." It's not surprising then to see a tray of spanking-fresh courgette flowers, picked from his Icklingham allotment that morning and now in the capable hands of sous chef James Carn-Pryor who is stuffing them with ricotta, neatly folding over the petals to form a round that will be coated in a light tempura batter, deep fried, and on the menu for lunch.

Justin talks while sliding oval platters in and out of his charcoal-fired oven, Bertha. She roars with appreciation as Justin levers open the door, oxygen fanning the flames and steam swirling round the tiny Pea Porridge kitchen. He slips in half a lobster, a handsome king scallop in its shell, and some trimmed spears of asparagus from the allotment. None of the ingredients has had more than the merest squeeze of lemon, a dribble of olive oil and seasoning. Silence falls as Bertha, the door closed on her belly-full of red-hot hazelwood charcoal, gets to work. Minutes later the food comes out and is sublime, finished perhaps with a few vivid-green samphire spears.

But back to Mick's rabbit. Both wild and farmed rabbit pop up on Justin's menu frequently, the various cuts used in ways best-suited to the respective meat. "Rabbit fits in with our ethos," he says. "It's plentiful, available year-round and I can cook it in lots of different ways – hearty in winter or lighter in summer. It's very lean and can take the middle-eastern flavours that I love really well too."

While farmed rabbit – plumper, white-fleshed, more delicately flavoured than wild – is best for dishes using the prime loin, leg or saddle, wild rabbit is perfect for mince or to use in a terrine. "Wild rabbit is a bit gamier and if you're not careful it can be dry. It's perfect for these Lebanese kibbeh, though, and they are a very popular starter here." The kibbeh, crisp minced meat croquettes

packed with fragrant za'atar, sumac and sesame and served with yogurt, fresh parsley and lemon [*see recipe*] are a perfect way of cooking wild rabbit. "They're a bit different, and I ring the changes by making them with pigeon or goat meat."

Rabbit liver and kidney – tiny nuggets of flavoursome offal – might be skewered onto a kebab and served with 'kohl' slaw made with kohlrabi and julienne chips while a shoulder could be allowed to absorb intense flavours in an overnight marinade of five spice, chilli, and garlic before being cooked slowly and left to enrich overnight. "The next day I pick it down to make rillettes. Perfect served with a few pickled girolles and a hunk of toast!"

You don't need to talk for long with Justin to realise that the warm, rugged flavours of middle-eastern food excite him. He pulls Sabrina Ghayour's book, *Persiana*, from a book-packed shelf. "I like this one; I don't follow recipes slavishly but they are a good starting point, give me ideas. I love trying new things, getting out of my comfort zone. I don't want to be labelled as a chef with just one style of cooking." Which probably explains the arrival this year of Bertha. The muscular, fiery, cast-iron beast of an oven thrives on the charcoal burnt by woodsman Graham Sayell from the hazel he coppices near Hadleigh. "Bertha is really an indoor barbecue," Justin explains. "I'm fascinated by the possibilities and I love the flavour cooking over wood gives – slightly smokey without being overpowering – and I love buying the wood locally from a sustainable source."

Steaks, and seared fillets of fish are an obvious fit with Bertha throughout the year, but when the embers are allowed to cool the oven is perfect for slow overnight cooking of wintry favourites

such as a lamb shoulder served with dauphinoise, greens, black pudding, lentils and salsify.

The urge to innovate also explains Justin's love of travel. He and his wife, Jurga, will often slip down to London on a Sunday and Monday when Pea Porridge is shut and eat at favourite spots: the informality of Duck Soup in Soho, and the Spanish flavours of Jose Pizarro's kitchens are places of choice.

Further afield, it will often be Italy, in particular if a trip includes natural wines. "I am so into them," Justin says, eyes alight, pulling out a bottle of Stefano Bellotti's biodynamic, natural, organic white wine sold under his Semplicemente Vino label. "There's a purity about wines like these because no chemicals have been added. It's completely different from drinking commercial wine, takes a bit of getting used to maybe, but so worth exploring!"

A predictable cooking comfort zone? Not here.

Wild rabbit kibbeh with tahini, sesame seed and coriander yoghurt

Stuffing

Olive oil; 1 onion, finely diced; 1 clove garlic, grated; 1 tsp cumin; 1 tsp cinnamon; 450g minced rabbit; Juice of a lemon; small handful coriander leaves, shredded; 2 tbsp sesame seeds

Shells

450g minced rabbit; 225g bulgur wheat, soaked; 1 onion, finely chopped; 1 clove of garlic, finely chopped; 1 tsp ground coriander; 1 tsp Chinese five spice; 1 tsp cumin; 1 tsp smoked paprika; olive oil for frying

Tahini yoghurt

500ml thick Greek yoghurt; pinch of smoked paprika; 1 tbsp toasted sesame seeds; 1 lemon; small handful coriander leaves, shredded; 1 heaped tbsp tahini

For the stuffing, warm up a large heavy based pan over a low heat, add a good glug of olive oil and lightly fry the onion and garlic to soften but not colour. Stir in the cumin, cinnamon and rabbit mince. Fry until golden brown, season to taste, remove from heat, allow to cool before adding lemon, coriander and sesame seeds.

For the shell, squeeze out excess water from the bulgar in a clean tea towel. Add with all the other ingredients to a food processor and blend, creating a firmish paste. Allow to rest in fridge overnight.

For the yoghurt, whisk all of the ingredients together and refrigerate.

To assemble the kibbeh, keep dividing the mixture in half until you get 16 balls. Flatten one ball on your wet hand. Place a teaspoon of stuffing in the centre. Bring the sides up to cover and seal, ending up with a rugby ball-shape. Repeat until shell mixture has all been used.

Over a medium-hot heat in a cm of hot olive oil, fry the balls for a minute or two on all sides. Serve on top of the yoghurt, with a wedge of lemon, a sprinkle of za'atar spice and a sprig of coriander.

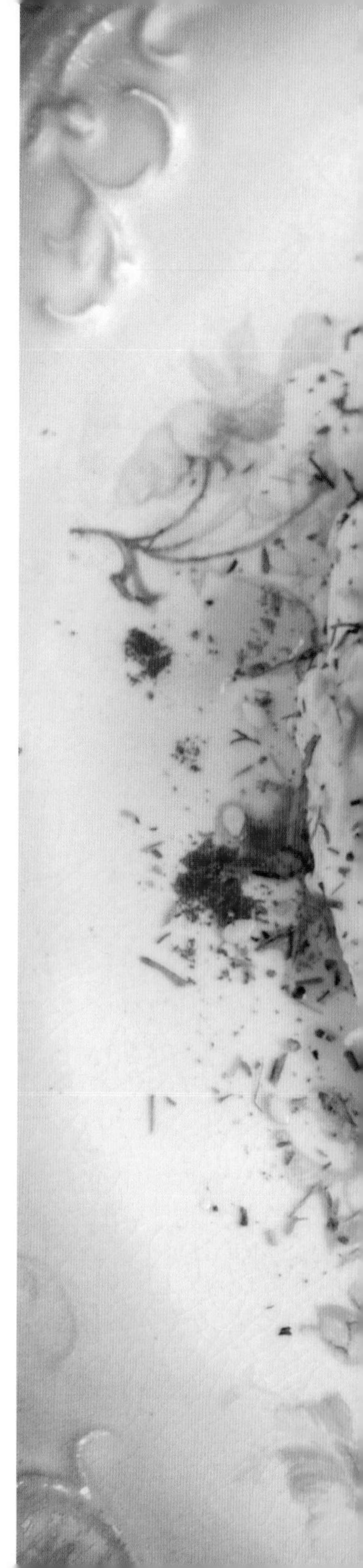

Sauté of snails, bacon and bone marrow and capers

A simple but delicious starter here since day one. Serve with good bread. (serves 2)

4 short pieces of sawn bone marrow; rapeseed oil; half a long shallot, finely chopped; 2 pancetta slices, in lardons; 12 extra large snails, ideally fresh or tinned; 100g fresh garlic butter

For the parsley salad
Quarter red onion, thinly sliced and lightly salted; small bunch of flat leaf parsley, picked and washed; 20 baby capers; olive oil; lemon juice

Pre-heat your oven to 200c and roast your bone marrow on a rack on a tray sprinkled with rock salt for 10 minutes, then turn and give another 5 minutes.

In a small frying pan with a glug of rapeseed oil over a medium heat, colour the pancetta, then add the chopped shallots and the snails and gently fry without colouring the shallots. Add the garlic butter and allow the butter to start to froth and gently colour. For the parsley salad, dress onion, parsley and capers with olive oil and lemon juice. Assemble by placing the parsley salad on a plate alongside the bone marrows and spoon the snails on top and around the marrows.

Tuscan-style pig cheeks

This eats well with wet parmesan polenta and crispy pigs ear fritters. (serves 6 generously)

8 pig's cheeks, trimmed; small handful of thyme stalks and rosemary sprigs; pinch Chinese five spice; 4 large garlic cloves, chopped; 4 bay leaves; 1 red chilli, deseeded and shredded; rapeseed oil; 2 carrots, 6 small shallots, 2 celery sticks, all chopped; 50ml red wine; 1kg baby plum tomatoes; 250g tin chopped tomatoes; 20 black peppercorns; 285ml chicken stock; 1 garlic clove; 1 lemon, zested; 1 tbsp flat leaf parsley, finely chopped

Marinade the pig cheeks overnight in thyme, rosemary, five spice, garlic, bay, chilli, seasoning and a splash of oil.

Pre-heat the oven to 180c. Take the drained cheeks and brown in an oiled hot hobproof casserole dish. Add the carrot, shallot and celery and colour these. Finish with the red wine and marinade ingredients. Add both types of tomatoes, peppercorns and stock. Simmer well and carefully cover with lid or a double foil sheet. Bake for 3 hours or until tender. Remove cheeks gently. Strain juices into a large saucepan and boil to reduce until a thick gravy texture and pour over the cheeks. Mix grated garlic with zest and parsley, to make the gremolata. Sprinkle over the pigs' cheeks.

Baked rice pudding

Good with Indian Alphonso mangoes available between May and July plus freshly-shredded mint leaves or with a berry compôte and mint. Also great cool but not fridge cold.

1 vanilla pod; 100g short-grain pudding rice; 100g caster sugar; 500ml milk; 500ml double cream; whole nutmeg and grater; 20g soft butter

Pre-heat the oven to 100c.

Split vanilla pod lengthways and scrape out the seeds into a medium saucepan with the pod too, add the rice, sugar, milk and cream. Mix together and bring to a boil over a medium heat, stirring. Cover and turn off heat. Leave for 30 minutes, whisking gently every so often to separate the grains.

Taking a deep wide casserole, smear with the softened butter and pour the rice mixture in.

Transfer dish to oven and bake for 30 minutes. Remove from oven and whisk. Bake for another 30 minutes and whisk. Bake for another 30 minutes. At this stage, whisk again and grate over lots of nutmeg to taste. Bake for a further 90 minutes.

Once time is up, switch off the oven and leave the pudding in there for 3 hours. Remove and serve or refrigerate.

Pea is for...

...good food made with good ingredients, nothing pretentious. Justin and Jurga Sharp use the words "simple" "neighbourhood" and "unfussy" a lot when talking about the food which Justin cooks and the cosy, welcoming 46-cover restaurant that they have run in the heart of the market town of Bury St Edmunds for the past six years.

Look around and the words are a fit: the old pine tables are cloth-less, the floor bare wood, everything's a bit mismatched, beamy, rustic. A black-leaded bread oven is a feature of one dining room (the building was a bakery in the 19th century), a rack of long-handled bakers' paddles hangs from the ceiling, and there's an inviting open fire in the other room.

Recipe books cram shelf spaces just as they might in the kitchen of any enthusiastic domestic cook, and Justin and his sous chef James Carn-Pryor do refer to them – they're not just for show. Tom Aikens, Rick Stein and Mitch Tonks lean up against Simon Hopkinson, Alastair Little, Richard Corrigan and Tom Kerridge, while books on conventional and natural wine hint at Justin's interest in that subject. The atmosphere throughout the place is relaxed; sitting down to a meal here feels a bit like going to a friend's for dinner.

It takes a bit of local knowledge to find Pea Porridge. The restaurant is named after the historic name for the square on which it sits, and the guides don't call it a 'hidden gem' for nothing. Don't be deterred, it's worth the winding walk through central Bury's Victorian residential streets to eat here.

Critics love the place. It has held a Michelin Bib Gourmand in recognition of serving good food at moderate prices since 2011 when it also won the Harden's award for best newcomer in the UK. A couple of AA Rosettes and consistently good reviews in the *Waitrose Good Food Guide* add to the accolades.

"This is where I'm making my mark," Justin says. "As a young chef I did the rounds of the good hotels around Aberdeen where I'm from – there were no stand-alone restaurants there 20 years ago – then had some time at Llangoed Hall in Wales and in various places in and around London including Chez Bruce. But this is where I am really cooking my sort of food."

"When we were looking for a change back in 2009, we had no particular reason to move to Bury, but the opportunity came up. It's as simple as that, and I'm really glad it did. We have found our niche here!"

Pea Porridge
28-29 Cannon Street,
Bury St Edmunds IP33 1JR
T: 01284 700200
W: www.peaporridge.co.uk
/Peaporridge
@peaporridge

Accolades: Michelin Bib Gourmand since 2011; Two AA Rosettes 2015; Harden's UK Best Newcomer 2011; *Waitrose Good Food Guide* 2015 score 4; Square Meal 2015

Cost: Carte £30 average; set L and D (L Thu - Sat, D Tue - Thu) two courses £14.50 / three courses £18.50; wine from £17.50

Open: Thu - Sat 12-1.45pm; Tue - Thu 6.30-9pm; Fri - Sat 6.30-9.30pm

Details: Private dining; children welcome

JUSTIN ON HIS...

QUICK SNACK OR MIDNIGHT FEAST?

Chips and béarnaise sauce! Or houmous and flatbread, or just some cheese and wine.

FAVOURITE LOCAL FOODIE PLACES?

I love eating at the Hawkeden Queen and the Thai St Café in Newmarket. The Old Cannon Brewery is literally on my doorstep and they do some great ale; for a coffee I choose Paddy & Scott's and a summer's evening drink by the lake at Tuddenham Mill is not to be missed! If I'm shopping for food, there's a great choice at the Suffolk Food Hall in Wherstead and I love Pinneys for smoked fish.

FOODIE NOSTALGIA?

Cristiano Guttarolo's amazing 2005 rosé reminds of pot pourri from my childhood and heather and honey from home in Scotland. Cristiano has vineyards in Puglia and this rosé is still drinking amazingly well.

FAVOURITE TIME OF YEAR?

Autumn and winter. I love the game season and slow-braised, hearty food with rustic flavours that work well with heavy red wines and cold nights by the fire.

WELL-THUMBED COOKBOOKS?

Pierre Koffmann's *Memories of Gascony*; *Book of Tripe* by Stephane Reynaud; the *Bocca Cookbook* by Jacob Kenedy from the Italian restaurant, Bocca di Lupo; and of course *Nose to Tail Eating: a Kind of British Cookbook* by Fergus Henderson of St John, a restaurant I love.

CHILDHOOD AMBITION?

I wanted to be an adult! And I always wanted to cook because my mum couldn't!

BEST DISHES EVER EATEN?

Salt-baked wild seabass in Duino, Italy; we were eating at a very simple restaurant on the tiny port watching a thunderstorm with the wine flowing – it was perfect! Mackerel rillettes at Chez Casimir in Paris: I've tried to emulate this dish but can't, the flavour was amazing, so fresh, subtle, simple and distinctly mackerel; carrot salad at Vejer in southern Spain: I still have no idea how they got carrots to taste like that! Outstanding!

TAKE FIVE RECIPE?

How about a quick guacamole? Just mash up avocado, lime juice, coriander, spread it on toast, and throw some crabmeat on top. Simple!

COOK'S CHEATS AND CHEF'S TIPS?

When making garlic mayonnaise, roast the garlic first, then squeeze it into the mayo – it makes it sweeter, less harsh. And when you're resting a roast chicken, stand it breast down so the juices run into the breast and keep it moist.

PERFECT DAY OFF?

We'll drive to the Crown & Castle in Orford, have lunch there which is always delicious, a stroll round the village, buy bread at Pump St Bakery, then fall asleep for a bit in the castle grounds!

CULINARY HEROES?

Pierre Koffmann is the master of amazing, ingredient-led, flavoursome food with zero gimmicks; Fergus Henderson, the hero of nose-to-tail eating, is also someone I admire hugely.

JUSTIN'S SIGNATURE DISHES

STARTERS

Lightly-curried lamb sweetbreads, kohlrabi, spinach

Grilled ox heart, dandelion, pickled walnut, French breakfast radish, shallot, caper, kohl slaw

Braised octopus, chickpeas, piquillo peppers, chorizo, new potatoes, romesco, smoked paprika

MAINS

English rosé veal osso buco, gremolata, saffron risotto

Tempura 'nero' cod cheeks, saffron aioli, lemon

Lobster cooked over charcoal in Bertha

PUDDINGS

Tarte tatin

Banana beignets, cinnamon ice cream, caramel sauce

Warm chocolate pudding, hazelnut praline parfait

Surf and turf:
Good food is the heartbeat of Aldeburgh and The Brudenell

Tyler Torrance hungers for local suppliers, especially flappingly-fresh dayboat fish

L-R: Dean Fryer, Tyler Torrance.

"Dean's our man, if anyone is going to talk Aldeburgh fish, it's him", affirmed Tyler. "35 years man and boy, well almost, he has manhandled fishing boats up and down this shingle beach, out to sea nearly every morning. His fish is caught daily, how more fresh and local could I possibly want" he continued as we walked up the promenade in the summer sunshine and along the High Street. Tyler Torrance is head chef of The Brudenell Hotel, on the southern fringes of Aldeburgh towards the Yacht Club, and delicious local fish is key to his insightful natural cooking. But it is far from all fishy; at The Brudenell's seafood and grill restaurant superb well-hung meats are the other half of the kitchen repertoire. Tyler diverts me via his artisan butchers' Salter & King en route, source of much of the delicious steak and lamb he enthusiastically promotes. Perfectly-aged Suffolk Red Poll sirloin from Gerard King is the turf to accompany Dean's surf of delicious local lobster on the menu.

Land and sea is also a big part of local fisherman Dean Fryer's daily routine, apparent while wandering to the north end of the town and the small clutch of boats high up on the beach, opposite the Brudenell's sister property, The White Lion Hotel and Brasserie Bleue in the TA Hotel Collection's stable of Suffolk establishments. From a distance, the yellow JCB bulldozer and trailer, with Dean's boat 'Spring Tide' mounted aboard, was clearly visible, satisfying my curiosity as to how exactly it went in and out of the surf from terra firma. A short stroll across the seafront around the unexpected boules pitch (all very continental, just like buying your fish direct from the fishermen) brings you to the black fishing sheds where around breakfast time, the eagerly-awaited varied catch from netting, long-lining and shellfish potting is dragged back up the shingle rise. Talking to Dean and other local skippers, one gets the impression that this is fishing at the tougher end of the spectrum. It's more than the physical graft of landing their crafts on shore rather than mooring in deep water; this is a profession where low fish stocks, by-catch restrictions, landing quotas, paperwork and competition of encroaching foreign trawlers all add to the strain.

With queues of eager customers building at the steps for the day's freshest haul, laid out in the shade, gleaming, bright-eyed and pink-gilled, it's clear that regulars know they are on to a good thing. The same goes for the seagulls who surprisingly patiently wait in the hope they can snaffle some of the remnants from Dean's cutting block as he swiftly guts and oven-readies whatever fish may be required.

This is family enterprise at its best with a team of husband-and-wife plus the next generation handling the retail at their charming simple shack. From white fish like sea bass, dogfish and codling, flat fish like skate and dabs to cooked lobsters, the variety was unexpected, despite the Fryers only selling their own catch. But it was the fine Dover sole we had come for. It is one of the most popular fish main courses on the Brudenell's seafood menus, and Tyler is a firm advocate of preparing it simply, to show off its firm flesh and delicate sweet flavour. After choosing two dinner-plate sized specimens, he

asked Dean to do the honours, a few swift knife strokes later, top skin and innards removed, it was back to Tyler's kitchen and under the grill. As the fish sizzled and griddled, we talked about his Canadian upbringing and globe-trotting culinary travels. While he has all the expected chef qualifications, it was clearly the hard work and unpaid stages (chef internship) at a galvanising age in his kitchen journey which inspired him most, amid the eateries of his native Ontario, the crucial time in his early career spent in the melting pot of the west coast Vancouver dining scene, with intermittent periods in the Cayman Islands and Kent. With dual nationality, (his British father was in the Armed Forces and married to his Canadian mother, hence Tyler living as a child and then working in Canada as well as the Caribbean). Well-earned retirement brought Tylers parents to the Isle of Wight where Tyler joined them in 2008, taking up UK residency with his wife Pauline. After several years at The Crown in Southwold, where they still live, Tyler moved to The Brudenell in 2014 where his ethos of simplicity, intensity and menu of thoughtfully prepared dishes is clearly welcomed in their Seafood and Grill restaurant.

Perhaps one of a kind on the East Anglian coast, Aldeburgh is a seductive smart resort, with antiquity and modernity in equal measure; the café culture and discerning retail in urbane art galleries, boutiques and smart eateries co-habits with the best of tradition in proper pubs and seaside fish & chips. The uniqueness comes from the town's relaxed air and natural simplicity, and its undoubted 'Padstow effect' (or replace the moniker with Ludlow or Bray), a sense of a good food co-operative, where the whole of this East Suffolk town, from locals, visitors, purveyors to chefs, unites in a meeting of culinary minds and appreciation. Its delightful array of great dining and drinking opportunities certainly satisfies the gourmand as much as the gourmet, capably catering for those seeking just a perfect coffee or delicious ice cream, as well as those wanting a fine dining experience.

One only has to look at some of the foodie icons here, not just notable in Suffolk terms but recognised nationally, the likes of Lawsons Delicatessen as winner of UK Deli of the Year, and the Aldeburgh Food and Drink Festival, celebrating its first decade, and aptly described as one of, the finest in the whole country ('There isn't a better, more enjoyable, more educational, more beautiful food and drink festival in Britain." Sheila Dillon, editor and Presenter of BBC Radio 4's *The Food Programme* said).
As a keen ally in the town's food and drink community, Tyler would most definitely agree this is a bounteous place to express Suffolk coast and countryside on the plate.

Aldeburgh-landed Dover sole, East Coast brown shrimps, Thorpeness asparagus & sea greens

Try this elegant main course for your next dinner party. It is such a simple technique but one to impress. Feel free to replace the greens with whatever is in season. Lemon wedges, new potatoes and a dressed salad complement this at the table. (serves 4)

East Coast shrimp butter

This would also work with prawns or even local crab. And of course, leftovers are great with toast or pasta.

500g unsalted butter, at room temperature; zest and juice of 1 lemon; 1 bunch flat leaf parsley, finely chopped; 1 long shallot, very finely diced; 1 blade mace, finely ground or 1 big pinch of ground; 250g shrimps, peeled

Beat the butter in a food mixer until very light and fluffy. Then gently fold in the zest, juice, parsley, shallot and mace plus seasoning to taste. Using a large double sheet of clingfilm, roll into a 4cm log and wrap tightly. Refrigerate to chill until needed.

Buttered asparagus and samphire

Prepare these after the soles are cooked through before adding the shrimp butter to the fish.

2 bunches asparagus, trimmed; 250g marsh samphire, trimmed; unsalted butter

In a large pan of boiling water, cook the asparagus until just al dente. Drain well, butter and season before keeping warm. Quickly repeat with the samphire.

To serve

The soles need to have head and fins removed before trimming and the dark top skin removed. The white underskin will hold the fish together. Cooking-wise it is best to use a grill but if yours is not very hot, then use the oven on maximum instead.

4 whole dover soles, prepared as above; Sea salt; 4 x 1cm-thick slices of shrimp butter

Pre-heat grill (or your oven) to very hot. Season the Dover sole and place on a solid baking tray. Grill or bake until the fish is flaking close to the bone and is opaque throughout. With a digital thermometer, you are looking for 55c in several places at the fishes' thickest parts under the bone. Allow to rest and cook the greens. Take your shrimp butter and lay on the highest part of the fish. Put back under the grill or in the oven. Bake until just softened. Remove and baste the fish. Serve with the greens.

Clam linguine vongole

Try and source British clams for this Italian classic. Prepare the clams by rinsing under a running cold tap for a few minutes. As with mussels, never cook open ones (tap them to see if they close) and discard any cooked closed ones. (serves 4)

Local rapeseed oil; unsalted butter; 200g pancetta, diced; 2 long shallots, diced; 3 garlic cloves, finely chopped; half bunch rosemary; 1 kg British clams; 300g cockle meats; 280g dried linguine; good glug dry white wine; 1 bunch flat-leaf parsley, shredded

In a heavy lidded sauté pan over a high heat, add a drizzle of oil and a large knob of butter. When bubbling, add the pancetta, shallots, garlic and rosemary. Fry until just browning, then stir in the clams and cockle meat and cover, shaking carefully every so often. Meanwhile drop pasta into a very large pan of boiling water. Stir well and simmer hard, setting time to the packet instructions for al dente.

Check on the clams, if all (except a few) are open, add the white wine and bring to a gentle simmer. While stirring, remove any closed ones and discard. Drain the pasta quickly and add to the sauté pan along with two good knobs of butter. Toss together and adjust seasoning of the sauce. Finish with parsley and serve in warm bowls.

Crispy plaice fillets and tartare sauce

We use local fish, usually from Dean's shed. Great fries and lemon wedges are essential. Any good fisherman will skin and fillet your fish for you. Panko breadcrumbs are found in good delis. (serves 4)

500g good mayonnaise; 100g chopped capers; 100g diced gherkins; 75g finely diced shallots; half bunch flat-leaf parsley leaves; half bunch tarragon leaves; zest and juice of 1 lemon.

Mix together. Season to taste and chill.

500g seasoned plain flour; 6 eggs, lightly beaten; 500g panko crumbs; 12 plaice fillets, skinless; rapeseed oil for frying

Pre-heat the deep fat fryer and oil to 170c and warm your oven. Prepare separate bowls for the flour, eggs and crumbs. Dip the fish into each bowl in turn (keep one hand for flour and eggs, the other for crumbs). Knock off any flour off lightly, dip into eggs, allow to drain, then into the crumbs. You need to push the crumbs in well on both sides. Lay on a tray as you go. Lower your fryer basket into the hot oil and drop in the fillets carefully. Fry until light-golden colour. Drain and lay onto kitchen paper. Serve warm, seasoned, with the sauce.

Surf & turf

Perfect mixed grill on the coast, the best of land and sea; served with proper chips, fine beans, tomato, mushroom and a red wine sauce. Feel free to use pre-cooked boiled lobsters (serves 4)

Garlic butter: 500g unsalted butter, beaten until fluffy, mixed with 1 bunch finely chopped flat-leaf parsley leaves, 85g minced garlic plus sea salt and white pepper to taste.

2 x 750g raw lobsters, humanely-killed and halved lengthways; good rapeseed oil

Pre-heat your oven to 200c and your char-grill very hot. Brush lobster on both sides with oil, place flesh-side down on your char-grill for a few minutes, then turn over and repeat. Place in an ovenproof roasting tin and glaze with garlic butter. Bake for 5 minutes in the oven, timing seafood and removing whilst you cook your steaks.

4 x 275g good sirloin steaks

Meanwhile oil and season your steaks before char-grilling to your taste on both sides. Based on 2cm thickness, it is approx. 2 minutes per side for medium-rare.

Rest the steak after cooking for a few minutes somewhere warm. Serve the beef with the lobster and a drizzle of garlic butter juices.

Cosmopolitan coastal chic

One of Aldeburgh's popular destinations is The Brudenell, rated in the top few hotels in East Anglia by VisitBritain, in recognition of its uniqueness and the calibre of hotel-keeping. Its alfresco terrace is a firm favourite in the local 'little black book' of essential addresses for those in the know, especially as soon as the sun breaks out, and the attractive restaurant is a special place to dine in style.

As with much of the Heritage Coast, Aldeburgh's popularity and custom is determined by the sunshine and the season. Come highdays and holidays, the well-known haunts around here buzz as you'd expect in light of their obvious tourist appeal. But out of peak times, the town meanders to a different pace, with more time for leisurely indulgent R & R, good conversation and more space for peace and quiet. With all the expected facilities and spacious accommodation, comfort and luxury are what The Brudenell does best, regardless of how popular it gets, even in the height of summer. Like the town, it has a contemporary upbeat feel yet underpinned with all the requisite sophistication and old-fashioned values of service and hospitality.

The Scandinavian 'cruise-ship' feel in the open plan cocktail bar and restaurant, split over two levels, takes in huge panoramic seaward views over the shingle beach and lapping waves beyond. If this cosmopolitan chic destination did not already entice, Tyler Torrance's stylish instinctive cooking, using the best of the coastal and Alde Valley produce on his doorstep, is a compelling reason to visit.

The Brudenell Hotel
The Parade, Aldeburgh IP15 5BU
T: 01728 452071
W: www.brudenellhotel.co.uk
/thebrudenellhotel
@brudenellhotel

Accolades: 2 AA Rosettes 2015; VisitBritain 4 stars hotel accommodation; Green Tourism award; *The Times* '50 Best Places To Eat Alfresco'

Cost: Carte £29 average; wine from £20

Open: Every day, all year; food served L 12-2.30pm (3pm Sat & Sun) and D (6-9pm Fri & Sat)

Details: 44 bedrooms; bar drinks; terrace; alfresco dining; private parties; car parking

BEST DISHES EVER EATEN?

At one of the many izakaya, or Japanese pubs (I forget the name but not the food), the best evening of my life started with sake and shoyu vodka. We ate like emperors for hours, all manner of grilled meats and savoury dishes. I wasn't dining, but working a stage at the Fat Duck with Heston Blumenthal in Bray, when I ate his pork loin with braised belly and black truffle macaroni, it blew me away. There are family favourites too - my mother's apple pie and Auntie Winnie's raspberry jam from her garden.

IF NOT A CHEF?

Definitely making things, I love working with silver, casting metal, producing jewellery and sculpture, so absolutely being an artisan silversmith.

FAVOURITE TIME OF YEAR?

Fall, or autumn as you say, the changing of the seasons, all the end of summer glut at its seasonal best to be preserved and bottled, jams, chutneys, pickles. The squashes and pumpkins leading in to all that wintry fare, absolutely lovely. And on a different note, I love wearing scarves and I get to grow my winter beard!

FOODIE DISCOVERIES?

It will sound a bit philosophical but it's sincerely meant, it is the willingness and openness of this generation to try new things, to develop an appreciation of new ingredients, flavours, textures, combinations. And the whole communal feasting thing, learning about food, everyone wants a bit at the moment, the whole foodie media explosion on TV and in books. And in the kitchen around me, these young chefs breaking out, learning like sponges, being able to teach them. It's a rosy future for good food.

INSPIRING SUFFOLK VIEW?

Has to be overlooking the river and sea, where they meet, any of the estuaries on the Suffolk coast. Here down by the Yacht Club in Aldeburgh it is just bliss to chill for a break between lunch and dinner services.

FAVOURITE PLACES TO EAT?

The Queen's Head at Blyford, I love the pub, family atmosphere, properly done; Delphine's here in Aldeburgh, a retro Fifties diner and a great fun burger joint; but I have to say I just want to be at home, eating with Pauline and the girls, her food is always the best.

MIDNIGHT FEAST?

A bowl of noodles! Japanese spicy ramen noodles, hot water and go...

CHILDHOOD AMBITION?

Always to be a chef. We were first asked in class aged 5 what we wanted to do when we grew up, my hand shot up and I said be a chef. Food has been my constant passion ever since then.

ULTIMATE DINING DESTINATIONS?

I must get back to Vancouver and my home country to see the food scene now, the old haunts and the new places. Ten years on it will be so different. Also I'd love to visit Hong Kong, I know I'd have the time of my life; my wife Pauline is part Chinese, Bengal, Punjabi and Portuguese, and I love their cuisine, proper authentic home cooking.

TOOLS OF THE TRADE?

I love knives, absolutely adore them, essential part of my working life. It's the sharp edge, the ergonomics, the craft, the transformation of produce. I've had my set for nine or 10 years, they are an extension of my hand.

LUCKY DAY OFF?

Predictable, but as I live on the coast, it will always be the beach, paddling in the waves, the four girls boogie boarding, in the water like mermaids all day. We'll have a picnic, fish & chips, ice cream, then go home happy.

TYLER'S SIGNATURE DISHES

STARTERS

East coast smoked mackerel pâté, beetroot relish, crostini

Suffolk ham hock terrine, pea purée, peas and shoots

Eggs Drumkilbo with east coast seafood and lightly-curried sauce mousseline

MAINS

Pan-fried hake, sea greens, crab-crushed new potatoes, pickled clams and cockles

Alde Valley lamb, olive oil mash, broad beans, peas, tomato and salsa verde

Local lobster and Blythburgh pork wonton noodle soup

PUDDINGS

Marybelle set cream, strawberries and strawberry sorbet

Elderflower cheesecake, English gooseberries

Dark chocolate ganache, raspberries and Turkish delight

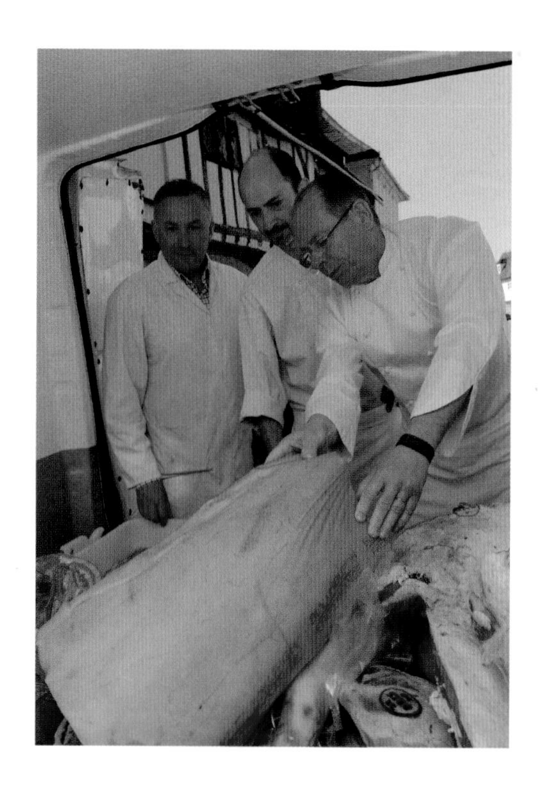

Free-range love:
Blythburgh pigs find Gallic champion

Régis Crépy and Enrique Bilbault on fashion, loyalty, taste – and fine Suffolk pork

L - R: Regis Crepy, Alastair Butler.

"Is that pig's head mine?"

"All yours, Régis."

Régis Crépy thanks his butcher and tucks the head under his arm. There's a bit of larking around for the photographer but it's clear that Régis is actually thinking pressed terrine, rillettes, maybe flavoursome stock. He puts the head carefully back in the butcher's delivery van; he'll be back to claim it soon.

The butcher, parked outside The Great House in Lavenham's unbearably pretty Market Square, is David Clarke of the family-run firm, Gipping Valley Meats, and if ever there was a close chef-supplier relationship this is it. "I've been selling meat to Régis since 1988," David says matter of factly, as if an uninterrupted 30-year business relationship were the most normal thing in the world.

Régis explains: "David always supplies the very best. He has great knowledge, knows exactly what cuts I like, how long I want beef to be hung [35 days rather than the conventional 28]. He'll find things for me too."

"And I'm proud to be associated with a restaurant like The Great House!" David adds. The company buys meat from local farmers topping up supplies with trips to Smithfield market particularly for popular prime cuts.

I break up the love-in and we talk pork. "I'd love to have a pig, don't you think it would be fun. A little one running around..." Régis waggles his fingers in a scuttling gesture; I try to imagine a pair of Kunekune pigs trotting around the beautiful Great House dining room – and fail. "No, one for the garden at home. They're wonderful animals," he insists.

A few hours spent in the company of Alastair Butler, marketing director at the family-owned firm Blythburgh Free Range Pork, confirms Regis' affection for these animals. He is eager to meet the piglets, happy to get in among them as they scamper across one of the fields on the sandy coastal fields around Blythburgh. "I'd love to bring my chefs here to see this and talk to Alastair. You learn so much about an ingredient this way." Alastair extends the invitation: he often hosts groups of chefs keen to find out what Blythburgh pork is really all about.

Pork features frequently on The Great House menu, and it is always Blythburgh meat. "I don't source ingredients locally at all costs," says Régis, categorically. "It's not possible to do that and maintain the standard my diners expect. But you can't beat Blythburgh pork, there's no need to go anywhere else."

He and head chef Enrique Bilbault watch as David expertly scores the loin making swift downward movements with a scalpel-sharp knife. The meat will be cut into chops or cooked slowly on the bone f or a staff meal. "Look at the amount of fat [there's not too much and it's hard and white], the colour of the meat, the dry skin... you can tell this animal was fed well and cared for," says Régis. "Of course the breed is important but it's really about how the animal lived. If it is fed well and never stressed – particularly at the time of slaughter – it will produce tasty meat."

Belly of pork is a favourite cut, but don't ever suggest that it's there because of mass popularity – Régis vehemently rejects 'fashion' in cooking. "I've always loved belly," he says, "maybe as a starter with gribiche sauce, dressed with crunchy pickled carrots, peppers and romanesco." As a wintry main it might appear with lentils, sultanas and tarragon, the skin crisped at the last minute after a fat-melting 36 hours in the oven.

"Pork shoulder used to go into sausages until Jamie Oliver came along, but now everyone's using it and it's become expensive; lamb shanks too." He fears the same will happen with belly pork. David agrees: "It's now one of the most expensive cuts because it's so popular. Beef cheeks are the same."

Régis looks up from tweezering, steady-handedly, slivers of beetroot onto a delicate carpaccio of beef that's been marinated in spices for 12 hours. "I think we'll come back to leg and loin soon. What do you think, David?" David puts money on shoulder of beef. "Lots of chefs are using featherblade but you'll only get eight portions from that joint and shoulder gives 20 or 30."

Don't get Régis onto the 'fashion' for molecular cooking, either. "I am influenced by many different styles of cooking, but not this one! Blobs here, blobs there, syringes for this and that," he waves a dismissive hand. "What's the point? If it makes sense, improves the taste fine; otherwise no, forget it." This is Régis at his passionate best. "A dish must have contrast in texture – so crunchy celery with a smooth pâté – and the flavours of individual ingredients must be crisp and neat and recognisable, maybe just three or four tastes on a plate."

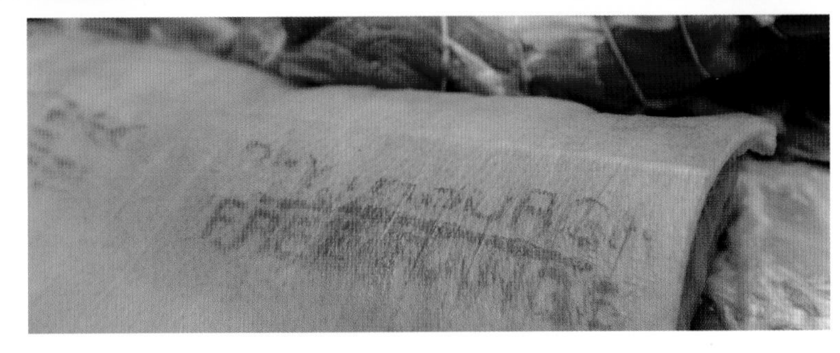

It's about colour and balance too. "I like my food to be light, modern, artistically presented, expertly seasoned." He's an advocate of nouvelle cuisine, but not the derided incarnation of that movement – minuscule portions at gigantic prices – more the game-changing lighter model championed by Michel Guérard in the 1970s.

Thirty successful years would suggest that Régis' philosophy is one his customers embrace too. Enrique, who has cooked for Régis for a staggeringly loyal 26 years, sums it up: "I love his passion for food, that he is a classic chef but innovates. He has always been supportive of my family too. We have a wonderful team, we are all friends."

Maybe that's the essence of The Great House: successful business partnerships *can* be founded on friendship. David has the last word. "I got married three weeks ago, and we had our wedding breakfast at Mariners [Régis' Ipswich restaurant]." He and Régis rattle off the menu – seafood gratin or smoked pigeon to start, fillet of beef or halibut to follow, a cheeseboard and dark chocolate gâteau to finish. You can bet your bottom euro that Régis made sure it was the happiest of days for David and his new wife.

Slow-cooked neck of Blythburgh pork with leeks, baby onions and celery fronds

A lovely, heart-warming midweek supper using great free range Suffolk pork, one of our best-known products. (serves 4)

200g young leeks, washed and cut into pieces; 100g carrots, 100g celery, 100g onion, all diced in 2cm cubes; 1 bay leaf; 2 sprigs thyme; 2 parsley stalks; 2 cloves; 10 whole black peppercorns; 100ml olive oil; 200ml chardonnay white wine; cold water; 600g joint of pork neck end

35g unsalted butter; 35g plain white flour; 150g whipping cream; 4 baby leeks; 12 baby onions; knob of butter; 1 tsp sugar; celery micro herbs to garnish

Pre-heat the oven to 150c. In a large hot pan over a medium heat, sweat the first nine ingredients with the olive oil for 10 minutes without colouring, then pour in the white wine and a splash of water. Simmer for 30 minutes to extract all the flavours. Strain the juices and discard the solid.

Season and lightly oil the neck end of pork and on a hot chargrill or dry frying pan, sear it on all sides.

Put the neck end in a snug heavy lidded casserole and cover it completely with the vegetable juice (adding water as necessary), put on the lid and braise in the oven for three hours.

Remove the meat from the casserole and keep warm on a hot plate. Pass the cooking juice through a fine sieve into a measuring jug. In a small pan, melt the butter and add the flour to make a roux, add 400ml of the juices and bring to a simmer whilst whisking. Cook gently for a few minutes, add in the cream and season to taste. Keep warm until required.

Take the neck end of pork out of the casserole dish, carefully dry well and cut into four equal pieces. Grill them on a hot griddle for one minute on all sides. Set aside and keep warm.

In a steamer cook the leeks until tender to the point of a knife. Set aside. Meanwhile in a small lidded saucepan, add the onions to the water, sugar and butter. Bring to a good simmer, cover and cook, stirring occasionally until tender and glazed, approx. 10 -15 minutes (if dry, adding more water). Keep warm.

To serve

Put a generous amount of sauce on four warmed deep plates, add the caramelised pork in the middle and decoratively arrange the leeks and baby onions around. Garnish with a few celery micro herbs.

"I like my food to be light, modern, artistically presented, expertly seasoned."

Régis Crépy

Carpaccio of local beef fillet

A local take on an Italian classic of marinated raw beef. We garnish ours with horseradish, berries and asparagus tips for contrast and freshness. (serves 4)

Marinade

2 litres of water; 200g coarse sea salt; 200g granulated sugar; 2 red chillies, halved and deseeded; 2 dried bay leaves; 10g whole black peppercorns; 10g fennel seed; 10g coriander seed; 10g dried mixed herbs

400g fillet of beef

Put the water, salt, sugar, chillies, bay leaves, peppercorns, fennel, coriander and mixed herbs in a saucepan and bring to the boil. Remove from the heat and leave to cool completely.

Cover the beef with the marinade and refrigerate overnight. Drain and dry the beef. Place on two sheets of clingfilm, roll up firmly into a tight cylinder before twisting and knotting the end. Chill once again.

To serve, remove the clingfilm and, using a very sharp knife, thinly slice the beef. Lay out to cover the centre of four chilled plates and add your chosen garnishes.

Guinea fowl suprême with sultana and tarragon mousse

A tastier alternative to chicken, giving a delicious elegant finish. We accompany this with an Armagnac reduction. (serves 4)

4 x 150g guinea fowl breasts; 15g salted butter; 150ml double cream; 30g sultanas soaked in hot water for two hours, then drained; 15g fresh tarragon, finely chopped; 2 tsp Armagnac

Trim each guinea fowl breast (keeping the trimmings for the mousse) and butterfly. Flatten each breast lightly between two sheets of clingfilm. Chill in the fridge.

Pulse the guinea fowl trimmings in a food processor with the butter until smooth. In a bowl over an ice bath, add in the cream, a quarter at a time, and mix vigorously with a wooden spoon until the mousse is firm and sticks to the spoon. Season lightly and mix through the sultanas, tarragon and Armagnac. Cover and refrigerate for 1 hour.

Unwrap the guinea fowl and spread the mousse down the centres. Roll up each breast lengthways and firmly wrap in cling film, twisting the ends tightly into a sausage.

Preheat the oven to 75c. Place guinea fowl on an ovenproof tray and bake for 40 minutes until fully cooked. Unwrap the guinea fowl before carving onto hot plates.

Lime and basil tart

A zesty dinner party dessert to cleanse the palate. For this you require pre-cooked pastry-lined tins. We make a dough with icing sugar, ground almonds and vanilla extract. NB this recipe contains raw eggs. (serves 6)

Filling

3 whole eggs; 170g caster sugar; 180g lime juice; 10 fresh basil leaves; 200g salted butter; 3 egg whites

Honey meringue

90g egg white; 100g honey; 150g whipping cream

6 small deep pastry cases, blind-baked until light golden

In a pan, mix the eggs, sugar, lime juice and basil leaves, heating to 82c and whisking continually. Pass the lime mixture through a fine sieve and leave to cool down until it reaches 45c. Beat in the cold butter with a hand mixer, little by little. Stiffly whip the egg white and fold into the lime mixture. Refrigerate for two hours to set properly.

Make the honey meringue by whisking the egg white until smooth and fluffy, and slowly adding the honey until firm. Whip the cream until stiff, then fold through the meringue. Spoon into a piping bag. Pipe the tart cases three-quarters full with the lime mixture and top with meringue, before carefully caramelising with a blow torch.

Gem of a place in a gem of a village

Push the heavy latched doors of The Great House, and you enter a little bit of France in the heart of the quintessentially English village of Lavenham. When it's quiet, when overnight guests have left and before lunch service begins, you'll rarely hear English spoken here as the sleek team goes about preparations in the kitchen and dining room.

It's an undeniably lovely place at any time though, striking an unflashy, balanced note between sophisticated French chic, and English country informality in both the interior décor and the natural, warm service. Inside, dark oak beams stand out against pale shades of dove-grey, white and taupe, tables are dressed with gleaming glassware, crockery, silver candlesticks. Outside, a charming patio area is popular for summer alfresco dining. Service throughout is glidingly unobtrusive and at the same time genuinely friendly.

The Great House was built in the 14th and 15th centuries by the Caustons, a local weaving family made wealthy thanks to Lavenham's then powerful position as a wool town. The Georgian façade was added in the 18th century and the property changed hands several times until the celebrated poet, Stephen Spender, and his artist-photographer brother Humphrey lived there in the 1930s, turning the house into a meeting place for notable artists and poets of the time.

Régis and Martine Crépy bought it in 1985, opening The Great House as a restaurant with rooms. Thirty years on, they have created a fixed gem of a place where elegant surroundings are matched by polished, complex and masterly cooking from the kitchen brigade led by Régis and head chef Enrique Bilbault. Régis likes to play it down: "We offer tasty, fine country dining," he says. "Yes, it is gourmet food but it is perfectly possible to offer a level of cooking excellence, source ingredients very carefully and locally if possible, and serve it in an relaxed, comfortable way." The extraordinary cheeseboard with its 30 or so mainly French cheeses has a nationwide reputation, and the wine list is magnificent, sweeping diners on a tour of the finest old and new world vintages, with occasional sidesteps to investigate the wares of less well-known winemakers.

The Great House
Market Place, Lavenham CO10 9QZ
T: 01787 247431
W: www.greathouse.co.uk
/LavenhamGreatHouseHotelRestaurant
@greathousehotel

Accolades: Three AA Rosettes 2015; 3 Michelin red forks; Top 100 UK Restaurants and Top 30 UK French Restaurants, *Harden's Guide* 2015; Editor's Choice Gourmet award, *Good Hotel Guide* 2015; Fabulous Food award, *Alastair Sawday's British Hotels & Inns* 2015; *Waitrose Good Food Guide* 2015 score 4.

Cost: Carte £45 average; set D (Tue - Fri) £35, set L (Wed - Sat) two course £19.50 / three courses £24.50; Sun set L £35; wine from £15.95

Open: Wed - Sun L 12-2.30 / Tue - Sat D 7-9pm (Sat 9.30pm). Closed: Sun D, Mon and Tue L. Jan and Aug (part)

FAVOURITE COOKING EQUIPMENT?

Simple: a mixer.

CULINARY HEROES?

Michel Roux Snr – he's hugely knowledgeable and changed the culinary landscape in the UK, I have enormous respect for him; Sir Terence Conran for his influence on design and style, and for his restaurant philosophy; and Jamie Oliver not only for what he has done for meals in schools and hospitals but also because he has encouraged people to cook at home.

LUCKY DAY OFF?

A walk on the beach at Aldeburgh with the wind blowing – wonderful!

INSPRING SUFFOLK VIEW?

I never cease to be in awe of our beautiful countryside whatever the season.

REGIS ON HIS...

FOODIE NOSTALGIA?

The aromatic smells of herbs and vegetables conjure up happy memories of the simple tasty food eaten on holiday in the south of France. Big, fat, juicy home-grown tomatoes, wild garlic, onions, shallots, thyme, rosemary and basil for local dishes such as ratatouille or bouillabaisse.

GUILTY SNACK?

One of my own brioches! Once you start eating it you can't stop but it's so light and airy that it doesn't feel like a guilty snack!

YOUR LAST SUPPER?

Of course there would be Martine my wife, our children Alexander and Amélie and two dear friends. We would eat salmon marinated with star anise, roast chicken or a good rare ribeye steak, and lemon tart.

COOK'S CHEATS AND CHEF'S TIPS?

Freeze horseradish so that you can easily squeeze out the juice when it defrosts. And to keep a pastry base crispy longer brush it with chocolate once it's cooked.

ULTIMATE DINING DESTINATION?

I'd love to go back to the restaurant of Jean-François Piège in Paris. He has two Michelin stars but is worth three in my opinion; he has amazing creativity and precision. I've been three times and I remember every dish I've eaten there.

IF NOT A CHEF?

I've always wanted to be a chef but if I had my time again I'd try to be an MOF Pâtissier. A MOF (Meilleur Ouvrier de France) is the top national accolade in any discipline and it takes enormous skill and dedication to achieve it.

WELL-THUMBED COOKBOOKS?

I have so many, but my favourite is probably the pastry book from the Ecole Hôtelière de Lausanne where I studied. Can I add my own, *Bon Appétit*, too?!

FAVOURITE TIME OF YEAR?

It has to be Spring – it heralds the change of seasons and the arrival of wonderful indigenous British produce and our cooking has to adjust to accommodate these sophisticated yet subtle flavours – spinach, spring cabbages, pea shoots, herbs, new potatoes, lamb, rhubarb and of course asparagus. And there's still the promise of more good produce and warm weather around the corner.

REGIS' SIGNATURE DISHES

STARTERS

Duck foie gras marinated in port and Armagnac, pistachios and sultanas, white balsamic vinegar and tarragon reduction, warm brioche

Scottish mackerel roulade, white wine and dill gelée, horseradish sauce, blackcurrant and Jerez vinegar coulis

Home-smoked chicken and sage ravioli, sautéed girolles, chicken jus infused with porcini

MAINS

Mint and marjoram-marinated lamb saddle, garden pea 'crémeux', lamb jus, port reduction

Marinated Gressingham duck, braised sweet potatoes, chestnut and Cognac sauce

Steamed fillet of turbot, glazed salsify, lemon and tomato butter sauce

PUDDINGS

Macaroons filled with white chocolate and lime mousse, strawberry coulis

Pistachio crème brûlée, raspberry marmalade, sablé Breton

Rum baba filled with crème pâtissière, confit pineapple, piña colada sorbet

A sense of place: Thinking local, delivering big

Southwold without Adnams would be like good food without great drink

L-R: Roger Middleditch, Rory Whelan, Jonathan Mitchell.

THE CROWN HOTEL RORY WHELAN

The days when the town's finest bitter was only for the refreshment of locals, as far as the horse-and-drays could drop the pins and firkins, have long gone. With a nationally-known beer 'brand', it is tempting to think that the family-owned brewers might lose sight of their roots. But a quick food safari down Southwold High Street and all is well with the world as the many arms of this multi-faceted business are revealed. The heady smell of malt hanging in the air at their East Green brewhouse; the coppery gleam and chromework of the distinctly 21st century distillery (the new kid on the block competing with the nearby Lighthouse and Pier for iconic status); the eco-friendly Adnams store, a haven for keen cooks and winelovers; and a convenient crawl of tied pubs within walking distance of each other. But it is the two flagship hotels at the heart of Adnams country, The Swan and especially The Crown, that interest us most here. This pair of historic coaching inns are the domain of softly-spoken executive chef Rory Whelan, whose dulcet Irish tones belie his passion and steely determination.

History and tradition are at the route of everything that Adnams has evolved into, over the past 200 years as the company grasp the 21st century firmly. Their carefully-considered and cleverly-crafted clutch of offshoot ventures stemming from the Southwold brewing roots demonstrate that forward-thinking innovation, but one still anchored on the integrity of the family name. Being a good company and demonstrating green industry are just two of the guiding principles which make their enterprise stand out.

The changing face of pubs and the rising costs of brewing mean clever diversification and re-strategy have been essential for the survival of our regional brewers, however fine their real ales might be. Modern marketing and social media have made Adnams a household name in hostelries and supermarkets for their great beers, certainly across London and the south of England and increasingly (inter) nationally.

The 'brand' evolution is told in the ever-expansive perspective of the beermats through the decades, as 'Southwold by the pint' became 'Beer from the coast' to the recent 'Let's talk beer', sharing the obsessive detail and creativity which makes their real ales stand out. However the ground-breaking 'Jack Brand' craft beers garner the best of the old in their long-forgotten Southwold Jack trademark of knight clunking bell with sword and the centuries-perfected foundation of brewing skills; but the new is predominant, influencing with exciting flavour profiling, the clever science and the free-thinking of the pioneering international brewing movement, which Adnams is helping to shape.

This brings us back to chef Rory. With three busy hotels and a pub-restaurant under his direction, it is a juggling act that tests a raft of skills, kitchen management and culinary direction as well as the more generic teambuilding and over-arching business direction. His is a similar fusion of the modern and the classical; he homed old school cooking techniques that Escoffier might be proud of

during his apprenticeship back in Ireland and ten years at Hintlesham Hall, one of Suffolk's grandest country house hotels; he worked on the former at the Michelin-starred L'Escargot in London's Soho and the contemporary chic of The Hoste Arms in Burnham Market, Norfolk.

The Crown, perhaps the more urbane of the two Adnams' Southwold hotels, is where we catch up with Rory. Local provenance, seeking out the best of land and sea from this rich area, is where it all starts. As much as the brewing and distilling start with the East Anglian speciality of prime malting barley, so Rory looks on his figurative kitchen doorstep to around East Suffolk for the finest producers and ingredients. Being on the larger size as food buyers go, servicing this busy group is not for the faint-hearted small-scale supplier or the micro-artisans out there. Needing the volume and consistency to ensure his brigades of chefs have the right raw materials on every plate, he works closely with farmers and growers to get the specialist supply in the sizeable quantities he needs. Step up the likes of Gressingham Duck, Marybelle Dairy, Stokes Sauces, Suffolk Farmhouse Cheeses, deservedly well-known names on our Suffolk roll of foodie honour.

And so we turn to Rory's favourite crop, and if the pages of this cookbook are a judge, clearly a favourite choice of many of our 20 Suffolk food heroes: fabulous asparagus. It's something this county grows so well; those purply-green shoots loved by chefs and diners alike as the 8 – 10 week season signals the welcome start of spring in late April. For his eagerly-awaited crop of "sparrowgrass" Rory heads to Priory Farm nearby in Wrentham, on the edge of the Benacre Estate, whose productive acres provide Sea Breeze Asparagus with the right soils and climate to excel. Here it is picked, washed, graded in six sizes and sold commercially and direct to the public at an honesty stall.

"There is something magical about asparagus," says Rory. "It comes up when and how fast it wants, it's a real expression of nature, it can't be held back, a true unpredictable harvest." We head over to one of the fields which is a busy hive of horticultural activity as an army of seasonal workers, mostly food-loving eastern Europeans, who follow the various seasonal food crops throughout East Anglia, arrive to start work. This is back-breaking stuff, pickers crab sideways down the mounded ridges, that house the productive crowns buried deep in the fertile loam, their quick-moving hands cutting the occasional mature spears. Not only are they bent double but they also walk a huge number of miles in a typical day to harvest this precious vegetable crop.

Back in his Southwold kitchen, Rory is all about letting the asparagus shine, keeping it clean but appealing, perhaps in a starter with tomato consommé and goats cheese pannacotta, perhaps for a warm salad with confit salmon and candied almonds or just griddled with sauce béarnaise. And lighting up the coals at home, he barbecues it alongside lovely marinated local meats and salads.

Good food doesn't get better than when fine Suffolk asparagus is put centre-stage.

Wrentham asparagus with posh egg and soldiers

An elegant starter or add some simple char-grilled poultry breast to make a fresh, tasty main course. The creamy base can be made in advance along with blanching the asparagus, but the other elements must all be prepared simultaneously. (serves 6)

Sauce

60g unsalted butter; 1 long shallot, shredded; 1 garlic clove, peeled and sliced; 50g leek, green part only, shredded; 380g finely cut asparagus trimmings; 250g milk; 340g double cream; 16ml Noilly Prat vermouth; 250ml double cream, whisked to soft peaks

Heat up two knobs of butter in a wide deep saucepan and fry the shallot, garlic and leek without colouring. Add the asparagus and cook until soft. Then pour in the milk and cream before simmering for 2 minutes.

Carefully blend in small batches and pour through a fine sieve into a large container. Measure out 400ml into the original pan, cool and refrigerate until required.

Return the 400ml of the base sauce to the heat with the vermouth, add the soft peak cream and bring to a simmer. Serve just like this or put through a gas-fired cream squirter.

Morel mushrooms

15 morel mushrooms or 1 large handful of other wild fungi; unsalted butter; splash of Madeira

Brush away any dirt from the morels and halve lengthways gently. In a small heavy pan, gently stew the morels in butter over a low-medium heat, and when starting to soften, add a splash of madeira, cover and keep warm.

Brioche soldiers

Brioche loaf, cut into 6 x 1cm thick slices

Lightly oil a small frying pan and over a low-medium heat, melt two large knobs of butter. Taking a three inch cutter, cut each slice into a round. Gently fry the rounds until crisp and turn over to do the same. Season lightly, remove and keep warm.

Duck eggs

6 duck eggs

In a lightly-oiled heavy frying pan over a low-medium heat with two large knobs of butter, add small metal rings and add an egg into each, before cooking until the white sets. Season lightly, remove and keep warm.

Asparagus

30 asparagus spears; local Hillfarm rapeseed oil

Pre-heat your char-grill. Warm soup plates. Drop the asparagus into fast boiling salted water, bring back to simmer for about 1 minute (less if thinner). Drain into iced water and pat dry on towel paper. Lightly oil and season. Grill until well-marked.

To serve

15ml truffle oil

Put a thin layer of the sauce onto your warm soup plates. Place the spears in the centre and place a soldier on top. Add a duck egg and scatter morels around, before drizzling with a few drops of truffle oil. You can serve more sauce in warm cups or top up the bowls.

Pulled Suffolk pork with cabbage and elderflower sabayon

Tart up your Sunday roast leftovers with this tasty dish. Preferably use a fresh, home-pickled cabbage rather than sauerkraut. NB protect vulnerable diners with pasteurised egg yolks. (serves 6)

50ml elderflower cordial; 5 egg yolks (or 100g pasteurised egg yolk); 150g dry fruity white wine; 100g caster sugar; 6 slices of foccacia, griddled; 600g shredded slow-cooked pork shoulder; chicken stock; pickled green cabbage, drained

Pre-heat your grill to maximum and warm up six starter plates. For the sabayon (a light, fluffy glaze), over a bain marie whisk together the first four ingredients until well-aerated, remove from heat and continue whisking as it thickens. Adjust seasoning and keep warm. To serve, heat up the pork in a little amount of stock. Remove meat with a slotted spoon and keep warm. Add the cabbage to the stock pan and warm through.

Place cabbage and pork onto the focaccia toast, season and coat with a little of the stock. Spoon over some sabayon and grill until browned.

Lowestoft cod fillet and minted parmesan cream

This works well with any good local white or oily fish, just bake or grill as appropriate. We serve this with fried spätzle pasta, peas, broad beans, red onions and watercress. (serves 6)

1 shallot, finely chopped; 250ml fish stock; 75ml double cream; 75ml soft peak cream; 100g parmesan, grated; small bunch mint, leaves only, finely chopped; 6 x 180g cod loin portions; rapeseed oil; unsalted butter

Put the stock and shallot in a wide saucepan, boil until reduced to a quarter. Add in the double cream and bring to a boil. Fold in the soft peak cream and simmer again. Whisk in the parmesan, heat through and fold in the mint off the heat. Adjust seasoning and keep warm.

Salt the skin of the cod; add a glug of rapeseed oil and knob of butter to a hot pan, fry skin-side down. When three-quarters cooked, turn over and turn heat down. Finish frying until opaque and flaking, before keeping warm. Serve with the sauce and garnishes.

Adnams gin, lime and white chocolate mousse

A colourful, elegant dessert for summer. NB if in doubt with consuming raw eggs, please use pasteurised ones. (serves 6)

125g white chocolate; 1 lime, zested and juiced; 2 egg yolks (or 40g pasteurised egg yolk); 2 egg whites (or 70g pasteurised egg white); 15g caster sugar; 1.5 leaves bronze gelatine, softened; 50ml Adnams First Rate gin; 250g soft peak double cream; 300g raspberries; raspberry coulis; baby or droplet meringues; basil leaves, finely shredded; white chocolate, finely grated; freeze-dried raspberries

Melt the white chocolate with the lime juice over a bain marie and keep warm. Whisk up the yolks, whites and sugar and warm in a bain marie. When blood temperature, remove and whisk again until light and fluffy. Whisk the gelatine into the chocolate, followed by the gin. Fold this mixture into the eggs. Mix in the cream and decant into a container. Refrigerate until lightly set.

To serve, toss raspberries in coulis and arrange with meringues on the plates. Place on a quenelle of mousse neatly with a hot dry spoon. Sprinkle with basil, grated chocolate and dried raspberries for texture.

Crowning glory

With a good claim on being one of the UK's original Nineties gastropubs the philosophy of The Crown back then still holds true: it is an exciting, informal combination of pub, small hotel and restaurant in the heart of the cosmopolitan seaside town of Southwold.

The relaxed, warm atmosphere exudes that 'something for everyone' appeal and comfort-fit menu. And it's not just Rory's skilled imaginative seasonal local food which entices but of course Adnams' focus on the excellence of the drink. Far from being limited to the expertly-brewed beers from just behind The Crown, it includes the well-known skills of the wine-buying team and the new distilling prowess with their international award-winning spirits and liqueurs.

With such a long association with the town, and its sheer popularity when the sun comes out especially during the holiday season, The Crown does have a must-visit label as one of the essential dining destinations for the discerning clientele in these classy parts.

And with the gastropub-style operation, the flexibility of Rory's menus and his dish styles have to suit the busyness of the place, from the weekenders staying for indulgent suppers, the day visitors wanting a light bite, the different generations who flock to the town en famille at the same time every year. All these varied needs and dining expectations are met with good cheer and well-catered for.

The Crown Hotel
90 High St, Southwold IP18 6DP
T: 01502 722275
W: www.adnams.co.uk/hotels/the-crown
/thecrownsouthwold
@crownsouthwold

Accolades: *Waitrose Good Food Guide* 2015 score 2; Suffolk Dining Pub of the Year 2013 & 2014 *The Good Pub Guide*; Green Tourism Gold

Cost: Carte L £25 / D £30 average; wine from £18

Open: 8am-11pm (10.30pm Sun); food served 12-2pm (2.30pm weekends) and 6.30-9pm (6pm Sat)

Details: 14 bedrooms; bar drinks; children welcome; dogs allowed in rear bar; parking

RORY ON HIS...

MIDNIGHT FEAST?

Cheese, any cheese, oh and pickled gherkins. Chocolate too, cheap milk, bitter dark, don't care! Cured herrings too. Not all together obviously...

LAST SUPPER?

Thai fish broth; rib eye steak, hollandaise, chips, all the trimmings; stewed rhubarb and custard; amazing cheeseboard. On the invite list – Kurt Cobain, witty foodie Stephen Fry, fishing guru Ali Hamedi, chef Raymond Blanc, rebel element in Eminem, and family of course, partner Anna and toddler son Tadgh.

WELL-THUMBED COOKBOOKS?

Recipes From Le Manoir Aux Quat' Saisons by Raymond Blanc; *Dough – Simple Contemporary Bread* by Richard Bertinet *Preserving* by Oded Schwartz; *Proper Pub Food* by Tom Kerridge *Larousse Gastronomique.*

FAVOURITE PLACES TO SHOP?

Emmetts of Peasenhall is a cracking place, I love it, they're just obsessive; Food Hall at Snape Maltings has a great range and quality, full of interesting stuff; and I adore the honesty stalls where I live in Wenhaston, brilliant cheap produce from back gardens and allotments.

FOODIE DISCOVERIES?

Getting into home-made wine, converting foraged and bartered fruits into a pretty passable glassful, my second batch of plum last year was rather good!

TOOLS OF THE TRADE?

At work, I love my gas solid top hob and Rationale combi bake/ steam oven; at home, a lidded cast iron pot does everything almost, steaks, stir-fries, stews, one-pot dishes.

COOK'S CHEATS AND CHEF'S TIPS?

Tempura – batter of one part cornflour, two parts self-raising, very cold sparkling water or good lager, mix with chopsticks to a lumpy single cream texture. Fruit compôte – marinate berries overnight in vanilla sugar, reduce drained juices to a syrup carefully, drop cold fruit into hot syrup but don't allow to cook.

'TAKE 5' RECIPE?

Herring bruschetta – griddle thick-cut baguette, garlic-rubbed, on a hot char-grill, then repeat with herring fillets in pieces, oiling and seasoning both first; toss fish with Adnams bloody Mary tomato relish, pile on bruschetta, sprinkle with chopped gherkins and smoked cheese (Suffolk Smokehouse), then glaze in oven; enjoy!

LUCKY DAY OFF?

Cycle and a walk to wake me up; fishing if I am allowed; lazy barbecue for the rest of the day, I love the alfresco vibe, the idea of relaxed, good company and communal slow feasting.

ULTIMATE DINING DESTINATIONS?

Per Se in New York's Central Park was memorable, 3 Star Michelin, really good tasting menu; Fat Duck in Bray, and Midsummer House in Cambridge or the imagination, detail and expression; I must visit Tom Kerridge soon at the Hand and Flowers in Marlow.

FOODIE NOSTALGIA?

Mum Eileen's spaghetti Bolognese. I remember being given the ingredients, aged about 13, and being told to make it as she rushed out, family actually ate it, wasn't half bad. The first thing I ever cooked by myself.

BEST DISHES EVER EATEN?

The vast array of delicious oysters and clams in Grand Central, Boston, just shucked with lemon; going to an Indian curry house in Malaysia, wonderful spicing of curries slow-cooked in the morning and reheated fast over red-hot coals.

RORY'S SIGNATURE DISHES

STARTERS

Cured herring, onion preserve tart, lemon mascarpone, cabernet sauvignon vinegar

Wild bass sashimi, Szechuan pepper and yogurt sorbet, lemon and ginger

Roast partridge breast, fried confit leg, parsnip crisps and velouté, cep mushrooms, bitter chocolate

MAINS

Baked cod fillet, slow-braised mutton in tomato and balsamic, griddled courgettes

Roast loin of Bunwell venison, roasted cauliflower and purée, crispy Savoy cabbage, pancetta and white chocolate

Wild sea trout, baked with lemon marmalade, griddled radicchio and chicory, dauphinoise potato, capers and dill pollen butter

PUDDINGS

Passion fruit and Greek yoghurt posset with white wine and ginger sorbet

Saffron and honey custard tart, caramelised pear and sorbet

Poached rhubarb soup, Greek yoghurt, custard ice cream

Aristocratic pickings: Accomplished Estate-sourced cooking

Stuart Pegg counts ingredients in food yards, not miles, at The Duke's Head, Somerleyton

Stuart Pegg

THE DUKE'S HEAD STUART PEGG

A gunshot stops our conversation about new season leaves mid-flow. "That'll be Matt," Stuart says. "Always a good sound to hear – it means muntjac, just what the salad needs!"

Matt Roe is the Somerleyton Estate's deerstalker, the man responsible for keeping The Duke's Head kitchen (and that of the Fritton Arms just over the border in Norfolk) supplied with game from the Estate. He goes out regularly, keeping the population of this diminutive deer in check year-round and sustainably controlling the numbers of fallow and red deer during the shooting season.

"It's essential work," explains Stuart Pegg, executive chef on the 5,000-acre Somerleyton Estate just a few miles from Lowestoft. "The deer cause damage to farmed crops as well as the landscaped parkland, and we also need to make sure we keep ground plants healthy as these are habitats for nesting birds and other herbivorous mammals. It's about creating a sensible balance. If they weren't controlled, deer would very quickly dominate."

The ultimate beneficiaries of Matt's deer management programme are the guests at the Estate's two pub-restaurants. Stuart who is in charge of food at The Duke's Head and the Fritton Arms as well as all event catering, wants to get as close as possible to sourcing ingredients 100% from the Estate, whether this be venison culled by Matt, beef from the herd of Welsh Black cattle, lamb from the flock of Norfolk sheep, eel and pike fished from Fritton Lake, or even ketchup made from home-grown tomatoes. It goes without saying that the Estate shoot provides pheasant, partridge and wild duck in season too. "I'm so lucky to have all this literally on my doorstep," Stuart says. "It really can't get any better for me as a chef." Stuart, whose professional career has taken him through the classical kitchens of London's Dorchester hotel and two-Michelin-starred Gidleigh Park in Devon where he worked under renowned chef Michael Caines, shows me the game chiller where a muntjac carcass hangs. It will soon be butchered, cooked and served perhaps as the warm venison salad with fresh leaves, zingy herb oil and pickled raspberries [*see recipe*] that is so popular in the summer months. At other times of the year muntjac might appear as a charred venison burger with Suffolk blue cheese and Walled Garden pickled pear or pan-roasted haunch with carrot spaghetti, chive oil, liquorice, fondant potato and port jus. "It's not surprising customers like this meat," Stuart says. "The flavour is sweet, not particularly gamey and the texture is delicately fine. It's also extremely healthy, low in fat and of course totally free-range."

Other popular meat dishes on The Duke's Head menu include roast pigeon with beetroot risotto, goat's cheese croquettes and toasted pine nuts; or slow-braised free-range pork belly with black pudding, braised peas and charred Little Gem lettuce. The burger is a high-rise beauty, succulent Welsh Black beef draped in Norfolk Dapple cheese,

all the colourful vegetable trimmings you'd expect and of course triple-cooked chips; Estate-reared lamb might appear as chops with pancetta and pea fricassée or as a pinkly-cooked sharing platter of loin, pulled and stuffed shoulder and kidneys.

As for non-meat ingredients, the Estate's rambling, relaxed, very English kitchen garden grows much of the produce for the daily-changing menu. Stuart works closely with head gardener Anna Outlaw to make sure the right crops of fruit, vegetables, salads and herbs are planted every year, and looks forward to opening boxes crammed with the best pickings that are brought to the kitchen door every week. "Look at these lovely new potatoes, courgettes, herbs everywhere," Stuart says as we wander through the stunning vegetable garden, its warm red-brick walls nurturing espaliered apples and pears, richly-mulched beds swollen with early summer abundance. Glasshouses and orangeries – they are the original, ornate Victorian ones designed by Crystal Palace architect, Joseph Paxton – burst with figs, citrus and peaches; cut-flower beds are dreamy swathes of romantic colour, many of the stems to be used for weddings, or in arrangements in the Hall which is lived in by Hugh, Lord Somerleyton, his wife Lara and their three young children.

Stuart clearly gets a huge amount of horticultural and foodie satisfaction from the relationship with his Estate environment. "To cook with such local, seasonal, ingredients as fresh and nutritious as you could hope for, harvested and delivered straight to the kitchen is what every chef dreams of! I spend a lot of time with Anna and the team checking what's ready to be dug, picked or cut. I particularly love tasting new varieties that Anna has grown – we are always trialling new things – thinking how best to put them on my menus." In the wider Somerleyton grounds, Stuart will often pick wild garlic, elderflower and even stinging nettles in early summer, and blackberries, damsons, sloes and mushrooms later in the year.

Food miles? This is a place to measure distance in gentle steps from the back door.

Warm kitchen garden salad with seared loin of Somerleyton muntjac, pickled raspberries and herb oil

An expression of the Estate, this is such a flexible friend. It combines the savoury rich meat with a mix of the vegetables and salads and the essential sweet-sour, fruity, fragrant edge to provide a little cutting contrast. So long as you stick to a similar balance to keep it interesting and fresh, it really is a 'mix and match' dish that works well with whatever you can harvest from your own vegetable patch or allotment and of course local farm shops. NB the empty pea pods make a delicious summer soup, softened with good stock, and finished with mint and spring onion, eaten hot or cold. (serves 4 - 6)

Pickled raspberries

100ml Aspall cyder vinegar; 100g caster sugar; 200g ripe raspberries

Melt vinegar and sugar over a high heat and boil carefully until reduced by half. Cool the syrup and then add raspberries before refrigerating.

Herb oil

10 basil leaves; 8 sage leaves; 8 mint leaves; few large sprigs of flat-leaf parsley; 4 thyme sprigs; 1 small rosemary sprig; 75ml local rapeseed oil

Remove the leaves from all the herbs and set aside. Gently heat the stalks and oil together in a small saucepan and leave on a low heat for 10 minutes. Strain oil through a sieve and reserve.

Meanwhile in a heatproof bowl, pour a little boiling water over the herb leaves to cover. Once wilted, drain leaves through a sieve.

Pulse the leaves in a processor and pour in the strained oil. Blend again until completely smooth. Season well to taste.

Advance preparation

500g new season potatoes, simmered until al dente, cooled and cut to bite-size pieces; 3 courgettes, halved lengthways and cut into 1cm diagonal half-moons; 500g freshly podded peas

To serve

1 whole loin of muntjac venison; oil; butter; 100g mizuna leaves or rocket, washed; 100g mustard leaves, washed; nasturtium leaves and flowers

Add a splash of oil to a hot frying pan, season the loin all over and lay in. Carefully seal until browned on all sides, turn the heat, add a good knob of butter, baste as it cooks until rare, perhaps two minutes on each side, check the pinkness and remove to somewhere warm to rest.

Warm dinner plates. Carefully wipe out the pan, fry the potatoes in a good knob of butter and a splash of oil over a high heat until just caramelising on the edges, add in the courgettes, stir well and leave to brown again, stirring occasionally. After a few minutes, add in the peas to heat through. Check the vegetables are tender. Fold through the mizuna and mustard to wilt for a few seconds.

Serve onto the warm plates. Carve the muntjac and arrange on top, before garnishing with the nasturtiums, drained raspberries and herb oil.

Crisp slow-braised pork belly

Proper Suffolk free range pork is perfect for this. We serve with honey-roasted carrots, fondant potato, braised cabbage and bacon. (serves 4+ generously)

1 litre dry Aspall Suffolk cyder; 500ml good chicken stock; 1 large piece belly pork, rind scored; 3 sprigs fresh thyme; 4 large cloves, unpeeled, crushed; 2 banana shallots, peeled and sliced; 2 sprigs of rosemary; 1 lemons, zest only

Pre-heat your oven to 140c. Bring cider and stock to a simmer. Place pork into a snug very deep roasting tin to fit, add in other flavourings and just cover with sufficient hot liquor.

Cover with baking parchment and then tin foil, carefully seal up tightly and bake for 5 hrs.

When cooked and very soft, remove from liquor and allow meat to cool. Strain liquor, reduce and season into a gravy. Put meat into a snug container, cover with clingfilm and press on another smaller container. Refrigerate meat with a weight on top to press down. When cold cut into portions. To serve, pre-heat oven to 180c, oil the pork on all sides and seal in a hot ovenproof frying pan then bake until heated through.

Sweet chilli beef

A taste of the Orient with super local beef like Red Poll or the Somerleyton Estate park-reared Welsh Black cattle. We make our own sweet chilli sauce.

250g plain flour; 50g each of ground cumin, ground coriander and cayenne pepper; 300g rump steak, very thinly-sliced; sweet chilli sauce; watercress

Mix the flour and spices together. Toss the beef in the flour mixture. Heat your deep fat fryer to 180c. Lower in the basket and carefully drop in the beef a few pieces at a time. Do not overcrowd the basket.

Shake gently as it cooks until crispy and golden. Lift basket, drain, tip onto kitchen paper and keep warm. Repeat until all cooked. Season to taste. Serve quickly, drizzled with chilli sauce. Garnish with watercress

Chilli sauce
The amount of chillies is up to you, a couple of medium-sized mild ones are best for beginners!

Red chillies, topped and de-seeded; 1 red pepper, topped and de-seeded; 100g caster or palm sugar; 100ml white rice vinegar; 100ml water

Simmer for 30 minutes. Carefully liquidise, boil and reduce to a sticky sauce.
Cool and refrigerate.

Shortbread

A great store cupboard treat to enjoy with most desserts for texture or just with good coffee or Earl Grey anytime of day.

180g plain flour; 55g sugar; 125g butter, room temperature

Pre-heat oven to 190c. Beat butter and sugar until smooth. Sift in flour and combine. Turn out on to floured surface and roll out to 1cm thickness. Cut into rounds or fingers and place on a greased lined baking sheet. Bake for 15 - 20 minutes or until light golden-brown.

Well-dressed Suffolk Duke

"Please park prettily" urges the sign on the barn wall at the top of driveway, politely.

It rather sums this place up. Pretty the red-brick Duke's Head pub most definitely is from the freshly-painted outside, while inside a stylish boho-chic feel is achieved with a mix of vintage decoration, inglenook fireplaces, antique furniture and old rugs. Wooden floors, mismatched chairs and scrubbed-pine tables give a comfortable, relaxed feel. It's the sort of pub that encourages lingering whether over a pint and bar snacks or a full three-course meal in the dining rooms or on the sunny garden terrace.

The pub is one of two on the Somerleyton Estate. Since 2013 both places (The Duke's Head is in Suffolk while The Fritton Arms is officially over the border in Norfolk) have been back under Estate management and the ultimate control of Hugh Crossley, Lord Somerleyton, himself a former restaurateur (he used to run the middle eastern restaurant, Dish Dash, in south London). Since bringing the pubs back into the fold, Hugh and his wife Lara have overseen the reinvention of both properties in terms of their interior design and food offer.

While the team has been careful to retain The Duke's Head's credentials as a welcoming 'local', they have also nudged it into the realms of destination pub-restaurant. It seems to be working, a loyal following eager to return for second helpings of the good food, cooked using Estate produce by executive chef Stuart Pegg, head chef James Santillo and the rest of the brigade.

Visitors often combine a bite to eat at the pub with a tour of magnificent Somerleyton Hall and its spectacular gardens, open to the public between April and September. Beyond the stateliness of these parts, a tour tells the story of a working Estate where modern land management and farming practices, a commitment to the environment, energy-efficiency and the surrounding community, are preserving this corner of Suffolk.

The Duke's Head
Slugs Lane, Somerleyton,
near Lowestoft NR32 5QR
T: 01502 730281
W: www.somerleyton.co.uk
/dukesheadpub
@somerleytonduke

Accolades: *Good Pub Guide* 2015; *AA Pub Guide* 2015

Cost: Carte £21 average; wine from £16

Open: 12-11pm (10.30pm Sun); food served 12-2:30pm & 6:30-9pm (12-8pm Sun)

Details: Bar drinks; beer garden; private parties; weddings; children welcome; dog-friendly; car parking

STUART ON HIS...

CHILDHOOD AMBITION?

I only ever wanted to cook, did so much as a child with my two Nans, constantly making things in the kitchen with Nanny Dolly; it was baking bread, roasts, offal; and with Nanny Peg it was pigeon pie, good family fare, stews, the best apple pie! I started working in Gasche's Restaurant in Weybourne, near Holt as a teenager.

ULTIMATE DINING DESTINATIONS?

Sat Bains in Nottingham is just brilliant, I love his food, and the sublime tasting menu; I must get to French Laundry in California's Napa Valley, Thomas Keller is a culinary genius; and here the same goes for Heston at The Fat Duck in Bray. I've heard so much, I want to see what it's all about.

TOOLS OF THE TRADE?

My solid top hob is my best friend at work. It holds sauces, rests meat, keeps garnishes warm. At home I have a bright red Kitchen Aid mixer for baking cakes and making pizza dough with my son.

WELL-THUMBED COOKBOOKS?

Dough and *Crust* by Richard Bertinet, his writing and bread recipes are so instinctive; *Nathan Outlaw's Fish Kitchen;* the Duck & Waffle restaurant cookbook and Glynn Purnell's too.

BEST DISHES EVER EATEN?

A 'rabbit BLT and liver lollipop' at Purnell's in Birmingham, awesome 1* Michelin dish. James Santillo, my head chef at The Duke's, made a brilliant red mullet and chorizo cream dish recently, just fantastic; my Nanny Peg's apple pie, sweetcrust pastry, Bramleys, real custard, which I've eaten ever since I was a child.

FOODIE DISCOVERIES?

Marsh Pig, Jackie and all her amazing charcuterie from Blythburgh Free Range Pork, her cured and smoked produce is unbelievably good.

LUCKY DAY OFF?

Taking my son, Stanley to build sandcastles on Lowestoft beach, bit of sea-fishing off the pier or maybe stroll around Southwold, fish and chips in the harbour. I don't drink, so I miss out on the Adnams!

FOODIE NOSTALGIA?

Pigeon and rabbit. Uncle Steven used to get lots on the farm where he worked for our childhood suppers. And also fresh fish from Granddad Richard's little outdoor boat.

INSPIRING SUFFOLK VIEW?

Sizewell B, may sound odd, but such a captivating modern icon.

MIDNIGHT FEAST?

Posh cheese on toast, we're talking prosciutto, mango, Mrs Temple's Copys Cloud cheese, always have those in the fridge just for this. It's also a favourite of Stanley's. Maltesers, it's a childhood thing, oh and Curly Wurlys; KFC on the run.

'TAKE 5' RECIPE?

Sticky Pigs, Duke's Head-style. Get really good cocktail-size sausages, wrap in half a rasher of streaky bacon, bake in a pre-heated 200c oven and roast for 15 mins until bacon is crispy. To dip, 200ml of good tomato ketchup, 75ml wholegrain mustard and 50ml of honey, mixed together. Happy days!

STUART'S SIGNATURE DISHES

STARTERS

Parmesan, lemon and herb-crusted monkfish cheek, pea purée, smoked tomato salsa, confit lemon, chorizo oil

Pan-roasted crown of Somerleyton woodpigeon, fruit and nut polenta bar, sweet and sour-pickled cucumber, raspberry dressing

Seared scallops, confit chicken wing, cauliflower purée, chervil oil and chicken scratchings

MAINS

Butter-poached lobster tail, carpaccio of braised Welsh Black beef tongue, smoked apple purée, slim fries, parmesan, brown shrimp butter

Cider-braised Blythburgh pork belly, basil and apple, black pudding croquette, poached langoustines, shellfish bisque

Seared loin of Estate fallow deer, smoked venison cottage pie, carrot purée, fondant potato, port jus

PUDDINGS

Assiette of black cherry: parfait, sorbet, compôte, dust, chocolate mousse and cherry garnishes

Port-poached Kitchen Garden Williams pear, smoked paprika honeycomb, Suffolk Blue cheese sorbet

Classic treacle tart, crème anglaise

More than just a pretty plate: Real flavours leap out at Wyken

'Home-grown' head chef Simon Woodrow displays a light touch with the exceptional ingredients on his doorstep

L - R: Simon Woodrow, Lady Carla Carlisle.

THE LEAPING HARE SIMON WOODROW

It takes me a while to catch what Lady Carlisle is saying, muffled up as she is against the keen Suffolk wind, head protected with her trademark hat. She hollers over the field: "Onze! Douze! Angelica!" but it's probably the rattling bucket of feed that brings the ewes and their lambs running rather than instant recognition of their names.

"I do have a handful of favourites, ones I've bottle-fed because they were orphaned or rejected," Lady Carlisle admits. She pauses, before adding in a stage whisper lest the unnamed lambs should hear: "Of course, we'll never eat them." Angelica, a docile Red Poll cow (one of Wyken's small herd), is also a favourite, though I take a little longer to warm to her after she makes a briskly trotting beeline for my bag which she proceeds to nibble determinedly.

These sheep, grazing fairly decoratively (many of the ewes are naturally shedding their fleece so look a bit raggedy) at the back of Wyken Hall, are hardy rare-breed Shetlands. Most of the lambs will spend a year romping on the fields around the estate before appearing on the menu at Wyken's Leaping Hare restaurant. It is an award-winning place, crowned Suffolk Restaurant of the Year in the *East Anglian Daily Times* Suffolk Food and Drink Awards 2015. There, head chef Simon Woodrow and his brigade turn the carefully-reared meat into dishes that taste as good as they look - maybe a lamb canon with buttered spring vegetables and crushed Jersey Royals or a rack of lamb with baby fennel and a fennel and tarragon risotto. He might equally explore some middle eastern flavours with a slow-cooked shank tagine with spring onion and apricot couscous and Marybelle yoghurt.

"The Shetlands have a fabulous, delicate flavour, not too fatty, and a lovely tender texture," says Simon. "The flavour means I don't have to do much to it to create a really tasty dish, and that's really important. At the core of any good dish is a good ingredient: if that's not right, then however pretty you make the plate, it will never taste great."

Lady Carlisle agrees: "We keep our lamb much longer than is common because it's a small breed. I think we eat lamb far too young in this country, before it has a chance to develop any depth of flavour. Lambs need to put on a bit of fat if they are to taste good."

Of course it's a privileged relationship; not many chefs enjoy the luxury of cooking ingredients reared or grown in their restaurant's backyard. But Simon revels in it, eyes lighting up as he talks of the bounty literally on the doorstep. Wild muntjac and rabbit is available year-round while other deer, pheasant and partridge are shot in season. At times there's beef from the Wyken Red Poll herd, in spring there's wild garlic and nettles to be picked in the woods, while summer and autumn bring apples and pears from the orchard, and onions, potatoes and other vegetables from the kitchen garden.

A new asparagus bed will start to produce spears next year too. "The gardeners bring stuff to me whenever they have it. I love using estate-grown ingredients," says Simon. "It's an exciting way of cooking and makes me and the team very inventive!"

If a main ingredient has been sourced from the estate itself, or within five miles of it, this is indicated with a two-star symbol on the menu; if the main ingredient is from East Anglia it earns a one-star rating. So a spring dish of marinated breast of Sutton Hoo chicken with smoked bacon, peas and broad beans earns a star; ditto a starter of Cromer crab, Rushford Estate asparagus, pea pannacotta ("I love crab but unfortunately I'm allergic!" says Simon); and a pigeon breast with pigeon and chorizo pastilla, carrot purée, pickled carrot and beetroot. Among the two-star dishes are a main of wild nettle and herb risotto with an Old Winchester and rocket salad; and a smoked and seeded haunch of venison with roast beetroot, salt-baked celeriac and salsa verde.

Herbs, if not picked in the kitchen garden, are from Phil Mizen at Langham Herbs who also sells his produce at Wyken's weekly farmers' market; and eggs are from Oak Farm free range eggs, a business run by Wyken farm manager, Will Reed.

It seems fitting that in a place known for its use of very local produce, that the head chef should also be home-grown. Brought up in Stanton (his grandmother was a housekeeper at Wyken for nearly 50 years), Simon worked on the estate as a teenager, painting or doing odd jobs. "I've been working here for 14 years on and off! At first I was saving for a trip to Australia where I spent seven months in 2005, but when I came home I started working in the restaurant as a kitchen porter and gradually worked my way up through commis, chef de partie, to sous chef. I did three months at the West Suffolk College, but I've really learnt to cook on the job."

When Jon Ellis, the Leaping Hare's head chef for the previous six years, moved on, Simon was the obvious replacement. He now works closely with Lady Carlisle, restaurant manager Francis Guildea and talented pastry chef, Steve Williams and the rest of the team to create a monthly-changing menu that celebrates the best that Wyken and its immediate surroundings have to offer.

Lady Carlisle, eagle-eyed and with an American directness only slightly tempered by nigh on 30 years living in the UK, is firm in her likes and dislikes, sharing her opinions with gentle authority. She has little time for "hypodermic needle" cooking. "I really don't want to see dots or foam on a plate of food; the simpler the better for me!

"What I like about Simon is that he has a light touch, but a great attention to detail. He's very focused, and has great love for and curiosity about food. To my mind that's the perfect recipe for a chef."

Pink-seared rump and slow-braised shoulder of Wyken lamb with pommes Anna and glazed baby carrots

At The Leaping Hare, we serve this in late spring with a thick onion and wild garlic soubise purée and simple asparagus. At other times, go with whatever delicious greens are in season. Use the braising liquor for a red wine sauce to accompany. (serves 4)

Pommes Anna

100g unsalted butter; 3 sprigs of thyme, bruised; 2 cloves of garlic, peeled and thinly sliced; 400g small new potatoes

Pre-heat the oven to 170c. Lightly oil 4 holes of a cupcake tin and line with greaseproof paper. Melt the butter in a small pan over a low heat with the thyme and garlic and leave to infuse for 10-15 minutes.

Finely slice the potatoes with a mandolin. Strain the butter into a large saucepan and add in the potatoes, season with salt and pepper and mix well. Layer the potatoes in the cupcake tin, going round in a circle until they protrude about 1 cm above the tin. Cover with foil and cook for 15 minutes, uncover and cook for a further 10 minutes. Remove from the oven and leave to cool, cover with greaseproof paper, a tray and some heavy weights before refrigerating.

Braised shoulder fritters

2 onions; 10 sprigs each of rosemary and thyme, leaves only; 1.5kg lamb shoulder (on the bone); 6 cloves garlic, peeled; 250g dried apricots; 1.5 litres of good red wine; 100g flour; 2 eggs, lightly beaten; 200g breadcrumbs

Preheat an oven to 150c. In a food processor, pulse the onion with the rosemary and thyme until coarsely chopped. In a very hot oiled frying pan, sear the lamb shoulder on all sides and place in a lidded casserole dish, adding the onion mix, garlic, apricots and red wine. Cover and cook for 3-4 hours until falling off the bone. Strain the juices and reserve for use in a red wine sauce.

Flake the meat from the bones, break up the garlic and apricots, season and mix together well. Roll mixture into small balls and leave in the fridge to firm up. To serve, pre-heat your deep fat fryer to 180c. Place flour, egg and breadcrumbs in separate soup plates. Dip balls in flour, then egg, then crumbs, pressing firmly. Gently remove the excess, then deep fry carefully until cooked. Keep the fritters warm before serving.

Lamb rump

4 x 200g lamb rumps; local rapeseed oil

Pre-heat the oven to 180c. Score the rump fat in a criss-cross pattern and season all over. Heat up an ovenproof oiled frying pan. Sear the meat fat-side down until colouring, next brown the meat-side all over and place in the oven for 12-15 minutes, depending on your personal taste for pinkness. Leave to rest for at least 5 minutes somewhere warm.

Glazed carrots

12 baby carrots; 1 tbsp salt; 2 tbsp sugar; 3 cardamom pods, flattened, seeds retained; 2 star anise

Peel the carrots and cover with cold water in a small saucepan, add the remaining ingredients, cover and bring to the boil. Remove from the heat and allow to cool in the liquor. To serve, bring back to a simmer and keep warm.

To serve

Pre-heat the oven to 200c and warm four dinner plates. Turn out the potato cakes onto a baking sheet, lined with greaseproof paper and reheat in the hot oven until golden along with the shoulder fritters if they have cooled. Plate the carrots, potato cake and fritters before carving the rumps and arranging.

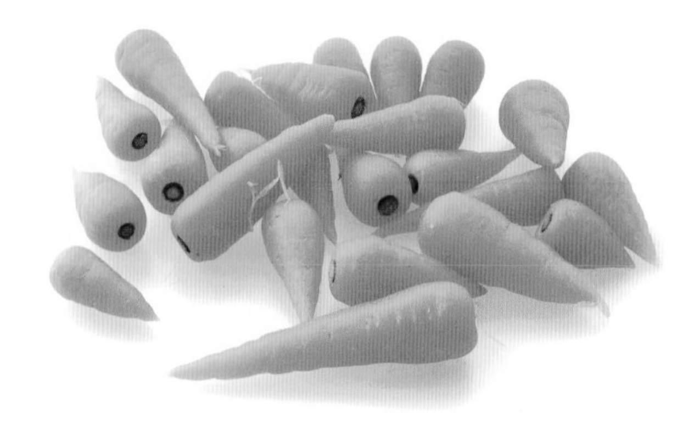

Sutton Hoo chicken and smoked bacon terrine

For this recipe, take a 2.5kg Sutton Hoo chicken, poach the breasts gently and confit the legs in duck fat. This eats very well with a Caesar-dressed salad and local quail's eggs. (serves 10)

Poached chicken breasts and confit leg meat; 1.25 litres good chicken stock; 600g smoked streaky bacon rashers, lightly-cooked; 8 bronze leaf gelatine sheets, softened in cold water; 300g leeks, finely sliced and softened in butter

Bring stock to boil and reduce to 500ml. Allow to cool. Line a clingfilmed terrine mould or loaf tin with the bacon, slightly overlapping the rashers and ends overhanging. Warm chicken stock and whisk in strained gelatine until dissolved. Flake chicken breast meat. Debone legs and shred separately.

Layer the breast meat inside the mould, followed by seasoning and chicken stock to cover, repeat with the leeks and then the flaked leg meat, and more chicken stock to finish. Allow to settle and top up if needed. Fold the remaining bacon over the top and cover with clingfilm. Weigh down overnight in the fridge to compress.

To serve, unwrap and cut thickly.

Smoked Gressingham duck breast with carrot purée and walnuts

We smoke our own duck breasts over vine prunings and aromatic tea leaves. Good addition are some pickled carrot and micro herbs. We like to use multi-coloured heritage carrots (serves 4)

2 cooked smoked duck breasts, preferably Gressingham; 50g butter; 1 long shallot, sliced; 1 tbsp Chinese five spice powder; 400g organic carrots, sliced; 300ml carrot juice; small handful of walnut halves to serve

In a sauté pan, heat the butter over a medium heat and fry the shallot without colouring for 2-3 minutes and then add the five spice and carrots, cooking for 2 more minutes. Pour in the carrot juice and simmer until very soft, for approx 20-30 minutes. Reserving the liquor, strain and purée the carrots, loosen with a little of the liquor if needed; taste and adjust seasoning. Keep warm.

Slice the duck thinly (we serve ours warm) and serve with the purée and a scattering of walnuts.

Vanilla Marybelle cream custards

Poached rhubarb (gently baked with vanilla pod, orange zest and grenadine) works well alongside honeycomb and crisp meringues.

700ml Marybelle double cream; 1 vanilla pod, split and seeds scraped; 1 bronze gelatine leaf, softened in cold water; 75g egg yolks; 60g caster sugar; 6g cornflour

In a deep saucepan, bring the double cream, the vanilla pod and its seeds to a simmer and remove from heat. Whisk in strained gelatine.

Whisk yolks, sugar and cornflour together in a large heavy bowl continuously whilst slowly pouring in the cream.

Strain, allow to cool and pour into clingfilmed small moulds. Leave to set in the fridge. Turn out and garnish.

A Utopia of sorts

To be told, "you have nothing, in the middle of nowhere" must be a downer for even the most idealistic of people.

"That's what the farm manager said when my husband and I moved here in 1986 and I started having ideas about diversifying the 1,000-acre farm. I could see it wasn't viable, and I'd always wanted to open a restaurant. But somehow, out of ignorance, comes confidence!" said Lady Carlisle.

Slow down on the ignorance, though. Lady Carlisle's grandparents were cotton farmers in the Mississippi Delta and she grew up aware of the challenges of agriculture, albeit those particular to the USA's Deep South. She also grew up to become a feisty civil-rights activist, a Vietnam protester, imprisoned briefly for her actions. "Have I created a reprieve from the real world here?" she wonders. "Does that fit with being an activist? Maybe not, but I like to see Wyken as a well-run community, a Utopia of sorts."

Lady Carlisle's activism may now be softer round the edges, but she has always insisted on running what she describes as a "humane" restaurant in the 400-year-old barn. "I wanted to create an asset to the community, and a place that is kind to the workforce – that's why we only open two nights a week, plus lunchtimes."

The fine dining restaurant operates alongside a café, open daily for breakfast, light lunch and afternoon tea. At both places, Lady Carlisle (who worked at Alice Waters' famed California restaurant, Chez Panisse, then in various Parisian restaurants and as Paris correspondent for the American *Food & Wine* magazine), is closely involved in the menu creation. Indeed, in the beginning she did the cooking herself.

Her years in France honed her vision for the vineyard, planted in 1988, just two years after her arrival in Suffolk and a year before the birth of her son, Sam. "I wanted to create a French vineyard," she says. "I knew we had south-facing slopes and sandy loam over chalk, and that the field cooked in summer – perfect for vines!" The seven acres, said to be on the site of a Roman vineyard, grow Madeleine Angevine grapes for Wyken's citrussy white wine, Bacchus for a more aromatic white, Auxerrois and Pinot Noir for sparkling Wyken Moonshine, and Triomphe d'Alsace for the rosé Wyken Pink. Visitors are encouraged to walk through the woods, and, in season, to enjoy the Hall's dreamy English country garden.

She's also closely involved in the farmers' market, open every Saturday morning, and in the Country Store with its tempting array of practical and beautiful homewares, clothing and books.

The Leaping Hare
Wyken Vineyards, Stanton,
nr Bury St Edmunds IP31 2DW
T: 01359 250287
W: www.wykenvineyards.co.uk
/leapinghareatwyken
@wykenvineyards

Accolades: Restaurant of the Year 2015, *EADT* Suffolk Food & Drink Awards; Michelin Bib Gourmand; *Waitrose Good Food Guide* 2015 score 3

Cost: Carte £30 average; set L £21.95; wine from £20

Open: 12-2.30pm daily; 7-9pm Fri and Sat; café is open for breakfast and lunch daily

Details: Breakfast; light lunches; afternoon teas; outside seating; gardens; woodland walk; Country Store; weekly farmers' market; car parking

SIMON ON HIS...

FOODIE NOSTALGIA?

Scotch broth! Peter Harrison used to make this and it was such a hearty, simple soup but with such depth of flavour. Tasting that was a turning point for me as a chef.

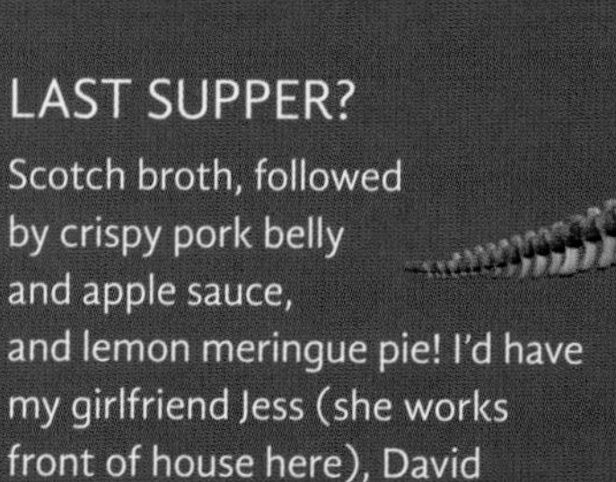

LAST SUPPER?

Scotch broth, followed by crispy pork belly and apple sauce, and lemon meringue pie! I'd have my girlfriend Jess (she works front of house here), David Attenborough (I think I've watched every one of his programmes!), Stephen Fry, Keith Richards and Billy Connolly.

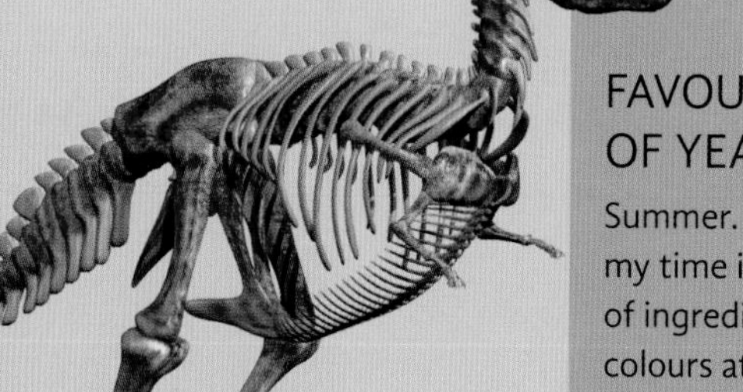

CHILDHOOD AMBITION?

To be a palaeontologist – I was obsessed with Jurassic Park and dinosaurs as a child! I've always loved science and nature.

FAVOURITE TIME OF YEAR?

Summer. Even if I spend most of my time in the kitchen, the range of ingredients available and the colours at this time of year really brighten me up.

FAVOURITE LOCAL FOODIE PLACES?

Pea Porridge for Justin's use of forgotten cuts, and Midsummer House for its faultless eight-course menu. I'd go back to both places in an instant. I love the local produce at Hillcrest Nurseries, and the scotch eggs at Gastronome in Bury St Edmunds. The Old Cannon Brewery in Bury does fantastic local ales, and Benson Blakes is the place in town for a burger!

COOK'S CHEATS AND CHEF'S TIPS?

Lightly grill a soufflé before putting it in the oven so the soufflé has something to rise against. Also, soaking a boiled quail's egg in a vinegar solution will make it easy to peel.

IF NOT A CHEF?

Probably something involving art or graphics. I did a National Diploma in Art and Design. It would be nice to play the guitar for a living too!

FOODIE DISCOVERIES?

Equilibrium brining. For example, with pork you basically weigh the meat and water needed to cover it and add 1.75% of the total weight in salt, then refrigerate. Because of the specific salt levels you can leave the meat in the brine for longer. It gives a firm texture and deep flavour and seasons the meat accurately. You can use the technique for fish too with a lower percentage of salt.

WELL-THUMBED COOKBOOKS?

I buy one a week I reckon! I'm constantly learning and I love reading about food as well as cooking it; Skye Gyngell's *A Year in My Kitchen* is great, and I love Tom Kerridge's *Proper Pub Food* for really reliable recipes and for developing the concept of Michelin-standard pub food.

BEST DISHES EVER EATEN?

A duo of pork at Pollen Street Social, London – it was an amazing belly and cutlet of suckling pig! A smoked eel and crispy chicken wing starter at Alimentum in Cambridge and I'll never forget eating roast grouse with pear and elderberry at Midsummer House also in Cambridge.

CULINARY HEROES?

Peter Harrison [former head chef at The Leaping Hare], I was his commis and he taught me to appreciate flavours, opened my eyes to what food can be, and gave me the foundation for my career. I also have huge admiration for Sat Bains and Raymond Blanc.

SIMON'S SIGNATURE DISHES

STARTERS

Whisky-cured salmon, pickled cucumber, horseradish cream, dill

Suffolk blue cheese and Wyken apple salad, yellow pepper dressing

Wyken venison carpaccio, white truffle oil, rocket, shaved parmesan

MAINS

Wyken pheasant breast, braised leg pithivier, Jerusalem artichoke purée, braised cabbage

Salsify, baby spinach and Old Winchester risotto, thyme pesto, salsify crisps

Roast Wyken partridge, shallot tarte tatin, cauliflower purée

PUDDINGS

Great Barton raspberry and peach parfait, white chocolate custard, toasted almonds, raspberry popcorn

Wyken elderflower and gooseberry jelly, lemon curd, lemon and poppy seed cake, lime granita

Wyken pear tarte tatin, ginger crumble, burnt orange and honey syrup, stem ginger ice cream

All about that bass: Fresh fish sings out at The Anchor At Walberswick

Sophie Dorber's coastal menu gleams with Lowestoft-landed seafood

L-R: Sophie Dorber, Danny Porter.

Cinderella

THE ANCHOR AT WALBERSWICK SOPHIE DORBER

"It must be strange to spend most of your working life under the moon and stars," says Sophie Dorber as we walk between blue crate after blue crate of flappingly-fresh catches at the Lowestoft auction. Morning is not long broken but the boats that have fished overnight are back, laden, eager to sell their fish. "I'm up early, but not that early!"

She's after some wild sea bass, North Sea-caught, for the lunch menu at The Anchor At Walberswick, the pub-restaurant she runs with her husband, Mark. The Anchor is busy with holidaymakers in the season – and locals year-round – and, as it is a lazy stone's throw from the waves, it is not surprisingly a place that champions fish in all its guises.

"I love cooking fish," says Sophie. "The flavours and textures of fresh fish are so subtle and fleeting that they demand every ounce of a chef's concentration and, dare I say it, sensitivity.

"I like to keep it simple, so maybe a fish soup with rouille and croûtons, or half a dozen oysters with shallot and sherry vinegar – you can't go wrong with those starters." Among the popular main courses are the inevitable fish and chips with hand-cut chips and a pokey jalapeño tartare sauce, razor sharp against the airy-light, crisp beer batter; and smoked haddock and salmon fishcakes with saffron aioli and peppery watercress and rocket. "I couldn't ever take those two dishes off the menu; there'd be uproar in the village!" she says.

She eyes the sea bass for sale. "I'm going to do it with some courgettes from the allotment, cut into ribbons, and with the flowers deep-fried in a light tempura batter [*see recipe*]. It'll go really well with a smooth, garlicky tomato sauce and crispy potato skins."

With perhaps a couple of hundred boxes to sell that morning, the pace of the fish auction is brisk, the auctioneer calling buyers, fishermen, the odd chef, to order. It's a bizarre process. A tight crowd gathers round the crates, a high-speed, familiar-but-alien tongue utters words that are baffling to an outsider. We are left unsure what exactly is for sale and how much it sells for; there's none of the loud announcement of an antiques' auction, no grand bidding gestures or gavel-banging; it's more a case of the odd twitch or raised eyebrow, and a rapid-fire string of numbers before the lucky buyer throws down a numbered ticket on the box and the group moves on. Local skipper Ove Jinkerson – or Ovey as he's known – explains: "You have the big buyers who might be processing and exporting fish, or even buying here to send to other auctions around the country for a quick profit. Prices fluctuate hugely; one species may make twice or three times more or less from one month or even one week to the next, and from one side of the country to the other. Price is determined by availability and that is dependent on very local weather conditions of course. We are working with a living, variable product, not something that is predictable."

Ovey sells his catch under contract to Sophie's fish supplier, the family-run Lowestoft firm, L&G Roberts so doesn't have to run the lottery of the daily auction, but Danny Porter, Roberts' fish buyer, is deep in bidding for other fish for customers. He delivers daily to The Anchor, bringing whatever Sophie requires for the day's menu.

She has a lot to choose from. The buyers move steadily between the boxes of codling, whiting and dogfish before moving on to skate, sole, oily herring and mackerel, and magnificent lobsters. Danny chooses some silvery-shiny sea bass and we head back to the company headquarters where Gary Roberts, the G of the family partnership, is busy preparing oven-ready fillets of smooth-hound, a firm-fleshed, boneless fish from the shark family that is spiking some savvy chefs' interest.

Preparing fish is a dying skill, they say. "Chefs don't really come to the auctions and plenty of them don't even know how to skin, gut and fillet any more," says Gary, quickly excluding Sophie from that category. "They just phone up and order the portions they need; they pay us to do the hard work! That's why fish is more expensive in restaurants these days. Then of course there's the supply and demand issue due to the lower stocks and pressure from other sources."

The plight of the local fishing industry has been well-documented. The number of fish buyers like Danny can be counted on a few hands and the home fleet of boats moored at the Lowestoft quayside on even fewer, though Danny does point out that other East Anglian crews regularly driver their catch ironically to be sold at Lowestoft.

Sophie hears the woes from Ovey as he shows us his boat, *Western Lady*. It's a story of danger, regulations, quotas, the cost of diesel, the time demands as smaller catches require ever-longer and more frequent trips out to more distant fishing grounds. But something makes him stick at it, and the conversation soon turns to the importance of offering unusual fish alongside the ever-popular types. Nurse-hound, for example. "It's a type of dogfish also called bull huss," Ovey explains with reignited enthusiasm. "It's known in fish and chip shops as rock salmon or rock eel and is often used as lobster pot bait but it has a firm flesh and it's not unlike expensive monkfish." Sophie leaves with a promise to order some from Danny and experiment back in The Anchor kitchen.

As we make our way back to the pub, Sophie reflects on the joy of cooking such fresh seafood: "With fish like this you really don't have to do much to it. It's the same with other local seasonal produce that I love to cook; you get much more impact by preparing it simply, using a few really good ingredients and keeping textures and flavours straightforward. There's no space to hide with this sort of cooking, though; you do have to trust your ability as a chef. Still, if you have an ingredient like this, the best thing for sure is to let the ingredient do the work!"

Wild Lowestoft-landed sea bass, courgette ribbons, tomato sauce

An earthy simple main course. We serve this with tempura courgette flowers and crispy potato skins for contrast. Feel free to use any other local white fish, sea trout fillets or even an oily fish like mackerel or herring. Best not to keep the courgettes waiting too long, so do not cook too far ahead. (serves 4)

Tomato sauce

Olive oil; 1 onion, diced; 3 garlic cloves, chopped; 750g ripe local tomatoes, roughly diced

In a heavy large saucepan, heat up a layer of oil, when hot, soften the onions and garlic without colouring. Next turn up to a high heat and fry the tomatoes until they break down. Remove and carefully pulse in small batches with a liquidiser. Sieve back into the saucepan and reduce the liquor by half on a rapid simmer. Taste and keep warm

Courgette ribbons

4 medium courgettes, quartered lengthways, seeds removed; good olive oil; unsalted butter

Using a potato peeler, shave the courgette quarters into ribbons. Heat up a deep sauté pan on a high heat, add a glug of oil and couple knobs of butter. Toss ribbons in, mix and season to taste before serving immediately.

To serve

4 sea bass fillets, skin-on; olive oil

Warm up four dinner plates. Pre-heat the oven to 200c. Oil the skin of the fish, score three times lightly diagonally and liberally salt. Heat an ovenproof frying pan until it's smoking, lay in the fish skin-side down and cook until browning after a couple of minutes. Season the flesh-side and turn over. Add two large knobs of butter and then bake for 2 minutes. Remember it will carry on cooking once off the heat. Remove as it starts to flake and rest for two minutes somewhere warm.

Serve fish on to a bed of courgettes with sauce to one side, along with chosen garnishes.

Anchor bread

We sell our bread from the bar every day. Handle dough with lightly-oiled hands in a cool place. (for two small baguettes)

Day before: In a very large bowl, blend 250ml blood-temperature water and 1 tsp fresh yeast, sprinkle in 175g strong white bread flour sprinkled in and mix well. Cling film and leave at a warm room temperature.

175g strong white bread flour; 18g sea salt; semolina for dusting

The next day: into a large bowl, add the flour and mix in the salt. Add the yeast mixture and knead with a dough hook for 8 minutes on slow (until very soft with a light shine and just comes away from bowl). If too sticky, add more flour; if too firm, add more water. Place on an oiled baking tray, cover very loosely with oiled clingfilm. Leave at warm room temperature. After 30 minutes, fold right in two-thirds and left over to right edge. Turn over, recover loosely and leave for another 30 minutes. Halve and shape into batons. Put oven on to pre-heat at 240c with tin of hot water on bottom shelf. On to tray, loosely cover again and sit for 30 minutes. Remove clingfilm, dust with semolina. Cut gently lengthways once with a serrated tomato knife. Bake for 12 minutes and check every 2 minutes until golden, cooked and hollow-sounding underneath.

Crab and rocket linguine

A quick and simple light lunch. Enjoy with your favourite dressed tomato salad. (serves 4)

4 tbsp olive oil; 4 garlic cloves, finely diced; 2 red chillies, finely diced; 2 large dressed crab; 285ml reduced fish stock; linguine, cooked al dente; 2 large handfuls rocket leaves; 1 lemon, zest and juice; lemon wedges, to serve

Warm pasta bowls. In a heavy large saucepan, warm olive oil, add garlic and chilli, and gently fry until golden, fold in the crab and then stir in fish stock gently. Drop in the pasta and gently turn over with tongs. Repeat with rocket. Add lemon zest and juice, taste and adjust seasoning. Serve with lemon wedges.

Sweet oatcakes

Perfect accompaniment for good ripe cheeses or just distinctly more-ish for great morning coffee.

100g pinhead medium oatmeal; 100g wholemeal flour; 40g muscovado sugar; 4g sea salt; half tsp bicarbonate of soda; 100g unsalted butter, melted; 40ml boiling water; heaped half tsp malt extract (optional)

Pre-heat oven to 170c. Combine dry ingredients, then add butter, water and malt extract. Mix well to a soft dough. If too moist, add more flour. On one large sheet of clingfilm, push out with oiled hand. Lay another on top. Roll thinly, ideally 1 – 2 mm thickness. Cut to desired rectangle size and place on lightly-floured baking sheets. Bake for 8 – 12 minutes until lightly-golden. Cool for a few minutes and transfer to a rack to crisp up. Cool completely and store in a sealed container.

The path to the beach (via the allotment)

The water tower just off the A12 is where you leave daily busyness behind. Walberswick requires you to do that – this is no place for frenetic activity. Time spent in the relaxed atmosphere of the Anchor at Walberswick helps the process of de-stressing beautifully.

This delightful seaside bolthole, just a salty sniff from the beach and the allotment where much of the kitchen's produce grows, is where Sophie and Mark Dorber have put down roots. They moved here back in 2004 to take over the lease on the 1920s Adnams property after over 20 years running the award-winning White Horse pub in London's Parsons Green. There, they had developed a reputation for a notable, globe-trotting cellar of beers and wines, chosen by Mark (he's co-founder of the Beer Academy which runs courses for enthusiasts and professionals), and paired carefully with Sophie's fresh, straightforward, ingredient-led food.

In Suffolk, Sophie's menu adapts constantly to cope with the ups and downs in the Walberswick population – in particular the summer swell. A wood-fired pizza oven has proved popular and the large terrace and safe garden area are magnets for families, not to mention one of the dining rooms with shelves of games and books to keep children entertained. At the front of the roadside property the team fires up a barbecue on summer weekends, there are popular Friday night curries, beer festivals draw lively crowds and there are regular fundraising events and exhibitions, not to mention private parties, training and tasting sessions, making good use of the adjacent flint barn.

Beer and wine are revered as much as the food at The Anchor, each dish on the menu matched – just as the couple did in London – with a glass of something vinous or hoppy. Should the draw of the sea, the freshness of the air and the lure of this gentle Suffolk village prove as tempting as The Anchor's myriad brews and vintages, then a night in one of the ten comfortable rooms, of which six are cedar-clad chalets in the pub grounds, is the perfect solution. The Dorbers also own The Swan at Stratford St. Mary, a freehouse inn by the banks of the river Stour on the Essex border near Dedham.

The Anchor At Walberswick
The Street, Walberswick IP18 6UA
T: 01502 722112
W: www.anchoratwalberswick.com

Accolades: *Waitrose Good Food Guide* 2015 score 3; Top 50 UK Gastro Pubs 2015 *The Publican Morning Advertiser*; 2011 Wine Pub of the Year, *Harpers Wine & Spirit Trade Review*; *Alastair Sawday's*, *Hardens* and *Michelin* guides

Cost: Carte £27 average; wine from £15.95

Open: 8.30am-11pm; food served 12-3pm & 6-9pm

Details: Bedrooms; bar drinks; breakfast; alfresco dining; sea-view terrace and pizza oven; gardens; parties and meetings; children welcome; dogs allowed; car parking

SOPHIE ON HER...

FAVOURITE LOCAL PLACES TO EAT?

Aldeburgh Market – I love Sara's place, has all the things I hold dear, the lovely, fresh mussels in the café; Pinneys' Butley-Orford Oysterage, more seafood, really local and seasonal, whole lobster caught by their boats, really decadent; Two Magpies over the river in Southwold High Street, their cheese melt sandwich is always a delicious treat when out with the kids.

LAST SUPPER?

On the menu – has to be on the beach, chilled fruits de mer, home-made aioli; char-grilled Dover sole, sausages, asparagus, good bread; and then for afters grazing on a good cheeseboard and pastel de nata, Portuguese custard tarts.

FOODIE DISCOVERIES?

Eating Yotam Ottolenghi's food from his London restaurant as a take-out at a friend's house, it was all about the food, simple true flavours and combinations of vegetables and spices.

MUSIC TO COOK TO?

Soul music, bit of a 'disco diva', I think it energises the team and makes them happy, but they may disagree!

CULINARY HEROES?

Raymond Blanc, Michel Roux Jnr, Steve Winter (guru baker from Norwich – Bread Source farmers' market stall).

LUCKY DAY OFF?

Long bike ride from Walberswick to Thorpeness for tennis, try and beat my personal best time of 52 minutes on the way there, seafood barbecue, great wood-fired pizza, sliced root ginger tisane in the garden afterwards.

ULTIMATE DINING DESTINATIONS?

Pierre Koffman's La Tante Claire was my first experience of 3 Star Michelin food; Moroccan street food in Essaouira, huge Dover sole cooked over a wood fire, breathtaking and cost peanuts, even forgave the plastic plate; Czech sausage shop in Prague early one morning, all sorts of extraordinary shapes and sizes. Must eat at Le Gavroche in London, The French Laundry in California and I wish I had eaten at El Bulli in Spain.

FOODIE NOSTALGIA?

Warm fresh baguettes with melted chocolate, in France as a child, always back to Banyuls sur Mer for the summer holidays.

'TAKE 5' RECIPE?

Ham bubble & squeak is a simple treat from the fridge. Mix together cooked mashed potatoes, blanched sliced greens and shredded Suffolk smoked ham, season well, heat an oiled frying pan and fry the mixture, adding duck fat or butter regularly as you slowly brown it.

IF NOT A CHEF?

I'd go back to ceramics, working in porcelain, in my own studio, throwing my own pots, producing beautiful bowls to eat from and a shop for a bit of a social life.

WELL-THUMBED COOKBOOKS?

The Constance Spry Cookbook, used by my mother and granny, really fundamental recipes; *British Larder: A Cookbook For All Seasons* by Madalene Bonvini-Hamel, written intelligently about what she knows and loves; Claudia Roden's *The Book of Jewish Food*, brings together so many cultures and cuisines.

SOPHIE'S SIGNATURE DISHES

STARTERS

12 hour fish soup, rouille and croûtons

Scallops with artichoke purée and pancetta

Asian sticky pork salad, dipping sauce

MAINS

Beer-battered fish and chips with Anchor jalapeño tartare sauce

Locally-smoked ham, bubble & squeak, mustard cream sauce and Maple farm poached eggs

Brazilian black bean and pork stew with chocolate and cumin, coriander and tomato salsa

PUDDINGS

Chocolate fondant

Toffee pudding, vanilla ice cream

Danish apple and almond cake, toffee sauce, Marybelle frozen Greek yoghurt

Pick of the crop:
Home-grown chef champions local fruit

Arron Jackson demonstrates a light touch with superlative ingredients at the Angel

L - R: Clive Williamson, Arron Jackson, Robert Gough.

Arron Jackson
HEAD CHEF

THE ANGEL HOTEL ARRON JACKSON

Some chefs court celebrity brashly; for others celebrity, uninvited, pursues them. For others still it's a case of 'no thank you, let me cook, that's what I do best'.

Arron Jackson is one of these, happiest in his spacious kitchen at The Angel Hotel in Bury St Edmunds where he has quietly led a brigade of 10 for the past 11 years. He's a chef who has proved himself by learning on the job after studying at the West Suffolk College. "I worked up through the ranks with Gough Hotels [the family owned parent company of The Angel] to be head chef at The Salthouse Harbour Hotel for five years before moving to The Angel in 2012. It's been a fantastic way of progressing my career and Robert [Gough] has really helped me broaden my love and knowledge of food."

Arron reluctantly emerges from behind the pass where he has put the finishing touches to dishes to be photographed. We are off to meet Clive Williamson of Maynard House Orchards, the family-run firm of apple growers and juice-makers based in Bradfield Combust, just a few miles out of Bury down the Sudbury Road. The Williamson family grows over 100 acres of, among others, Bramley, Cox and Russet apples, turning the fruit into juices that are sold to retail outlets, delicatessens, farm shops, hotels and restaurants.

"Have you visited the Maynard orchards before?" I ask Arron. "No," comes the reply, and I get the feeling he really would rather be back in the kitchen. It turns out, however, that he loves growing his own produce, and that he gets enormous value from visiting suppliers like Clive. "I'm trying to turn the garden at home into a fruit, flower and veg garden," he explains. "I've got a couple of Cox and Spartan trees, some Conference and Williams pears, raspberries and rhubarb. Maybe I'm thinking back to where I lived as a child in Long Melford, surrounded by orchards. I still love the smell of apples and used to go scrumping after school all the time!"

"We grow some fantastic fruit in this part of Suffolk, especially apples, and I've always loved bringing this produce into my cooking. It's important to see production first hand so I can properly understand it and why it's so good." He has used the Maynard House apple juice in recipes for over seven years; it might appear in popular dishes such as seared scallops with slow-braised pork belly, apple and fennel salad; pheasant poached in cider with chargrilled red chicory, caramelized walnuts and wild mushrooms; or tarte tatin with cinnamon ice cream.

"I love the fact that the apples were grown and processed just a few miles from the restaurant, and the juice really is fantastic, the right combination of sweetness and acidity, and a great product to cook with as well as drink. With the pork dish *[see recipe]*, I braise the meat in the apple juice for three hours so it's melting and sweet. Any saltiness in the layered potato and black pudding terrine is offset by an apple and celeriac purée, again made with the juice," Arron says.

As we walk among the still blossom-laden trees, arranged in tidy rows along the neighbouring A134 road, Clive explains the production process, the close care that goes into ensuring every tree is healthy and productive, the insistence that fruit is picked at the right point in its maturity to ensure fullest flavour, and that it is pasteurised only gently to ensure shelf life without ruining taste.

Importantly, it is a family business too. This strikes a meaningful chord with Robert Gough whose own family celebrates 50 years of owning The Angel (and its sister hotel, The Salthouse Harbour Hotel, Ipswich) in 2015. "I have huge respect for family businesses because successful ones are inevitably run with passion and real expertise, whether it's running a hotel or growing apples or producing a fine wine. We always try and partner with supplier businesses with a similar family-centred ethos to our own."

And so the conversation moves to Italy. Arron's menu is heavily influenced by Italian cooking, and Robert has made sure that his head chef has experienced first-hand the simple, real flavours of Italian cooking. "I've learnt such a lot from trips to Tuscany and Piedmont, and doing stages at the Capezzana, Fontodi and Leonardo vineyards," says Arron. "I love the way Italian cooking doesn't tamper with ingredients but takes really good ones, like a fantastic Capezzana olive oil or perfectly-ripe tomatoes, and prepares them simply."

Robert, pouring a glass of amber-coloured vin santo, agrees. The sweet wine is honey-filled and nutty, full of Christmas spice and enough acidity to balance the sweetness. It's the product of – naturally – a family-run operation, Capezzana, based in the Tuscan hills not far from Florence.

"It really is an eye-opener visiting places like Capezzana," Robert adds. "They are so connected to the land – there's literally mud under their fingernails! – they are very small businesses making small quantities of fabulous products. We always have sensational food, always very simple, very real and using the very best of the ingredients they have to hand. You can't beat it and I am so happy that Arron is able to bring that ethos to customers here at The Angel."

Apple-braised Blythburgh free range pork belly, celeriac purée, black pudding terrine, cabbage and bacon parcels

A hearty but elegant, celebratory assiette of great Suffolk pork. We garnish the dish with arty pork crackling wafers for texture along with apple sauce. NB Make the black pudding terrine and the cabbage balls the day before serving. (serves 6)

Black pudding terrine

1kg potatoes, thinly sliced carefully on a mandolin; 150g butter, melted; 280g black pudding, thinly sliced

Pre-heat the oven to 180c. Toss the potatoes in the melted butter to coat. In a deep gratin dish, layer potatoes overlapping three thick, season and then add black pudding slices singly, just overlapping. Then repeat with triple potato layer, seasoning and more black pudding.

Repeat, ensuring your final layer is potato. Place the dish in a larger tin, half-filled with boiling water (a bain-marie) and bake for 1 hour or until tender. Remove, cool for an hour, cover with clingfilm, weigh down with a board and tins before refrigerating overnight.

Cabbage & bacon balls

1 large savoy cabbage; 150g streaky bacon, shredded; rapeseed oil; 1 large leek, finely sliced; 100g butter

Remove the cabbage's tough outer leaves and then carefully take off 6 large leaves. Blanch the latter in a large saucepan of boiling salted water until just tender. Retain simmering water and drop leaves into a bowl of cold water. Drain and reserve.

Finely shred remaining cabbage and add to the pan to blanch, then drain well in a colander.

In a heavy deep sauté pan, fry the bacon in a small glug of rapeseed oil and when browning, add the leeks and keep cooking until tender. Add the butter and blanched cabbage, before mixing and seasoning to taste. Lay the leaves separately on larger sheets of clingfilm. Split the bacon mix on each, and wrap up into a tight parcel and twist film to seal. Leave overnight in fridge to set.

Pork belly

A snug deep roasting tin is required to accommodate the vegetables, pork and covering liquor

1.3kg piece of belly, skin-on but de-boned; 1 bottle of Maynard apple juice; home-made chicken stock; 1 large onion, diced; 1 large carrot, diced; 2 celery sticks, diced; 1 leek, diced; few sprigs of thyme

Pre-heat your oven to 170c. Put the apple juice and three times the same volume of stock in a large saucepan to come to the boil and turn off. Oil and season the pork belly all over. Brown in a very hot dry frying pan until lightly seared all over. Place the vegetables in your roasting tin with the thyme, place on the pork. Pour in enough juice/stock mixture to come three-quarters up the pork. Carefully seal tin with a double sheet of foil. Bake in the oven for approx. 3 hours or until tender. Remove meat from the tin and set aside covered, somewhere warm to rest. Strain the juices into a saucepan. Skim off fat and then boil down, reducing to a good gravy consistency. Keep warm.

Celeriac purée

250g celeriac; 100ml double cream; 100g butter; 100ml milk

Storing in water as you work, peel and dice the celeriac into 3 cm rough cubes. Wash well and place in a lidded saucepan with milk, cream and butter. Simmer for 15 – 20 minutes until tender. Drain the celeriac, reserving liquid. Carefully blend in a food processor until smooth with extra liquid to achieve a creamy texture. Reheat slowly, stirring well with a spatula over a gentle heat and keep warm.

To serve

Pre-heat the oven to 190c. Cut the black pudding into portion sizes, pan-fry in hot foaming butter on both sides, place on a baking tray and bake for 8 minutes to heat through. Meanwhile simmer the cabbage balls in a saucepan of boiling water for 5 minutes. Warm six dinner plates. Carve two generous slices of pork belly on to each plate. Drain the cabbage balls and snip away the cling film before plating, along with the black pudding. Garnish with the warm purée and the gravy before serving.

Deben mussels with leeks, Suffolk pancetta and apple Juice

A really simple, easy one pot starter. Best with home-made bread such as a warm granary loaf. (serves 4)

Rapeseed oil; 100g pancetta, chopped; 1 small leek, diced; 1 medium onion, diced; 2 cloves of garlic, peeled and finely chopped; 200ml Maynard apple juice; 1 kg Deben mussels, cleaned and de-bearded; bunch of flat-leaf parsley, leaves shredded

In a heavy big lidded saucepan, over a medium-hot heat, add a glug of rapeseed oil and when heated, fry the pancetta until golden brown. Add the diced vegetables and keep cooking until softened. Pour in the apple juice, turn up to high heat and once boiling, carefully tip in the mussels, cover with a lid, shaking every now and then until all the mussels have opened.

Sample the liquor and season to taste, before sprinkling with parsley.

Early summer pasta

A lovely quick alfresco lunch dish with the first tender vegetables of the year. Dried ribbon pasta is better than fresh, perhaps tagliatelle or fettuccine. Co-ordinate the asparagus and sauce to be ready as the pasta drains.

500g dried ribbon pasta; good olive oil; 100ml double cream; 200g frozen peas, cooked and warm; 100ml olive oil; 50g parmesan, grated; 2 tablespoons mint leaves, finely chopped; 1 bunch asparagus, woody ends removed; 200g fresh baby peas; 200g broad beans, podded; 100g baby spinach leaves; basil leaves; good olive oil; 100g parmesan

Put the pasta on to cook in plenty of salted boiling water with a glug of oil, timed to the directions for al dente and start your timer. Refill the kettle for asparagus. Process the next five ingredients – cream, peas, oil, parmesan and mint – together to a purée. Warm up in a wide saucepan. After five minutes on the timer, simmer the asparagus in boiling water for 4 mins, drain and cut each spear into three pieces. As the pea purée warms up, season to taste and slowly add the other peas, broad beans and spinach. Once all the ingredients are cooked, fold in the drained pasta, drizzle with oil, rip over the basil and shave over the parmesan with a potato peeler.

Apple jelly with apple sorbet

A delicious orchard dessert with a zingy apple freshness, a superb way to finish a heavier or spicier meal. Trimoline is available online easily but a light honey will work, albeit with a different flavour. You will need small moulds or a glass bowl to set the jelly.

2 Bramley apples; 500ml Maynard apple juice; 175g trimoline syrup; 11.25g gelatine or 7 small leaves; 750ml Maynard Apple Juice; 50g sugar; raspberries for garnish

Peel, core and dice the Bramley apples and place in a pan with the 500ml of apple juice. Bring to the boil and then simmer until the apples are soft. Pulse together into a rough purée and then strain the mix through muslin over a wide colander and saucepan. Add the trimoline and stir well. Place all the ingredients into an ice-cream machine and churn until sorbet-like. Decant to a covered plastic container and freeze.

For the jelly, cover the gelatine in cold water to soften. Warm up the 750ml of apple juice and add the sugar and drained gelatine. Stir until fully dissolved. Place small amount of the juice mix into the moulds and place a raspberry or more in for garnish. Refrigerate to set, checking regularly and occasionally stirring the remainder in the pan. Once set, fill up the moulds and refrigerate.

Bury's ivy-clad grande dame

If you could corral the famous people who have spent time in The Angel Hotel in Bury St Edmunds – perhaps into the 16-cover private dining Green Room with its magnificent silicone 'dripping candle-wax' chandelier – you'd have a dinner party to remember. Angelina Jolie would rub celebrity shoulders with Russell Brand; John Major and Martin Bell might have a political chinwag; and Charles Dickens would look on from a corner, perhaps making character notes for his next blockbuster (Dickens stayed at the Angel several times and it features in his novel *The Pickwick Papers*).

The guests may well sit down to a pre-dinner drink in the Lounge where eclectic art and artefacts – there's plenty here that's quirky, beautiful or unusual – a vast open fire and squashy armchairs encourage lingering. Dinner, if not in the Green Room, would be in the Eaterie where today Arron Jackson's modern Italian-inspired menu tempts diners at lunch and dinner seven days a week. They would finish the evening in the decadent Wingspan cocktail bar in the medieval vaults where all things flight-related are celebrated: there's a table made from a plane's door, a bar fashioned from an aircraft engine, a trio of flying pugs on one wall and a showily-pink feathered wreath on another. They might try a Wingspan Cosmopolitan, a shaken or stirred combination of Belvedere Citrus vodka, Cointreau, Aperol, cranberry, lime, cranberry bitters, and egg white.

The Angel's wine list is one to savour; and you can dip into all sorts of vinous treasures here thanks to the Enomatic wine preservation system which keeps bottles in pristine condition for four weeks after opening, thereby increasing to around 20 the number of premium wines that can be offered by the glass. It has transformed wine sales, according to Robert Gough.

Family-owned Gough Hotels, which marks 50 years in the hospitality business in 2015, comprises a trio of properties: The Salthouse Harbour Hotel, created from a renovated warehouse on Ipswich marina, fun-packed Southwold Pier where there are plans for a brand-new art deco boutique hotel, and of course the ivy-clad Angel. Robert and Clare Gough's love of art and design in all forms is evident throughout the properties, dramatic pieces of modern art, sumptuous antiques and eccentric kitsch catching the eye at every turn.

The Angel Hotel
Angel Hill, Bury St Edmunds IP33 1LT
T: 01284 714000
W: www.theangel.co.uk
/TheAngelHotelBury
@AngelHotelBury

Accolades: Two AA Rosettes 2015

Cost: Carte £32 average; set L one course £9.95 / two courses £13.95 / three courses £17.95; Sunday L two course £17.95 / three courses £21.95; wine from £18.90

Open: All year

Details: Private dining; bar drinks; children's menu; afternoon tea; car parking

ARRON ON HIS...

FAVOURITE LOCAL PLACES TO SHOP?

The Suffolk Food Hall has the best of local food and a wonderful setting by the Orwell Bridge; I also love Ruse Butchers in Long Melford – guaranteed quality; and the Chapel & Swan Smokehouse in Exning for the unique flavours (wood pigeon is a favourite!).

ULTIMATE DINING DESTINATIONS, A PLACE YOU'D LOVE TO GO TO?

I'd love to explore the street food of Thailand, trying local fresh ingredients cooked right in front of you.

TAKE 5 RECIPE?

A fresh take on bruschetta: toast some focaccia, pile it high with grated courgette, spring onion, chopped parsley or basil, a squeeze of lemon juice and some parmesan. OK, that's six ingredients, but who's counting!

INSPIRING SUFFOLK VIEW?

I know a secret way to get on top of The Angel Hotel and you get the most magnificent views across to the Cathedral and Abbey Gardens, plus the varied landscape of the Bury rooftops.

CHILDHOOD AMBITION?

A chef I'm afraid! I started working in a local Indian restaurant at the age of 12 – it was the only place that would employ me at that age legally! To be honest, my mum wasn't the best cook so I wanted to learn to cook for the family. She was the first to encourage me!

IF NOT A CHEF?

I'd be an international rugby player! I've followed Leicester Rugby Club since I was very young.

CULINARY HEROES?

Fergus Henderson for his 'nose to tail' eating and fascinating use of different ingredients, I love the whole St John's ethos of simplicity and great flavours.

FAVOURITE PLACES TO EAT LOCALLY?

Of course Southwold Pier for fish and chips and a family day out, and the Salthouse on Ipswich marina for the buzz of the restaurant and great wine list; elsewhere, I love the Company Shed on Mersea Island for oysters straight from the sea, the way they are supposed to be eaten.

PERFECT DAY OFF ?

I'd go on a walk over the water meadows near Sudbury, pushing the buggy with my two young kids and our cocker spaniels, Austin and Seth, followed by lunch maybe at the Waggon and Horses in Sudbury where my brother-in-law is a chef.

FAVOURITE TIME OF THE FOODIE YEAR?

Spring and summer, I'm inspired by fresh, local ingredients – beans, wild garlic, peas, it goes back to what I've learnt in Italy about fresh flavours that don't need to be tampered with.

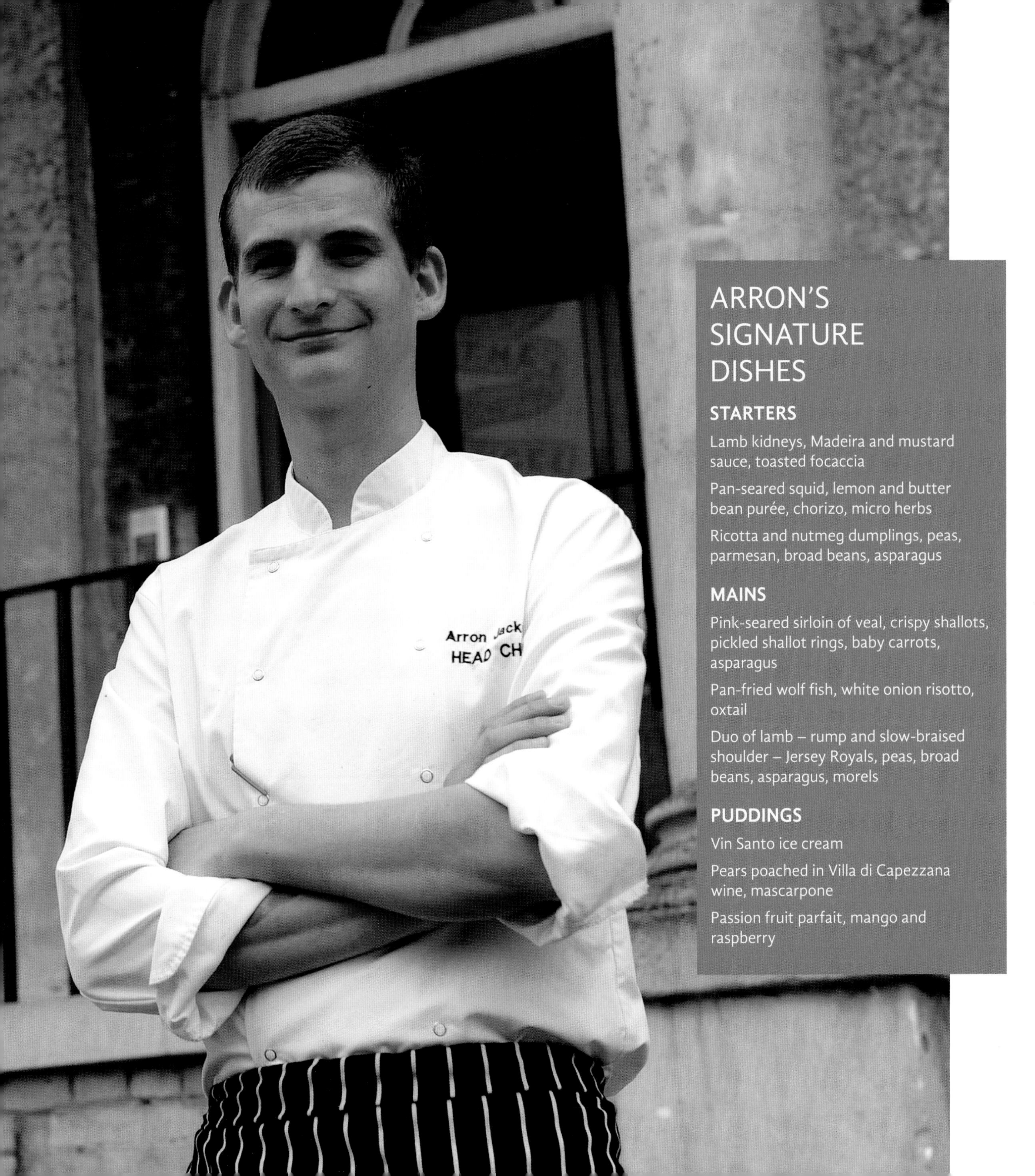

ARRON'S SIGNATURE DISHES

STARTERS

Lamb kidneys, Madeira and mustard sauce, toasted focaccia

Pan-seared squid, lemon and butter bean purée, chorizo, micro herbs

Ricotta and nutmeg dumplings, peas, parmesan, broad beans, asparagus

MAINS

Pink-seared sirloin of veal, crispy shallots, pickled shallot rings, baby carrots, asparagus

Pan-fried wolf fish, white onion risotto, oxtail

Duo of lamb – rump and slow-braised shoulder – Jersey Royals, peas, broad beans, asparagus, morels

PUDDINGS

Vin Santo ice cream

Pears poached in Villa di Capezzana wine, mascarpone

Passion fruit parfait, mango and raspberry

Comfort food: The Bell At Sax' menu rings with local artisan flavour

Jonathan Nicholson cooks Baron Bigod brie with Suffolk pride for his Saxmundham diners

L-R: Jonny Crickmore, Jonathan Nicholson.

THE BELL AT SAX' JONATHAN NICHOLSON

"Not entirely sure about getting to know my produce this well," Jonny Nicholson jokes as we nervously step down into the milking well of the cattle parlour at Fen Farm Dairy, near Bungay.

As if on cue from high above us, a beautiful red-brown and white pied Montbéliarde cow decides to share her good life, as it were. "Well at least that's a sign of a proper grass diet; smells rich enough!" Jonny quips.

He is soon in conversation with dairy farmer Jonny Crickmore, whose herd of so-called Montys provides the raw material for the unpasteurised milk and Brie-style Baron Bigod cheese that the award-winning Fen Farm Dairy sells. The cattle, a strong, long-living Alpine breed known for the creaminess of their milk, graze lush lowland on the Waveney Valley meadows, enjoying a healthy diet of grass, forage and home-grown hay. "The high protein and butterfat content of the Montbeliarde milk are ideal for what we need," says cheesemaker Jonny who runs the farm with his wife, Dulcie and the wider family. "The breed is sturdy and sure-footed too, which makes them easy to look after on our land".

He heads off with us in tow to call in the next group of cattle for milking, an event that happens twice a day, every day. This batch is down on the water meadow drinking from the brook; they wander up the hill towards the parlour, slowly responding to farmer Jonny's behest. Chef Jonny watches. "They really aren't intensively reared, are they – they look so happy grazing and chewing the cud, they're in no hurry to be milked!" As the animals approach, he enjoys the closeness to the beautiful, gentle animals: "They are so placid and friendly, so inquisitive and in such fine condition. It's really not surprising the milk and the cheese are so delicious."

Later in the cheese maturing room, cave-like and filled with rounds at different stages of the eight-week ripening period, farmer Jonny explains what makes Baron Bigod distinctive. "Much of it is down to four key things: good land, great cattle, an historic French recipe method and secret mould cultures." He won't be drawn on what the latter are, but chef Jonny is a fan: "Whatever it is, you're clearly getting it just right," he says, nibbling on an irresistibly soft slice. "It's golden, creamy, unctuous. Superb."

In his kitchen at The Bell at Sax', Jonny incorporates Baron Bigod into his menus at any opportunity. "I love it perfectly ripe and ready, runny almost, and also when it is slightly immature, with that acidic chalky edge. It's a very different cheese when it's young. It's great on a cheeseboard of course (I serve it with other local cheeses and some sultana-walnut crostini, apple, celery and home-made chutney), but I might also grill it on a bruschetta or put it with a spiced cranberry relish in crisp-fried filo. It's incredibly versatile." Other favourite uses are to glaze a risotto with the cheese, brown it under a grill to top a classic French onion soup, or melt it over beans on toast for his hungry children.

"It is so good having such a superb local cheese like Baron Bigod on offer," he says, "with it's wonderful farmyardy, almost mushroomy flavour that I love and it creates a talking point with customers. There's something very special about an ingredient made so locally and by a small family business, and as a chef I think it's right to champion ingredients like this whenever possible."

The small family business in question at Fen Farm started selling milk raw, unpasteurised and unprocessed, fuelled by a belief that the best product comes from the happiest animals. "There's no question that the best milk comes from cows who are unstressed and live a peaceful, contented, grass-fed life," says Jonny Crickmore. "Our cows aren't under pressure to produce certain amounts of milk; they live and produce as nature intended."

From raw milk the Crickmore family expanded into cheesemaking – a natural step – and the creation of Baron Bigod, the UK's only traditional farmhouse brie-style cheese made by the farmer. It was named after the Norman family, which owned the medieval stronghold of now-ruined Bungay Castle and, once upon a time, were the landowners of Fen Farm. Soon to come to market, Jonny says, will be their own dairy butter, the next stage of their business development.

Fen Farm sells Baron Bigod to chefs like Jonny, but also to specialist delicatessens and farmshops – and at their own farmgate cow-print shed where the Crickmores have installed an honesty box and ingenious vending machine to sell the cheese and milk; the latter dispensed to order into bottles. "The storage vat never lasts more than 48 hours at any time, so it really is milk fresh from the farm," says Jonny.

"When you think that commercial milk is pasteurised, homogenised, standardised, processed, sanitised, not to mention transported for miles before getting to the shop shelf, it's not surprising that our milk tastes different," he adds. "It hasn't been through any of those processes at all. Lots of customers are taken aback by the taste. Maybe it's back to milk as they remember it. Lots of people love seeing the line of cream that's risen to the top too. We're a forward-thinking family business, but there's a lot of nostalgia in what we make!"

Roast East Coast cod with tartiflette of Suffolk smoked bacon and Baron Bigod brie

The whole seafood and smoked bacon combo with creamy potatoes works so well. We serve this with wilted seasonal greens such as kale and some dressed leaves such as pea shoots for freshness and texture (serves 4)

Tartiflette

This Alpine potato gratin is a classic, best served warm, not hot. It is flexible to the time of year or occasion and you can mix and match the ingredients to what is in the fridge, even using leftovers from the Sunday lunch. NB The brie skin is lovely in the final dish so I suggest leaving it on before cubing. And for prettiness, you can use a gratin dish to bake it in, rather than the frying pan. Leftovers do reheat well.

800g cleaned unpeeled potatoes, in 2cm rough chunks; rapeseed oil; 2 tbsp unsalted butter; 200g smoked streaky bacon lardons; 1 medium onion, peeled, halved and finely sliced; 1 - 2 cloves raw garlic, peeled and finely chopped or flesh from a slow roasted bulb; few sprigs thyme; two bay leaves; 200g Baron Bigod brie in thumb-width cubes; 1 - 2 tsp good Dijon-style mustard; 250ml good Marybelle double cream

Pre-heat the oven to 175c fan or equivalent. Put the potatoes on to simmer, covered in salted water. Cook until just starting to go tender, approx. 10 – 15 minutes. Meanwhile put a large ovenproof sauté pan over a high heat, add a splash of oil and the butter, when bubbling, stir fry the bacon for a minute or two. Then add the onions, stirring until they lightly brown on the edges. Stir in the garlic, the thyme and bay leaves. Cook for a couple more minutes over a low heat. Set aside to keep warm.

Drain potatoes well and put back into their empty pan on the hob, heat turned off, uncovered to dry for a few minutes. Add potatoes to the bacon pan and, stir around. Nestle in the cheese. Whisk up the mustard, cream, a little salt and generous pepper and pour over the pan contents. Bake for 25 – 30 minutes or until golden and bubbling.

Roast cod

Local fish from one of the in-shore dayboats such as at Felixstowe, Aldeburgh and Southwold is unbeatable.

4 x thick cod steak portions, skin-on; rapeseed oil; unsalted butter

Place a heavy frying pan on a high heat. Add a small glug of oil and a good knob of butter. Dry and season your fish.

Once bubbling, place the fish skin-side down in the pan and leave for 2 minutes. Gently check to see if it is golden, if so, turn over or give another minute. When sufficiently browned, turn over and cook for 2 – 3 minutes on the flesh side. Once the fish flakes and looks opaque throughout, it is cooked.

Tarragon cider cream sauce

A simple flavoursome reduction adds some depth of flavour.

150ml dry Aspall cyder; 150ml good fish or chicken stock; 150ml Marybelle double cream; 1 - 2 tsp Dijon-style mustard; good pinch chopped tarragon leaves

In a wide heavy saucepan on a high heat, reduce the cyder and stock by half. Add the cream and reduce again until a rich thick sauce texture. Flavour with mustard and seasoning to taste. Take off heat and whisk through tarragon.

To serve

Plate up cod onto warm dinner plates, pour some sauce around, along with chosen vegetables and leaves for garnishes. Best to have tartiflette in the pan on the side to feast on communally.

Crisp salt and pepper sprats with harissa mayonnaise

A simple fishy starter. Allow 125g of sprats per person, approx. 12-16. Garnish with lemon wedges, more smoked paprika and flat-leaf parsley sprigs. (serves 4 generously)

Good mayonnaise; smoked paprika; lemon halves for juicing; harissa paste

Lightly blend four good spoonfuls of mayonnaise with seasoning, smoked paprika and lemon juice. Taste and adjust before whisking in harissa bit-by-bit, sampling as you go until fairly piquant.

Rapeseed oil for deep frying; 100g of plain flour; 50g polenta flour; 1 tsp fine sea salt, black pepper, cayenne pepper, smoked paprika, sumac, garlic powder; sprats; Marybelle milk

Heat up your deep fat fryer with oil to 180c temperature, basket lowered. Mix flours and spices together in a large bowl. Soak the sprats with milk in a container and leave for a minute or two. Drain well and drop into the flour mix, toss the fish to cover fully, lift out and shake off excess. Carefully drop into the hot oil for around two minutes or until crisp and floating, lift basket and drain. Remove onto kitchen paper, dab and then serve, sprinkled with sea salt.

Braised pork faggots

These form part of a trio we do of fabulous Blythburgh free range pork. They do eat well on their own with mashed potatoes and seasonal veggies. We make the dry forcemeat mix but Paxo is good! These reheat well as left-overs. (serves 8)

Rapeseed oil; 170g pack sage & onion stuffing mix; 500g pork shoulder, diced; 300g fresh pigs liver, trimmed; half tsp ground mace; 1 tbsp sunflower oil; 2 onions, thinly sliced; 2 tsp sugar; 1 tbsp red wine vinegar; 3 tbsp plain flour; 850ml beef stock, warm; handful flat leaf parsley leaves, shredded

Pre-heat oven to 160c. Lightly oil a very large roasting tin. Make up the stuffing with 500ml boiling water. Pulse the pork and then the liver in a food processor until finely chopped. Add to the stuffing with the mace, salt and plenty of black pepper. Stir well. Shape the mixture (it will be very soft) into 24 large faggots and put in the prepared tin.

In a hot frying pan, sauté the onions with a little oil until starting to brown. Add the sugar and stir often, until well-caramelised. Add vinegar and stir. Mix the flour with two tbsp of water. Pour the stock into the onions, then whisk in the flour paste, stirring until smooth and thick. Pour into the faggots tin, cover with foil and bake for 1 hr until cooked. Serve sprinkled with parsley.

Easy blueberry & orange cheesecake

A quick and easy pudding to make in advance. We garnish this with mint leaves, candied orange zest and blueberry coulis (serves 4+)

3 tbsp good marmalade; 3 small punnets of blueberries; 300g good cream cheese; 300ml Marybelle double cream, in soft peaks; 5 tbsp icing sugar (or more to taste); 50ml Cointreau; 1 lemon, juiced; 6 digestive biscuits; 50g unsalted butter

Melt the marmalade in a saucepan and stir in 2 punnets of blueberries, stir over a medium heat for a minute or so until the berries pop, then cool and refrigerate.

Fold the cream cheese, soft-peaked cream, icing sugar, Cointreau, remaining blueberries and lemon juice together. Decant to a plastic container, cover and chill to firm up for 4 hours.

Crush biscuits and melt butter before mixing into a crumble mixture.

To serve, place circle of crumble on a plate, and with a dry hot large kitchen spoon, scoop out a neat quenelle and place on the crumbs, spooning over the blueberry compote. Garnish and serve.

Striking accord in Saxmundham

A laid-back charming restaurant-with-rooms, The Bell At Sax' stands tall on the High Street of this pretty market town, close to RSPB Minsmere and roughly halfway between the cosmopolitan delights of Southwold and Aldeburgh.

The grand façade belies the warmth and relaxation of this welcoming bolthole within and The Bell Hotel paintwork still remains, but chef-proprietor Jonny Nicholson is swift to point out "We are very much not a hotel, we may have comfortable, lovely bedrooms, a stylish bar and two intimate restaurants, and of course a friendly, helpful team around me, but it is all about being far more relaxed and less pretentious than a hotel."

That perhaps belies the quality of the cooking and the passion which goes into it; Jonny, once senior sous chef for Marco Pierre White in his younger days, has owned and run a number of very successful *Good Food Guide*-listed hotel-restaurants and other food businesses before. It is clearly working here in Saxmundham, Jonny hit the ground running at the end of 2013, re-opening it within a week and hasn't looked back; it's now a thriving business for locals and regular diners as well as the many visitors here to enjoy the Heritage Coast delights.

"What we offer is simple, the kind of food I like to eat, hearty but elegant, all about great local seasonal ingredients with a bit of global interest thrown in, home-made bread and ample portions; we never want anyone going home hungry, and above all, we keep it good value."

The ten bedrooms upstairs make a lovely bolthole for a few nights' precious 'R & R'.

The Bell At Sax'
31 High St, Saxmundham IP17 1AF
T: 01728 602331
W: www.thebellatsax.co.uk
@thebellatsax

Cost: Carte £24 average; set menu two courses £10 / three courses £13.50; pot luck main course and drink offer, Sun dinner and Mon lunch & dinner £10; wine from £15.95

Open: 8am-11pm; food served 12-2.30pm & 6-9.30pm (restricted Sun evening and all day Mon)

Details: Bar drinks; two dining rooms; ten bedrooms; breakfast; private dining at The Bell and in Market Hall next door; children welcome

JONATHAN ON HIS...

FOODIE NOSTALGIA?

Marmite, on toast, eaten it since I was knee high, especially as soldiers into dippy eggs; fish & chips growing up in lovely Hunny (Hunstanton in North Norfolk).

LAST SUPPER?

On the menu – eggs Benedict with smoked salmon and crusty sourdough; aged Red Poll sirloin steak, Café de Paris butter, dripping chips, all the trimmings; Roquefort, apple and oatcakes with lots of port; toffee apple bread & butter pudding, whisky custard.

CULINARY HEROES?

Delia Smith, she made it so accessible and understandable; Jean-Christophe Novelli, a great take on French cuisine; Raymond Blanc, a true culinary hero, taught all the greats.

FAVOURITE LOCAL PLACES TO EAT?

I tend to stay local so perhaps Pinneys of Orford for simple delicious oysters and smoked fish platter at the Oysterage; or might head up to The Crown & Castle just off the square; or back to Southwold where I used to live, probably fish and chips in Blackshore harbour, the best-fed seagulls.

UNFULFILLED DREAM JOB?

Food producer, probably a goat farmer making dairy products and cheeses, and charcuterie.

TOOLS OF THE TRADE?

A dishwasher, human or machine; decent steel for sharp knives, essential; heavy chopping boards, wood is best at home; Thick-bottomed saucepans.

MIDNIGHT FEAST?

After work, lots of my favourite East Anglian cheeses, home-made relish or Branston's finest, forget the biscuits! Or a bowlful of creamy mussels or a Bell burger, the boys do cook a good one; and I will admit to a proper chicken kebab from Pete the Greek's take-away Zorba's up the street, he also uses Clarke's of Bramfield butchers, so good stuff.

SOCIAL MEDIA?

We tweet @thebellatsax and I follow the trendy London restaurants, whoever is doing good stuff, keep up with what is happening in the food world.

BEST DISHES EVER EATEN?

Marco's chicken liver and foie gras parfait at Harveys, it was perfect; oysters in San Fran' off the barbecue in a seaside seafood shack, somewhere off the beaten track; Mark Jordan's white chocolate mousse when we worked together at Congham Hall (now at the Atlantic on Jersey).

FOODIE DISCOVERIES?

Our monthly lunch club on a different cuisine theme lets me research and develop fun menus. I love playing with new authentic ingredients and dish styles; just made spicy rich Massaman paste, huge list of amazing layered flavours, ready for a Thai peanut curry.

ULTIMATE DINING DESTINATIONS?

Southwold Pier, the Boardwalk restaurant, one of the best locations ever; around Cannes in the south of France, all those lovely beach seafood restaurants; Phuket and the smaller islands off Thailand, the amazing fish curries.

LUCKY DAY OFF?

On Southwold beach, down towards the dunes, fun for the kids, swimming, burying me in the sand, boogie boarding in the waves.

JONATHAN'S SIGNATURE DISHES

STARTERS

East Coast fish bouillabaisse with rouille and croûtons

Fresh peeled prawn cocktail with Bloody Mary dressing and crunchy gem lettuce

Baked Baron Bigod brie and cranberry bruschetta, with ruby grapefruit, fennel, red onion & pistachio salad

MAINS

Crispy confit lamb shoulder, champ potato, savoy cabbage, bacon and rosemary gravy

Char-grilled steak burger, smoked Shipcord, bacon, ciabatta bun with fries, 'slaw and chipotle relish

Roast sea bass fillet with Deben mussel, pea and bacon chowder

PUDDINGS

Double chocolate brownie, praline chocolate mousse

Vanilla pannacotta with raspberry compôte and lemon shortbread

Eton Mess strawberry ice cream sundae with meringues and marshmallows

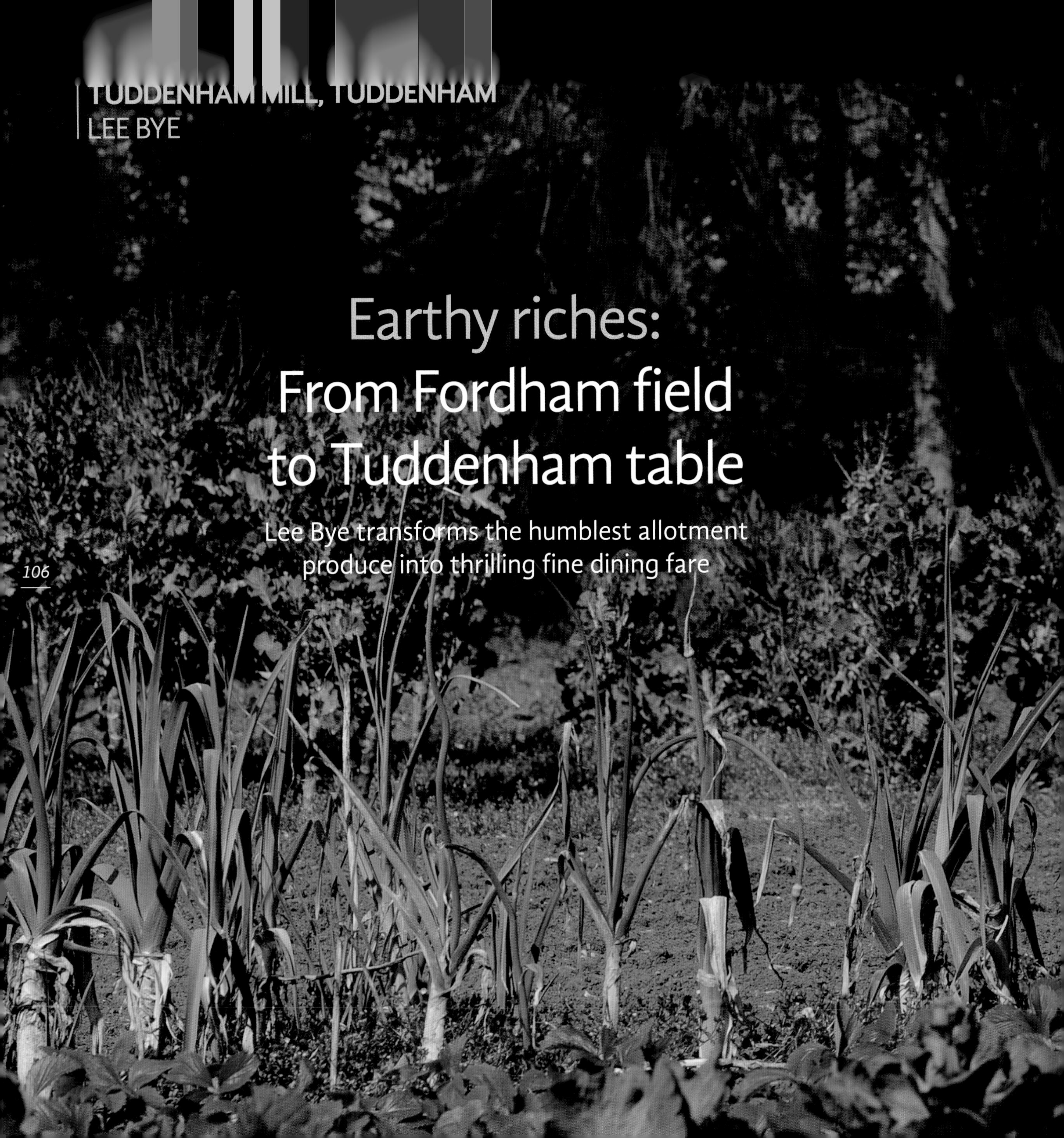

Earthy riches: From Fordham field to Tuddenham table

Lee Bye transforms the humblest allotment produce into thrilling fine dining fare

L - R: Rob Doe, Lee Bye.

"Got any leeks, Granddad?"
"Might do," comes the slightly gruff reply.
"What about some of that white sprouting broccoli?"

"You've had the last of that; it's bolted, I dug it up." Lee eyes a patch of strawberries, coming promisingly into leaf. "You can't have all them, you'll have to share with the others," his granddad warns, wagging a mock-stern finger. By 'others', Rob Doe means Lee's siblings, parents, his cousins and probably an aunt or uncle or two. Rob's produce is in demand.

We are at a bungalow in Fordham, a few miles from Tuddenham Mill. From the front it looks just like the other neat, well-tended omes in the row with pots tumbling with flowers and the odd stone ornament. Round the back is a different story. In between scattered ride-ons used by visiting grandchildren, an apparently still-functioning tractor, a pond with tinkling water, a troop of Pekins and Japanese bantams busily pecking, the washing line and a few garden seats, and sheltered from the whipping Fenland winds by tall pines, is Rob Doe's allotment.

"I put 'Rob Doe broccoli' or 'Rob Doe leeks' on the menu and people think it's some fancy supplier – but it's my Granddad!" says Lee. "I love having that connection. I drop in several times a week to see what he's got." Lee, still on a high after winning the 2015 *East Anglian Daily Times* Suffolk Chef of the year title, works the produce into daily-changing menus, perhaps including it as a red lentil dhal with charred Rob Doe leeks, or Goosnargh duck, Rob Doe's white broccoli, glazed beets, almonds, smoked garlic. Bashed berries, frozen from last year's crop and not pretty enough for Eton Mess, are the perfect ingredient for the hotel's homemade breakfast jam, and the kitchen team enjoys the hens' eggs most mornings for what Lee describes as a "proper breakfast, with bacon and HP sauce".

"I take what Granddad has grown – onions, spuds, carrots, leeks, hens' eggs – and what he can spare," says Lee. "I don't ask him to grow particular stuff. That would spoil the relationship, and this way I feel I can really celebrate the ingredient. I've loved using the white sprouting broccoli; it has a slightly different taste from the purple, less cabbagey, more delicate."

We walk round the allotment. There are raspberry canes coming into leaf, bamboo structures where broad beans and peas will soon scramble, and tiny carrot seedlings protected from scratching hens and hungry rabbits under a plastic poly-tunnel. Rob plunges a fork into the soil surrounding some of the last of the Musselburgh leeks, shakes the loose earth from the roots and hands Lee an armful. "There you go, that should do." This fits well with Lee's style of cooking, and his family-centred personality (most of his immediate family live nearby and he appears to be close to them all). "Granddad's allotment has come to mean a lot to me in recent years. Even as a young chef I didn't really appreciate it, but now every time I come here, it juices me up. I understand how privileged I am to have these ingredients available, and I want that to come through in my food. We have a fine dining menu but that doesn't mean ingredients shouldn't be real, earthy."

We are back at the Tuddenham Mill kitchen where Lee is preparing a pile of the white broccoli, trimming quickly, setting the leaves aside to blanch them and carefully leaving the heads, like tiny tight cauliflowers, intact. He talks bent over the work surface, focusing closely on the delicate stems, the last of the crop, picked the previous day. "When Granddad saw me pick off the leaves so carefully he said 'what the bloody hell do you do that for, who wants to eat the leaves?'" Lee laughs. "He must think I'm mad! But when produce is as good as this it deserves to be looked after. To me, these broccoli

"I put 'Rob Doe broccoli' or 'Rob Doe leeks' on the menu and people think it's some fancy supplier – but it's my granddad!"

stems are just as important as the piece of lamb or beef they will accompany, so they get the same care."

You get the impression chatting with Lee that this really does mean a lot. "I love it when I drop in at Granddad's and there's a carrier bag on the kitchen table for me! I have a similar relationship with Tuddenham Nurseries over the road. I'll text an order for asparagus to Gary [Tilbrooke] the night before, he'll cut them first thing, and it's on the set lunch that day." The spears might appear as a starter of Tilbrooke's asparagus, pecorino, watercress, escabeche oil or on the tasting menu with pheasant egg and dill oil.

Lee's kitchen life began at the local pub. "I started on pot-wash, enjoyed it, and went to study at Cambridge College." He worked a t Tuddenham Mill under Gordon McNeill, an important influence on Lee, then spent two years as Paul Foster's sous chef. After brief stints elsewhere, he returned to the Mill as head chef in February 2014. "Following Paul was not easy. So I decided to scrape it all back and start again with my food. Anyway, foraging isn't my thing."

So what is your thing, I wonder? "I'm essentially a 'meat and two veg' chef. I'm a country Suffolk boy. Home cooking is my inspiration. I love nostalgia, hearty flavours, but using modern techniques if that improves a dish. I love taking beautiful carrots, potatoes, simple ingredients, and making them into something guests at a boutique hotel restaurant want to eat."

"Chefs talk about having 'soft hands' and for me that is crucial. I try not to manipulate food: why mess around with ingredients that are already perfect?"

Local wild mallard duck with Rob Doe's white broccoli, Elveden beets, wilted kale and almonds

I use a locally shot mallard for my recipe but any good quality duck breast such as Gressingham will work in this recipe. Cooking on the crown keeps it moist. Cook the garnishes whilst the duck is underway. (serves 4)

300ml strong Aspall cyder; 150ml good chicken stock; 2 crowns of mallard breasts, skin-on and trimmed; rapeseed oil; 4 cooked beetroot, cut into quarters; local honey for glazing; 12 white broccoli or other calabrese florets; curly kale; knob butter; toasted flaked almonds to serve

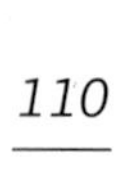

Reduce the cyder (reserve one tablespoon) by half to concentrate the flavour then add the stock. Boil to reduce down to a syrupy consistency, add in reserved cyder.

Pre-heat the oven to 180c equivalent.

Heat up a frying pan with a glug of oil over a high setting. Season the crowns all over and brown on all sides using tongs. Place on a baking sheet standing up and bake for around 8 minutes. Leave to rest somewhere warm for 5 – 10 minutes before carving.

Meanwhile place the beetroots in a small saucepan with a little water, cover and bring to a simmer. Turn off and leave for a few minutes. Drain well and glaze with a little honey.

And at the same time, simmer the broccoli florets in salted water until the stems are tender, approx. 5 minutes. Drain and keep warm.

Cook the kale in a knob of butter, seasoning and a splash of water in a very hot pan. Stir up with tongs until it wilts down after a few minutes. Drain and keep warm.

Carve the duck onto four hot plates, garnish with the beets, kale and broccoli, adding almonds for texture. Sauce each plate lightly.

Assington Farm strawberries, goat's milk granita, basil and Giffords Hall limoncello fizz

This is a great dish if you are entertaining friends and fantastic on a hot English summer's day.

500ml full fat goat's milk; 100g caster sugar; local strawberries; fresh basil leaves; chilled Giffords Hall limoncello liqueur and sparkling wine

Mix the goat's milk and caster sugar in a suacepan. Warm and fully melt whilst stirring, then pour into a shallow container. Cool and freeze down to a solid. Fork as it starts to set before freezing further. Fork again when almost completely set.

To serve, de-hull the strawberries and cut into quarters or eighths depending on size. Lay out in soup plates, scatter over torn basil leaves. Fork milk granita and scrape generously over the strawberries.

Fill chilled champagne flutes a third-full with limoncello and top with fizz slowly.

Serve together.

Suffolk pig's head terrine

Enjoy with asparagus, avocado mayonnaise and crackling wafers.

500g caster sugar; 1 garlic bulb in cloves; small handful of thyme sprigs; 1 pig's head, cleaned and singed; wholegrain mustard

In a snug heavy saucepan to fit the head, caramelise caster sugar over a medium heat to an amber brown with garlic and thyme. Carefully add warm water. Place head in and top up to just cover. Put lid on and bring to a rapid boil, skim and hold at a simmer for 3 - 4 hours.

At this point, meat should fall off the bone. Remove and allow to cool. When handle-able, remove inedible parts and season to taste with salt, pepper and wholegrain mustard. Clingfilm a deep baking tray, press the pork into it and refrigerate overnight.

To serve, cut the terrine thickly, place onto chilled plates and garnish with your chosen salad ingredients.

Meadowsweet pannacotta, English raspberries, bitter chocolate

I use meadowsweet in this recipe, a wild summer flower. Vanilla extract or tonka beans achieve a similar flavour. Firstly the pannacotta will need to be prepared and poured in small oiled moulds. I have simplified the recipe to make the garnishing easier.

250ml semi-skimmed milk; 250ml double cream; 25g caster sugar; 10g dried meadowsweet (or 1 vanilla pod, scraped or 2 tonka beans, finely grated); 3 gelatine leaves, soaked in cold water; fresh raspberries; dark chocolate to grate

Bring milk, cream, sugar and meadowsweet (or alternative) to a light simmer, whilst stirring constantly. Once simmering, remove and whisk in the drained gelatine. Pass through a sieve, cool and pour into moulds. Leave to set in the fridge.

To serve, turn out and garnish with raspberries and finely grated dark chocolate.

Where there's a Mill...

Tuddenham Mill is one of those picture-perfect settings that visitors travel to England to see. It's got the millpond, a towering chimney, the swans, at times with cygnets in tow, the dipping weeping willow, magical reflections; it's got the ancient cast-iron waterwheel – there's apparently been a flour mill on this site since the 11th century – flower-filled meadows and riverside walks.

Look beyond the brick and (freshly-painted) white weatherboard exterior of this converted 18th century building, and there's a smartly-contemporary interior. Muted tones, squashy sofas and plenty of wood and glass create the stylish but relaxed atmosphere – the website calls it 'rustic chic' – that pervades the property.

The original waterwheel is the focal point of the ground floor bar, its mechanism preserved behind glass and illuminated colourfully in the evening. This is a spacious area to enjoy pre-dinner drinks, a light lunch, or Lee's early-evening dinner option.

Upstairs, in the main dining room, tables are candlelit in the evening (the best overlook the dreamy water) and are a sleek backdrop for Lee's adventurous but hearty, Suffolk-rooted, cooking.

Overnight options are luxurious. Double-ended baths in the Loft and Mill rooms can, we are told, fit three; there's a Bose sound system in every room, an Apple tv, Missoni dressing gowns, and enough fluffy pillows on the six-foot beds to soothe even the tenderest of heads. For extra peace and quiet, the Water Meadow rooms might fit the bill, set a few paces from the main building and with their own terrace.

Tuddenham Mill is the glamorous poster-property of Agellus Hotels, the East Anglian-based group that also comprises two food-led pubs: the Westleton Crown and the Ship at Dunwich.

Tuddenham Mill
High Street, Tuddenham,
nr Newmarket IP28 6SQ
T: 01638 713552
W: www.tuddenhammill.co.uk
/tuddenhammill
@Tuddenham_Mill

Accolades: Two AA Rosettes 2015; *Waitrose Good Food Guide* 2015 score 5 and Editor's Best Set Lunch 2015

Cost: Carte £36 average; tasting menu £49.50; early evening D £19.50; set L £15.50 - £19.50; Sunday L £19.50 - £24.50; wine from £19.95

Open: All year, all week L 12-2.15pm; D 6.30-9.15pm; early D (not Sat) 6.30-7.30pm

Details: Private dining; afternoon tea; children's menu; bar drinks; terrace; car parking

LEE ON HIS...

YOUR SECRET MIDNIGHT FEAST OR GUILTY SNACK?

To be honest, I'm normally sick of the sight of food at the end of the day and I go to the gym most nights after service, so I'll have something quick like houmous or muesli.

YOUR LAST SUPPER?

I'm not cooking anything! I'm in Watson's Bay, Australia, eating lots of fresh cold shellfish, sinking lots of VBs [Victoria Bitters] and smoking Havanas. I'll be with partner Holly, my children Evelyn and Leo plus Winston, the dog; Sir Alex Ferguson, the Gallagher brothers and Ricky Hatton will be there too – that's a good knees-up!

WELL-THUMBED COOKBOOKS?

Kitchen Confidential, by Anthony Bourdain; and *The Perfectionist* by Bernard Loiseau.

FAVOURITE LOCAL PLACES FOR FOODIE SHOPPING

La Hogue in Chippenham is a brilliant farm shop, and there's great coffee at the Two Magpies bakery in Southwold.

PERFECT DAY OFF?

I'll be somewhere quiet, maybe Santon Downham.

BEST DISHES EVER EATEN?

Mackerel, white artichoke, cresses, a starter by Brett Graham at the Ledbury. Best main ever is my nana's midweek roast dinner, and to finish it would be white chocolate, celery, cobnuts by Simon Rogan at L'Enclume.

COOK'S CHEATS AND CHEF'S TIPS?

Cook fresh! It's crucial!

FAVOURITE COOKING EQUIPMENT?

I love my Vita-Prep blender and my Shun knives.

ULTIMATE DINING DESTINATION?

I'd love to go to The Three Chimneys on the Isle of Skye

FAVOURITE PLACES TO EAT LOCALLY

My mum's for a crumble, Pea Porridge in Bury St Edmunds for Justin's tarte tatin, and the Thai Street Café in Newmarket because they do amazing duck noodles. I always get a good belly full at these places!

CULINARY HEROES?

Gordon McNeill, my first head chef, who taught me at a young age how to understand my palate, and Marco Pierre White. I never got to work in his kitchens or try his menu but I am always inspired by his philosophies and approach to ingredients.

LEE'S SIGNATURE DISHES

STARTERS

Beef short rib, hazelnuts, sour onions, soy

Watermelon, feta, celery, pumpkin seeds

Speckled sea trout, fried pheasant egg, monks beard, dill oil

MAINS

Angus beef bavette, English onion, Madeira, bone marrow

Stone bass, Tilbrookes' asparagus, brown shrimps, coastal herbs

Lamb rump and shoulder, burnt aubergine, ricotta, red kale, St Peter's ale

PUDDINGS

Croissant pudding, gooseberries, toffee, Earl Grey ice cream

Bitter chocolate tart, basil ice cream, peanuts

Baked Denham pear, lemon curd, muscovado syrup, oats

BUXHALL COACH HOUSE, STOWMARKET
HONOR TOWNSEND

For the love of steak: Seasoned simply, rested well

Honor Townsend pours heart and soul into her menu that bursts with real Italian flavours – and local Red Poll meat

L - R: Roger Carter, Honor Townsend, Mark Hammond.

BUXHALL COACH HOUSE HONOR TOWNSEND

Sometimes, when you ask a chef a simple foodie question, you get more than you bargained for; you get an answer packed with enough flavour, passion and memory to open a deliciously rich story all by itself.

"So what would be your final meal?"

"Bistecca fiorentina, cooked on an open fire outside, in Italy, with a salad correctly dressed with olive oil and red wine vinegar on the side. Oysters, with a dash of Tabasco and some diced shallots, and Champagne; maybe bruschetta with fresh tomatoes, garlic, some first-pressing olive oil."

"Honor, what about your tris di pasta – tagliatelle with 'nonna's' ragù, penne all'arrabbiata, strangozzi al tartufo..."

"Fresh pecorino cheese with just-podded fava beans... Vin santo with biscotti alle mandorle."

I'm with Honor and Sarah Townsend, sitting round a scrubbed pine table at the Buxhall Coach House, Honor's Italian restaurant near Stowmarket. At times, mother and daughter talk over each other or finish each other's sentences, clearly sharing an obsessive love for and deep understanding of Italian food.

It being just after 11am, Sarah insists on a glass of prosecco. Honor disappears, returning with a plate of peppery finocchiona and wild boar salami, and what she mock-grandly describes as 'fat on toast' – crisp fingers of ciabatta with sweet-salt, syrupy, melting lardo di colonata with a sprinkle of fennel flowers.

Even though her menu is Italian through and through, Honor champions local beef with carnivorous gusto. "I've always loved a good steak," she says, "especially a bistecca fiorentina." These vast steaks, a good four inches deep and huge (Sarah uses her hands to indicate the size as if boasting about a fish she'd caught), are ideally grilled on an open fire, seared well on the outside, rare in the middle, drizzled with oil, seasoned and, vitally, rested well enough for the juices to relax back evenly into the meat so that blood does not run onto the plate.

To be truly authentic, the beef should be from a Chianina bullock, a big white beast typical of Tuscany, but here in Suffolk, Honor chooses Red Poll. She buys the meat of local farmer Roger Carter through M&M Butchers in Stowupland. "I stipulate Roger's meat as it's always tender and flavoursome and the marbling is wonderful. I love the fact that it was reared so locally too." Mark Hammond at M&M, it goes without saying, makes sure Honor gets what she wants.

At Roger's farm we see the fields where cattle graze, sheltering on this wet day under trees. "My great grandfather had a herd of milking Red Polls," Roger explains, "but when Friesians came in we moved out of dairy. Now we have a breeding herd of 25 Red Poll." Animals are reared slowly on grass and meat is hung for 28 days.

"For me, steak is the test of a restaurant," says Honor. "I'm very picky. Often it's either too thin or not rested or overlooked." Sarah interjects: "It's because it hasn't been made with love or respected and understood properly."

Honor's favoured cut for the restaurant is a ribeye for two, a deep 20oz steak served with tiny potatoes sautéed with garlic and rosemary or sautéed spinach.

If she's not pouring culinary care into a steak, Honor could well be making her signature oven-baked pasta dishes, maybe traditionally with a ragù, or tomato and basil, or truffle and porcini mushrooms. "My menu would be naked without a good al forno dish! And preparing pasta always makes me happy." She learnt the skill from her Italian mother-in-law and neighbours, and she stubbornly sticks to the authentic ragù ingredients. "I use minced pork alongside the beef to give depth of flavour and a soft texture, then what Italians call 'odori' – carrot, celery and onion – some tomato passata, red wine, bay leaves, nutmeg, salt and pepper. I let it tremble on top of the Aga for hours. It's always better the next day. Oh, and there's no garlic, no oregano, no bacon, no mushrooms!"

She almost thumps the table as she dictates the recipe. There's a lively directness about her, her hands are those of someone that uses them all the time, her forearms have a chef's trademark scratches and burns. She's honest, a bit of a rebel and, I suggest, not much of a diplomat. "That's why I'm a chef!" she laughs.

She wasn't born to the job, however. "I wanted to have children and get married! I loved cooking and I knew university wasn't for me, so my mother suggested Prue Leith." A one-year course under her belt, Honor worked in various restaurants and travelled before landing a job at Simon Hopkinson's London restaurant, Bibendum.

"His cooking isn't pretentious, it's all about flavour and ingredients, and I loved that. I was terrified of him, but adored him at the same time. It was a tough kitchen. I remember picking over trays and trays of crab meat in search of pieces of shell, and going through vats of sweetbreads. Philip Howard [chef patron of the two Michelin starred The Square] was there then too; he was so supportive when I came back from Italy. Philip and Simon are my touchstones."

Honor moved from her native Suffolk to Italy in 1991, first to study old master drawing techniques in Florence, then to cook at her mother's first boutique hotel near Cortona. There, she immersed herself in the rich local gastronomy and married an Italian with whom she had two daughters.

The end of the marriage coincided with Sarah opening her magnificent Palazzo Terranova hotel in Umbria after a long renovation. Honor ran the kitchen there until the Townsends sold the property in 2006 and returned to the family's rambling Suffolk home, Buxhall Vale, where Honor opened her current restaurant (with her mother the consummate host) at the beginning of 2012.

There's more change in the offing now and Honor's thoughts are turning to a fresh challenge. "I'd love to cook on an open fire, maybe have a trattoria," she muses, thoughtful. "I'd love to put an 'arrosto misto' [a mix of roast meats, often poultry, game and sausages, served together] on the menu – of course using Roger's Red Poll – but I'm not sure how Suffolk would take it!" I urge her to try it and see.

Grilled ribeye of Suffolk Red Poll beef

Less is more with very good heritage beef. In the style of her Italian-influenced cooking, Honor's cuisine is all about showcasing delicious simple ingredients at their best; her masterclass in steak cookery underlines this perfectly.

Find a helpful independent butcher who works with local farmers and look for matured dark red flesh, well-marbled for succulence and creamy-yellow surface fat from grazing pasture.

Cooking over a wood or charcoal-fired grill adds a unique flavour to the cooked meat but a good solid griddle pan and a very hot gas hob will deliver great results too.

Take the beef out of the fridge 30 minutes before cooking to allow it to reach room temperature.

Best eaten on its own with just some home-made crusty bread to mop up the juices, and of course a good glass or two of red wine!

(serves 2 generously)

To serve

1 x 20oz ribeye of beef;
the best extra virgin olive oil you can find, preferably Italian

Heat up your grill bars or griddle pan until very hot. Warm up your dinner plates and a serving dish.

Rub the beef all over with a very little olive oil. When the griddle is smoking hot, lay on the beef and leave it, without touching, for about 3 minutes. Lift one corner to see if the beef is well-coloured. If not, leave it for another minute. Next turn the ribeye over and sprinkle liberally with salt. Leave the beef to similarly caramelise well on the reverse for 3 – 4 minutes. Turn it over again but rotate the meat 90 degrees before placing on the grill again. Sprinkle the other side with salt and leave for 2 minutes. Turn it over again with a 90 degree twist and leave another 2 minutes.

NB The cooking time is approximate as it depends on the thickness of the steak; serving rare to medium-rare gives the best results.

Remove the steak onto a warm serving dish and drizzle generously with olive oil. Leave the beef to rest for at least 10 minutes. Then carve into 1cm slices and serve, with the resting juices and olive oil poured over, before tucking in!

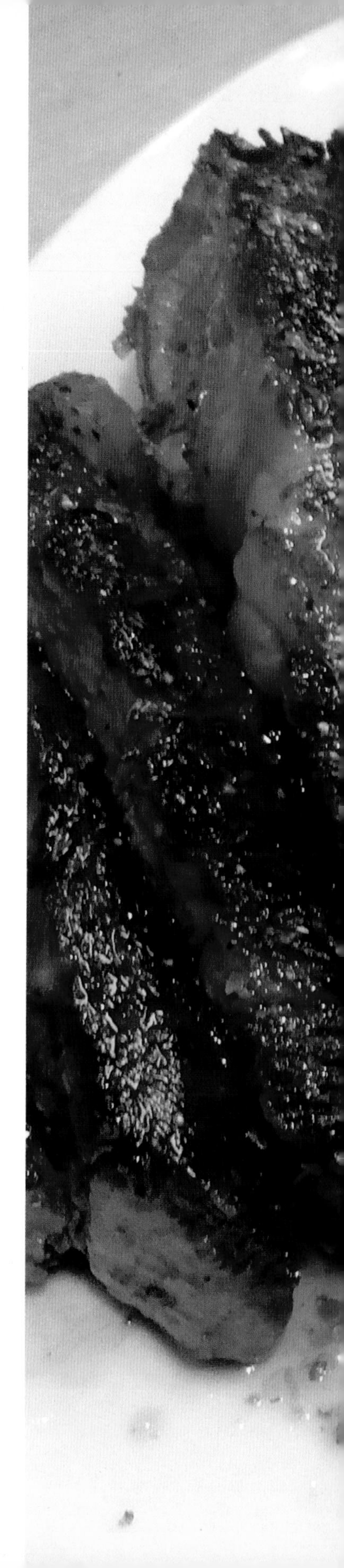

Risotto agli asparagi con pancetta – Asparagus risotto with pancetta

An Italian classic, best enjoyed with soft poached hen's eggs. (serves 6)

300g fresh asparagus; 1 onion, finely chopped; 2 garlic cloves, finely chopped; olive oil; unsalted butter; 150g cubed pancetta; 300g risotto rice; 250ml dry white wine; 2 litres hot chicken stock; sprig of mint or flat leaf parsley, chopped; 150g parmesan, grated; 1 large tbsp mascarpone

Cook the fresh asparagus in boiling water for 2 minutes then plunge immediately into iced water. Chop the cooled asparagus into half cm rounds, saving the tips for decoration.

In a heavy sauté pan, over a low heat, fry the onion and garlic gently in a little olive oil and a knob of butter with half the pancetta. Add the rice and toast over a medium-hot heat for 1 minute, then add the wine and simmer. Once evaporated, add a ladle of stock, stirring. As it's absorbed, continue to add and stir in the stock, keeping a 'porridge-like' consistency.

After 10 minutes, add chopped asparagus. Continue adding stock until the rice is 'al dente', approx. 20 minutes. Season well off the heat, adding chopped herbs, parmesan, a knob of butter and the mascarpone.

Pasta fresca all'uovo – Fresh egg pasta

1 kg durum '00' pasta flour; 10 whole eggs or 8 eggs and 6 yolks

Either by hand or with a dough hook, mix the flour and eggs to a smooth, firm dough. Wrap in cling film and chill for 30 mins. For ravioli, take a quarter of the dough, squash into a rectangle and roll it through a pasta roller twice on every setting until the second to last setting to obtain a thin sheet.

Ravioli di aglio selvatico e ricotta – Wild garlic and ricotta ravioli

500g wild garlic, blanched and squeezed; 500g fresh ricotta cheese; 150g parmesan, grated; nutmeg; eggwash

Chop or pulse the wild garlic until fine and mix with the cheese and parmesan, adding nutmeg and seasoning to taste.

Taking the pasta sheet, brush eggwash all over one half lengthways. Place teaspoons of filling at 5cm intervals. Fold the other half of pasta over the fillings. Gently press down around each mound to remove all the air. Cut into ravioli with a knife or round cutter and lay on a floured surface. Cook one as a test in boiling salted water for approx. 3 minutes to check the timing before simmering the ravioli to serve.

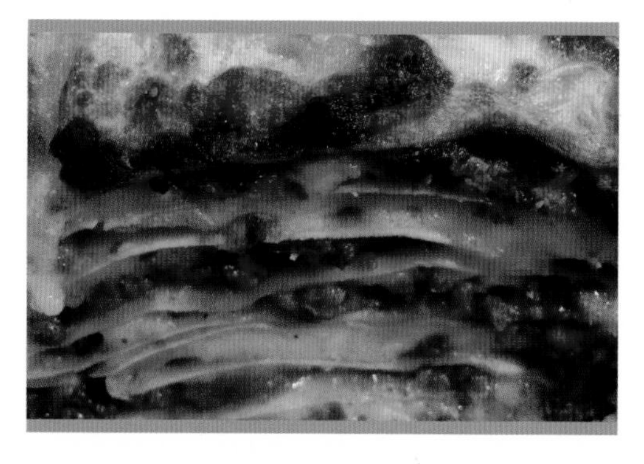

Honor's Italian ragù

Works well with ribbon pasta or penne shapes and perfect for pasta al forno interleaved with fresh sheets of pasta, a savoury white béchamel sauce and grated parmesan

250g lean Red Poll beef, minced; 250g pork shoulder, minced; good olive oil; 1 large glass of red wine; 1 large carrot, 1 large onion, 1 stick of celery, all finely diced; 300ml of good beef stock; 2 tins of peeled Italian tomatoes, puréed; 1 small carton tomato passata; ¼ tsp nutmeg, freshly grated; 2 bay leaves, fresh

In a hot deep sauté pan, heat up a glug of olive oil and fry the mince in batches , allowing it to brown and breaking it up as it cooks. Transfer to a deep lidded saucepan when ready along with the wine. In another hot sauté pan,fry the diced vegetables similarly until softened and well-coloured and add them to the saucepan. Add the rest of the ingredients.

Cover and bring to a simmer on a low heat, cooking for four hours, stirring regularly. Add a little water if necessary for a thick sauce texture. Adjust the seasoning and it's ready to use. Cool, refrigerate, use as required.

Italy comes to Suffolk

This corner of Suffolk is just about as English as it is gets. Here, East Anglia rolls a bit, narrow lanes wind, cottages are pretty and the relaxed, slightly dishevelled feel of Buxhall Vale – home of Honor Townsend's Buxhall Coach House restaurant – is a perfect fit.

Sit down to eat here, however, and you'll find yourself in Italy (and more particularly in Umbria) faster than you can say 'prosciutto crudo'.

It's a story that started almost 20 years ago when Honor's mother, Sarah Townsend, started renovating properties in Italy to rent out to italophiles. "I studied art back in the early 60s," Sarah explains, "so of course I spent time in Italy. I fell in love with the country and decided to direct my creativity into renovating dilapidated properties. Our biggest project by far was Palazzo Terranova which we completely refurbished and opened in 1999 as a 14-bedroom hotel and restaurant."

Honor, who by then had earned her cooking stripes, gradually took over the cooking at the Palazzo, running the kitchen at this stunning hillside property for almost a decade.

Accolades poured in during the late 90s and 2000s, but the family decided to sell the Palazzo in 2006 and move back to Suffolk.

The imminent reinvention of the Buxhall Coach House business will see Honor concentrate on doing private parties for groups of eight or more guests rather than the conventional restaurant format. "They will be bespoke events with private use of the restaurant and a menu that will be planned closely with the client," Sarah says. Honor says she will always have particular days and occasions for her regular guests and friends so they won't miss out! A series of Italian cookery courses is also in the pipeline.

"We've had endless family pow-wows and we all agree that this is the best way forward for everyone. "The life of a chef is not compatible with bringing up children," Honor says, "and it's particularly hard given that I'm on my own, even though the girls are now teenagers and have been incredible waitresses at the restaurant! I would also like to work more normal hours so I can catch up with friends.

"Whatever I do it will always involve food, and it will be very personal, creative and true to my vision. I'm open-minded, I see this point in my life as an exciting opportunity."

Buxhall Coach House
Buxhall Vale, Stowmarket IP14 3DH
E: honortownsend@btinternet.com
(initial enquiries by email please)
W: www.honorsflavours.com
/BuxhallCoachHouse
@simplysugo

Accolades: *East Anglian Daily Times* Suffolk Restaurant of the Year 2012; Michelin Guide 2015; *Waitrose Good Food Guide* 2015 score 1

Cost: Carte £40 average; wine from £19.75

Open: All year

Details: Private dining; children welcome; wheelchair access; parkland walks; heated alfresco dining; car parking

HONOR ON HER...

SECRET MIDNIGHT FEAST?

A goat's cheese, tomato, red onion and fresh chilli toastie! I've been known to go to bed with a bowl of chickpeas with garlic, olive oil, chilli and rosemary too.

FAVOURITE TIME OF YEAR?

Autumn, maybe because of my time in Italy. I love the coolness after the hot summer, the freshness of the rain that comes as such a relief, and the fact that tourists go away! I love foraging for mushrooms (especially porcini), roast chestnuts, the grape harvest and olive picking, going out hunting or shooting, lighting fires and getting cosy, and all the 'sagre' or local religious and food festivals that seem to happen at that time of year in Italy.

CHEF'S TIPS?

I'm not really that 'cheffy', I just do what I love and what comes naturally, but my tips would be to always make your own stock; and learn how to make a perfect omelette and creamy scrambled eggs too, easy and luscious life-savers for unexpected guests and hungry teenagers.

MUSIC TO LISTEN TO AS YOU COOK?

I have a very eclectic taste in music so it varies according to my mood, but jazz, folk and singers such as Madeleine Peyroux or Dave Brubeck are always good. I still like my Eighties playlists too!

IF NOT A CHEF?

Something creative. I take all my own food pictures and love photography. My mother is an artist so perhaps I get it from her.

FOODIE NOSTALGIA?

Rosso di Montalcino is my favourite red wine and reminds me of the happiest days in Italy and the best steaks I've ever eaten, cooked on open fires. A perfectly-aged prosciutto nostrano with fresh salt-less Tuscan bread; a bistecca fiorentina and the ripest tomatoes, freshly-pressed olive oil and home-grown chillies have to be the tastes that evoke happiness and memories of my favourite people and places, even the simplest times which are often the best.

WELL-THUMBED COOKBOOKS?

Marcella Hazan's *Classic Italian Cookbook*, and Claudia Roden's *The Food of Italy*. At the time, they were the most authentic Italian cookbooks. Once I learnt to speak Italian I loved Pellegrino Artusi's classic bible of Italian food, *La Scienza in Cucina e l'Arte di Mangiar Bene*. I also love Simon Hopkinson's *Roast Chicken and Other Stories*.

FAVOURITE PLACES TO EAT LOCALLY?

The Shepherd and Dog at Onehouse is my local and a lovely, friendly pub run by a very hard-working all-woman team. Orissa in Bury is great for tapas-style Indian food, and LP is definitely the place in town for a pizza fix - their thin crust pizzas baked in a wood-fired oven are fantastic!

ULTIMATE DINING DESTINATIONS?

Kitty Fishers in Shepherd Market, London – it looks like my sort of place with open fire cooking and has had some amazing reviews; and Amaya, a smart, authentic Indian restaurant just off Sloane Street in London, where chefs prepare food in a fantastic show kitchen of open grills and authentic tandoor ovens. Nearer to home, Midsummer House is a wonderful spot for a special treat, and in Italy, I have two favourites: La Capannaccia in Arezzo and the Trattoria Sostanza in Florence for a bistecca fiorentina, but really there are too many to mention!

CULINARY HEROES?

Simon Hopkinson, who took me on at Bibendum when I was straight out of Prue Leith and taught me the importance of cooking things as simply and perfectly and honestly as you can. I was there only for three months in 1989 (at the same time as Philip Howard and when Henry Harris was sous chef), but I learnt such a lot and feel privileged to have had that experience.

HONOR'S SIGNATURE DISHES

STARTERS

Roast Piedmontese pepper, tomato, garlic, basil, grilled goat's cheese

Pan-seared scallops, cauliflower purée, crispy smoked pancetta, pea shoots, truffle oil

'Crostini neri' – traditional Tuscan toast topped with warm chicken liver pâté

MAINS

Pan-seared cod, Umbrian lentils, peperonata, salsa verde

Pasta al forno with Umbrian pork and beef ragù, béchamel sauce, parmesan

Rack of lamb, roasted with garlic and rosemary, Mediterranean vegetable compôte

PUDDINGS

Caramel and vanilla pannacotta with fresh strawberries

Apple tarte tatin with vanilla ice cream

Honor's truly Italian tiramisu

THE SWAN AT LAVENHAM
JUSTIN KETT

Elegant indulgence: Classical cooking and artistic flair in Lavenham

Justin Kett's refined cuisine and local earthy ingredients define The Swan's menu

L-R: Greg Strolenberg, Justin Kett, Gareth Doherty.

THE SWAN AT LAVENHAM JUSTIN KETT

"I can promise it will only be a few food miles from field to fork today!" followed by "walk this way to meet the butchers", are the first words on arrival in Justin's kitchens at the seriously historic and plush surroundings of The Swan Hotel.

Sitting right at the heart of this chocolate box medieval village, built by the famous wool merchants, this revitalised grande dame of Suffolk hotel-keeping showcases Lavenham in its fifteenth century beamed glory. With an original Guildhall at the heart of this beautiful seamless blend of picturesque properties, it is easy to see why it is such a magnet for well-heeled tourists (the American and Japanese travellers seemingly mesmerised by its charms) and weekenders seeking a luxurious bolthole for a few days. Top flight awards recognise The Swan's excellence as a pinnacle of hotel-keeping on a national scale.

As we walked out into the sunshine, there quite literally across the iconic High Street sat Lavenham Butchers, Justin's favoured game supplier, just yards from his kitchen door. And what a meat purveyor it was, all rare breed, high welfare and locally-sourced, the usual prime suspects foodies seek in the county, Blythburgh free range pork, Sutton Hoo chickens, Lavenham Brook Red Poll beef and Suffolk lamb. But we were here to source wild game, harvested by Justin's own fair hand. A well-practised shot, Justin took the rare opportunity to accept the invitation from Gareth and Greg, our hosts and owners of the butchery, to go out decoying that late afternoon for spring woodpigeons, as they were damaging the oil seed rape on a local farm. Leaving the tourists, the tearooms and the boutiques behind us, within a few minutes we pulled into a dusty farmyard in the middle of nowhere, overlooking a verdant wooded valley. As we unpacked the hide equipment and Justin shouldered his gunslip, the plump birds were already lifting from the well-pecked crop behind the farmer's house, their meal interrupted.

En route to our planned ambush point, a good 'sitty' oak tree, which is a natural vantage the birds head for before circling and landing in the field, our hosts talked more about the land we were on. Several blocks of woodland and the surrounding arable acreage compiled their stalking rights, where they would sustainably control the local deer numbers to help protect crops and supply their shop with fine venison. They explained pest control was also the reason we were pigeon shooting today to minimise the damage to the maturing rape; looking around it wasn't hard to see whole swathes where its leaves were stunted to ground level compared to the several feet high growth in other parts. After building our camouflaged shelter and laying out our convincing dummy birds to fool their live cousins

into coming closer, we sat and waited. Clearly patience is an essential virtue required in shooting and today was no exception. But it enabled us to appreciate the beauty of the great Suffolk countryside and take the time to talk pigeon asking Justin and the butchers how they like to cook this game meat. Clearly of like mind, keeping it simple was the preferred manner, serving it pink and tender, as breasts in a warm salad, Justin's suggestion with black pudding, pancetta and wild mushrooms; or on a cassoulet, maybe tomato-braised lentils and chorizo; or for a main something more substantial as a roasted crown, perhaps with thyme mash and salt-baked beetroots. Knowing where his ingredients come from is key to this passionate chef and also having the opportunity to get out with his suppliers hands-on and to understand products' origins.

"There!" came the firm whisper as we immediately stood stock-still, out in front a small flock of pigeons floating in on the wind from our right, having left one of the woods to feed. A few jinxed away, these are some of the hardest quarry to get near to, but a couple circled around, felt the danger had passed and set their wings to come into our pattern of decoys and within range. Quickly despatched, Justin went out to retrieve his bag. The pigeon's plump breasts a sign they had been unfortunately eating all too well at the farmer's expense recently. We didn't get many more that day but a sense resonated that apart from the obvious need to control numbers, there were simpler personal pleasures in taking something home for the pot, being an honoured guest in nature's own environment amidst a typical Suffolk rural scene.

Back at The Swan kitchens, Justin pulled out a couple of oven-ready birds, prepared by the butchers earlier, after they had been hanging for a few days, whilst commenting "I wish people would realise how great value local game is and find a good independent butcher like Gareth and Greg across the street, who will supply them prepared for the pan. Just as good, if not often better than farmed livestock, with their good and happy life, truly wild meats are slow-maturing, well-bred by Mother Nature and too well-fed, of course!"

Justin's interest in cooking and love of local ingredients was piqued by shooting, aged perhaps 13 or 14 with his father at Blythburgh, where he farmed. "I soon realised that suffering at dawn in the cold was so worth it to bag your birds as dawn broke. And much of my love of the countryside and game is down to rough-shooting and pigeon-decoying through my teenage years. The non-shooting public don't realise how much of our countryside is protected by shooting, it really is largely all about conservation." Local seasonal produce is key to Justin's food and it shows in his considered, well-thought out dishes. Cooking seems to be in his blood, not wavering since an early age in his desire to be a chef; he recounts nostalgic anecdotes of baking with his Mum and Grandma, good old Suffolk rusks, cakes, scones, sausage rolls and cheese straws (savouries remaining a favourite to this day) as well as licking the bowl to his mother's distaste. She would get her own back by making him help gut pheasants and rabbits, shot for the pot by his father. Good food like pigeon shooting takes passion, patience and practised skill.

Roast breast of local woodpigeon, summer vegetables and carrot purée

For this, crowns of woodpigeon are required, the ribcage with two breasts on the bone, skin-on. A good independent butcher can provide these for you oven-ready. (serves 4)

4 large carrots, shredded; 1 garlic clove, sliced; 1 long shallot, sliced; good vegetable or chicken stock; unsalted butter; rapeseed oil; 4 woodpigeon crowns; thyme; red wine; 8 each of spring onions, asparagus tips and halved baby turnips; 100g peas; 100g broad beans, podded

Pre-heat the oven to 180c. Peel the carrots, chop thinly and then place into a pan with the garlic and shallot. Cover with stock and cook until falling apart, if pressed with a spoon.

When the large carrots are ready, remove the carrots from the stock and purée in a blender with salt, pepper and a good knob of butter until nice and smooth. Add some of the liquor to achieve the right consistency. Keep warm.

Heat up a heavy ovenproof frying pan and add a splash of oil. Over a high heat, sear the seasoned pigeons on both breast sides until golden. Bake for about 6 - 8 mins until cooked. Remove the pan.

Place crowns on a board somewhere warm. Add a good covering of red wine to the pan with a sprig of thyme and gently simmer the pan juices on the hob until sticky; keep warm.

Bring a pan of salted water to the boil and blanch your spring onions, asparagus and turnips for a couple of minutes. Remove and plunge into iced water. Warm up dinner plates.

Cook the peas and broad beans until al dente. In a frying pan, add a splash of stock, salt, pepper and a knob of butter until hot and return all the vegetables until heated through.

To serve
Carve the pigeon breasts from the crowns. Put a swipe of carrot purée on to the plate and place vegetables around. Finish with the sliced pigeon breasts and pan juices.

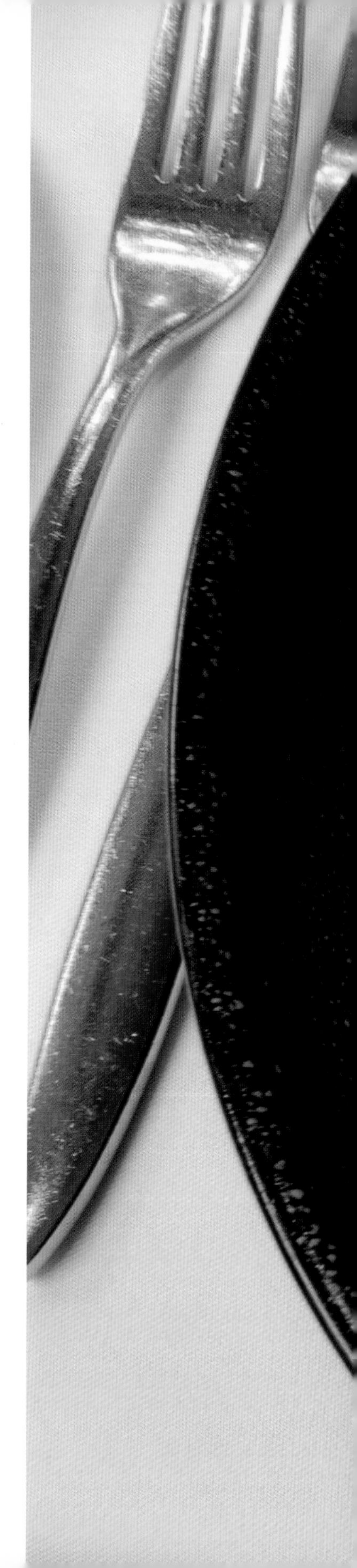

Roast pork belly, apple and pea purée, frisée and dandelion leaves

A smart dinner party starter. Bake the pork the day before. Store your leaves in iced water. (serves 4)

1kg piece of belly pork, skin-scored; olive oil; 3 Bramley apples; 40g sugar; 10g butter; 300g peas, cooked and warm; 100g broad beans, cooked and warm; frisée and dandelion leaves, separated and washed

Pre-heat the oven to 180c. Oil the meat of the pork and generously rub in salt and a little pepper into the pork skin. Place in a snug roasting tin and bake for 2 ½ hours. Remove, cool and refrigerate.

To serve, pre-heat the oven to 200c. Roast the pork for 30 minutes. Meanwhile peel, core and chop the apples. Simmer in a snug pan with the sugar, butter and a splash of hot water. At the same time, simmer 200g of the peas in salted water for 2 ½ minutes. Drain and immediately process until smooth, keep warm. When the apples are nice and soft, too purée them.
Put the broad beans and remaining peas in a pan with salt, pepper and a knob of butter to warm them through. When the pork is cooked, slice into pieces. Serve surrounded by the two purées and the whole peas the beans. Dry your leaves on kitchen paper and scatter around. Drizzle with oil.

Pan fried scallops with gem lettuce and apple salad

Please avoid over-cooking the scallops so they become rubbery. They need to be tender and just opaque in the centre. (serves 4)

60g cashew nuts; olive oil; 20ml honey; 1 lemon, juiced; olive oil; 1 green apple, cored; 12 large fresh scallops, trimmed; 1 gem lettuce, leaves separated and washed; pea shoots

Pre-heat the oven to 180c. Rub the cashews with a little oil and sea salt before roasting on a tray until golden.

Warm the honey and lemon juice to melt together. Remove and whisk two or three parts olive oil to make a dressing and adjust the seasoning. Core and slice the apple into matchsticks.

Take a wide heavy frying pan and heat until very hot. Dry the scallops on kitchen towel, oil and season them. Place the scallops in the pan in a circle, remembering where you started. After approx two minutes (less for smaller scallops), check they are golden and then turn over the first one and continue round until all are flipped. Cook for one more minute.

Plate the scallops and place the lettuce and shoots around them, garnishing with the nuts. Dress before serving.

Blue cheese and salt-baked beets

Seek out a good local firm blue cheese or Stilton. (serves 4 generously)

250g blue cheese; 200ml port; 200ml red wine; 10 egg whites; 250g salt; 4 large beetroots, trimmed; 2 punnets raspberries; 50ml grenadine; 50ml framboise; 3g agar agar powder; 750g caster sugar; 150ml water; 40g walnuts; 20 blueberries

The day before, soak the blue cheese with the port and red wine in the fridge.

Pre-heat the oven to 160c. Whisk the egg white and salt until stiff peaks. Use to cover the beetroot completely. Bake for 3 hours until cooked and remove the crust. Once cooled, peel the beetroots before chilling. Bring 1.5 punnets of raspberries, the grenadine and framboise to a simmer. Sieve into a clean pan, whisk in the agar agar and simmer for 30 seconds. Cool in a plastic tray and chill. When set, liquidise into a gel with a splash of water and refrigerate.

Bring the sugar and water to the boil then add the walnuts, simmer for 3 – 4 minutes, turn off and leave to crystallise.

Arrange sliced beetroot on four starter plates then sprinkle over some walnuts and cheese, drizzle with raspberry gel and garnish with halved blueberries and raspberries.

Swanning around in luxury

Sense of occasion and cosseting would be far from glib descriptors of what to expect when entering the historic surrounds of The Swan Hotel. In modern days when customer service can at times lack the sense of the guest 'being king', it is reassuring that in these walls, all is well with the world of hospitality. This is a place where waiting at table and serving generally is treated as a professional craft, with the clientele valued accordingly.

Befitting one of the highest-rated hotels in East Anglia, there is much for guests to indulge in whilst staying here. This is a collection of delightful properties which have been cleverly incorporated to make a sympathetic oasis, full of intimate nooks and hidden courtyards, among the range of dining and drinking options. Upstairs, the desirable array of 45 very individual bedrooms and suites are full of home comforts and modern touches plus inherent quaint charm from 400 years of innkeeping.

New for 2015 has been the conversion of the Weavers' House, converting an adjoining property cleverly into a spa with cool, calm spaces, an escapist bolthole to soothe and restore. There are six treatment rooms, relaxation areas and an outdoor vitality pool, complemented by lounges and break-out areas. A swish private alfresco terrace makes a secluded spot for peaceful pampering.

Detox and a healthy regime might be the order of the day after a few days of being spoilt by Justin Kett's cuisine. With not one but two restaurants, his elegant thoughtful menus indulge diners in style amid the suitably atmospheric and baronial Gallery, often with a pianist tinkling from the upstairs minstrels balcony. Like the whole of The Swan, this is replete in its period feel, exposed brickwork, leaded lights, beams of Mary Rose proportions, not forgetting the requisite inglenook and vaulted ceiling. The more relaxed Brasserie offers an equally delicious but lighter choice, covering most tastes and occasions. Another addition here to coincide with the Spa opening has been Justin's raw foods menu, for healthy dining. The hotel naturally buzzes come afternoon tea and there is a well-stocked Airmens' Bar (recalling the Second World War and the American allies). The Swan makes a romantic wedding venue and several function rooms are kept occupied with parties and meetings.

The Swan At Lavenham
High Street, Lavenham CO10 9QA
T: 01787 247477
W: www.theswanatlavenham.co.uk
/swanlavenham
@swanlavenham

Accolades: Two AA Rosettes 2015; Four AA Red Stars; VisitEngland Gold award; *Good Spa Guide* Five Bubbles award

Cost: Set carte three courses £39.50; set L two courses £16.95 / three courses £21.95; set Sunday L 3 courses £26.95; wine from £22

Open: Every day; food served L 12-2pm; D 7-9pm

Details: 45 bedrooms; spa; 24 hour room service; bar drinks; restaurant and brasserie; breakfast; afternoon tea; parties and weddings; children welcome; car parking

JUSTIN ON HIS...

LAST SUPPER?

On the menu – crispy whitebait, garlic aioli, lemon to squeeze; char-grilled rib-eye steak, Heston's recipe mushroom ketchup, beef fat matchstick fries, tarragon béarnaise; I love savouries, so baked brie with walnut toast and apple; ginger shortbread, vanilla and lime cheesecake; and mustn't forget bread, great sourdough and salted butter. On the invite list – Kairi, my partner, always enjoyed my best meals with her; Thierry Henry, Arsenal player, footballing legend; Gordon Ramsay, the first chef who amazed me; Michel Roux Jnr, the polar opposite to GR, just a calm, equally talented cook; parents Susan and Thomas, who influenced my cooking and supported me.

FOODIE DISCOVERIES?

Raw food is fascinating, so interesting and healthy, and tastes so great too; it's been fun developing a raw food menu for the new Weavers' House Spa here at The Swan.

FAVOURITE PLACES LOCALLY?

To eat – The Packhorse at Moulton, near Newmarket, really good food, a proper chefs' place; Aqua Eight in Ipswich, really diverse, I love their black pepper squid and the whole vibe; Pea Porridge in Bury, real rustic brasserie, great lunch menu.

LUCKY DAY OFF?

Long dog walk, with the cocker mutts Bear and Sprocket, by the river; back for barbecue of course with friends, real charcoal, probably Kairi's griddled Estonian pork marinated in chunks with vinegar and crème fraîche.

COOK'S CHEATS?

Always rest cuts of meat after cooking to get the juices back into the flesh, not on the chopping board. Finish sauces with a squeeze of lemon or lime, for less fatty and cleaner flavours.

WELL-THUMBED COOKBOOKS?

Gordon Ramsay's *A Chef For All Seasons*, the style, cooking technique, the pictures; *Essence: Le Champignon Sauvage* by David Everitt-Matthias, photos, cleanliness, simplicity; *Rhodes Around Britain* by Gary Rhodes, one of my first books and still the benchmark for classic recipes.

SOCIAL MEDIA?

I tweet as @justinkett and follow good chefs like Chris Lee, Nigel Haworth, Tom Aikens, Daniel Clifford and Sat Bains.

INSPIRING SUFFOLK VIEW?

The marshes around Aldeburgh and Blythburgh in that late winter sun or the fields after the harvest on my drive to work; I love how the county's colours change from plough to green to golden to stubble.

ULTIMATE DINING DESTINATIONS?

I recently ate at The Goring in Belgravia London, old-fashioned trolley service, impeccable. Must get to Gordon Ramsay Royal Hospital Road, Chelsea soon as well as my old head chef friend Richard Guest, who's got Augustus back in Taunton.

BEST DISHES EVER EATEN?

Chateaubriand in Málaga, southern Spain, huge roast fillet of beef, béarnaise and chips, simple heaven; the smoked prawns and garlic aioli at the Oysterage Café in Orford's main square; marshallows after a great meal overlooking Hyde Park at Galvins with Windows, the best freebie!

MIDNIGHT FEAST?

Crisp sandwiches, ready salted, crusty white bread, lots of salted butter, childhood thing; scrambled eggs, lots of black pepper on buttered white toast, heaven...

JUSTIN'S SIGNATURE DISHES

STARTERS

Scrambled duck egg with locally smoked salmon and curry oil

Chicken liver parfait, Cumberland sauce, toasted sourdough

Pea and broad bean risotto, wild garlic flowers

MAINS

Fillet of beef Wellington, thyme-creamed potatoes, carrot purée and nutmeg spinach

Roasted pork belly with apple sauce, roasted roots and wilted kale

Baked fillet of halibut with tagliatelle, heirloom tomatoes and caviar

PUDDINGS

Cherry chocolate fondant and clotted ice cream

Vanilla pannacotta with peppered strawberries and basil

White chocolate and croissant bread & butter pudding, crème anglaise

Bangers on trend: Farm to fork hits new heights at Ben's

Jim Sloman scours Suffolk and the smallholding of restaurant owner Ben Hutton to prepare crowd-pleasing dishes

L - R: Ben Hutton, Jim Sloman.

BEN'S RESTAURANT JIM SLOMAN

Sausage and mash. Surely there can be few dishes that more loudly shout 'eat me!' than a plate of very good sausages, some creamy mash and maybe syrupy-sweet onion gravy?

The cry of 'eat me!' gets even louder at Ben's Restaurant, one of the newest additions to the Bury St Edmunds restaurant scene. Here, rare breed pork sausages, made by family-run Long Melford butchers Ruse & Son from pigs reared on restaurant owner Ben Hutton's smallholding, are cooked by head chef Jim Sloman with no less care than he would use were he handling the most lah-di-dah of fine dining ingredients.

It's a textbook demonstration of farm-to-fork principles, and one that diners in Bury are clearly enjoying. "We've been busy from day one," Ben says. "There's such an interest in food provenance and we tap right into that."

When we meet at Ben's smallholding on the edge of Ixworth, Jim and Ben are talking pig in the company of Marigold and Phoebe. The two Oxford Sandy & Black sows nuzzle, gurgle and grunt throatily, clearly enjoying the attention on this sunny morning. In the next pen, Big Ginge, Ellen and the two Large Blacks, Blossom and Bubbles, pace the fence noisily, eager for attention too.

The sows – Ben has these plus six Kunekunes and an Oxford Sandy & Black boar – each produce a litter of ten or so piglets once a year. The young are raised in outside pens for 12 months before slaughter at Ruse's small abattoir. "Ruse will butcher the animal to give us whatever cuts we want, but we generally order about 50lbs of sausages, a mix of pork and Stilton, classic Old English, pork and chilli, or whatever Jim needs for the menu. Much of the prime cut meat goes into the sausages which is why they're so good, but occasionally Jim will get some to use in a braised pork suet pudding with root vegetables and Aspalls cyder jus, perhaps herb-crusted loin or chargrilled chops." Any shortfall in prime cuts is filled by Blythburgh pork which is used for all Jim's belly pork dishes.

We watch as sausage-maker Lewis Williams scoops out the rusk. "We put far less rusk than goes into a commercially-made sausage," he says, before adding the seasoning mix for a fresh batch of sausages. As the mincer grinds the hunks of meat, he mixes the dry ingredients with water before combining the paste and the minced meat and transferring the lot to the sausage machine. "I usually spend a day and a half per week making them for the shop and for customers like Ben and Jim," Lewis adds, carefully feeding the meat into the fine skins before twisting them deftly into loops.

Jim finds it reassuring to watch the process. "I love knowing how the meat I cook is reared and that there are no additives in the sausages" says Jim, "and it really does make a difference to the taste if an animal is slaughtered in a stress-free environment like the one here."

Kunekune pigs might not be rarebreed, but their meat does make fantastic sausages because they have the right proportion of fat, Jim adds. "I love the taste, there's none of the blandness that commercially-made sausages can sometimes have. Put that with some delicious mashed potatoes and you've got an English classic, food that makes everyone happy!"

If he's not in the mood for mash, Jim might ring the changes with Puy lentils cooked with red wine, rosemary and garlic, or add herbs to sausage meat to make Sunday roast stuffing. "I'll put some juniper to go with a muntjac dish, sage if I'm doing pork or fresh horseradish with beef."

Jim quite happily turns his hand to lamb, game or fish too. In keeping with the restaurant's local sourcing ethos, lamb is either from Ben's flock of native breed Jacob's sheep or Justin Hammond's Culford Flock and appears on the menu typically as a trio of braised shoulder, grilled cutlet and pan-fried liver, or as a pulled breast served in a brioche bun with fresh mint and redcurrant jelly.

Game is a favourite too. If not muntjac [*see recipe*], it could well be a rabbit and chorizo casserole or venison from the local estates in season. "I love the subtle, sweet flavour of muntjac and the fact it's available year round from a sustainable source. Venison shoulder is great casseroled, the bones make a great stock, and I'll do medallions from the fillet. I get the meat from independent stalkers on local shoots and top up with supplies from the Wild Meat Company near Woodbridge if necessary."

Jim learnt to cook largely on the job – "I've always worked hard and listened to the good chefs around me" – and has also travelled widely. From a first job in Kent, he moved to North Berwick to open a delicatessen and outside catering business before setting up the Lobster Shack on the harbour with a friend. "It was a cracking place – still is! We were licensed to buy straight from the fishing boats and we'd get line-caught mackerel, crab, langoustines, mussels, that we'd then cook to order.

"Cooking in the Alps, the Pyrenees, New Zealand and Spain has also influenced my cooking hugely. I've always loved the meat and fish combo – pork belly and white fish for example – which is a very Spanish taste. I love doing a fillet of hake with chorizo, saffron potatoes and a white wine reduction. And my confit rabbit wontons with chilli jam are a bit different, a good combination of local game and eastern flavours."

And though he's happily settled behind the stove at Ben's (Suffolk family ties pulled him this way two and a half years ago), his mind fizzes with ideas. "I'd love to have a lobster and shellfish tank here. Right there, in that alcove," he indicates the ideal spot. "I love the simplicity of lobster, it's quick, fresh and delicious!" He pauses, looks round the dining room. "I'm just getting going here. There is so much potential," he says, almost to himself.

Ben's 'bangers and mash' with shallot jus

The signature sausage dish from Ben's home-reared pork. Source the best-quality sausages possible, ideally bought from Ben's Restaurant (when available) or your good local independent butcher. The mashed potato can be flavoured with interesting additions, such as apple or quince compôte and a good pinch of chopped flat leaf parsley, or try some wholegrain mustard, shredded sage and spring onions. We garnish the dish with pea shoots. (serves 4)

For the shallot jus

200g shallots; olive oil; Maldon sea salt; 20g caster sugar; 50g salted butter; 25g plain flour; 200ml red wine; 500ml beef or chicken stock; five sprigs thyme

For the mashed potatoes

1kg Maris Piper potatoes (or a good floury equivalent), peeled; large knob of butter; cream; chosen flavourings (optional)

For the sausages

12 good butchers' sausages; 1 hispi cabbage; 4 rashers smoked bacon, finely-sliced; 40g toasted flaked almonds; unsalted butter

Pre-heat the oven to 180c. For the shallot jus, peel the shallots, cut lengthways and slice thinly widthways. Add the shallots to a large heavy saucepan with a drizzle of olive oil and salt. Cook on a low heat for a good 15-20 minutes to really concentrate the flavour. Stir regularly so they are slightly coloured. Add the sugar and butter and stir until melted, then add flour to form a roux. Cook out for a further 2-3 minutes, whisking continuously. Add the red wine and continue stirring until smooth Leave on a low heat for a further five minutes to cook out the alcohol in the wine. Add the stock and drop in the thyme. Season to taste and leave on a low heat while you prepare the other stages.

For the mashed potato, put the potatoes in a saucepan of cold salted water and place on a high heat for 15-20 minutes until soft and tender but not overcooked. Remove from the heat, strain into a colander and give them a shuffle. Put them back into the pan and return to a low heat for 2-3 minutes to steam off any excess water. Add the butter and cream and mash until smooth. Try not to overwork the potatoes as this will release too much starch and leave the mash 'gloopy'. Keep the potatoes warm until ready to plate up.

Put the sausages in a large roasting tray and cook for 12-15 minutes until nicely coloured and cooked through in the centre.

Discard any course outer leaves and stalk from the cabbage. Shred the lighter leaves finely and rinse in cold water. Drain and simmer in salted boiling water for four minutes.

While the cabbage is cooking, gently fry some bacon and add the almonds. Strain the cabbage and stir into the pan with a knob of butter and pinch of cracked pepper. Mix gently.

To serve, plate up your mash using a large clingfilmed serving spoon (the mash will just slide off), top with the cabbage, then rest three sausages around the side. Finish with shallot jus.

Suffolk lobster and salmon rillettes

This eats really well with a beetroot-horseradish chutney and beer bread crostini.

200g salmon fillet, poached in seasoned milk until just cooked; 200g cooked lobster meat; 100g unsalted butter, at room temperature; 2tbsp flat leaf parsley leaves, chopped; 2tbsp dill leaves, chopped; 2 pinches smoked paprika; juice and grated zest of half a lemon

Flake the salmon and lobster meat, mix well with all the other ingredients.

Lay out a large piece of clingfilm on a flat surface, spoon the mixture along the centre, bring the sides one over the other to roll the mixture into a thick sausage-shape cylinder. Wrap around another long sheet to secure. Tie the ends of the cling film and place in the fridge to set.

When ready to serve, cut finger-width slices of the rillettes, remove the cling film from the outside and place on your toasts.

Loin of wild muntjac with a bitter-sweet chocolate and port reduction

A lovely tender lean cut, we serve this with creamy mashed potatoes and local vegetables.

4 x loin steaks of muntjac venison; 50ml port; 150ml good beef stock; 10g bitter chocolate; 2 sprigs fresh thyme, leaves only

Season the venison on all sides.
Oil a non-stick frying pan and heat up over a high setting. Place the venison in and turn the heat down to medium, cook for approximately two minutes on each side or to taste. Remove from the pan and leave to rest somewhere warm.

Place the pan back on the heat and deglaze by adding the port and leave to simmer for 1 minute. Add the beef stock, bring to the boil and reduce by a quarter. Add the chocolate, thyme and seasoning to taste.

Serve the venison, carved alongside your chosen accompaniments and spoon over the sauce.

Raspberry, custard and vanilla tarts

A lovely dessert full of great Suffolk dairy and fruit goodness matched by the Alder Tree tayberry luxury cream ice. (serves 6)

6 egg yolks; 100g caster sugar; 525ml whole milk; vanilla pod, split and seeds scraped; 20g plain flour; 20g cornflour; 6 sweet pastry cases, blind-baked, in their tins; 280g raspberries; 2tbsp good raspberry jam

Whisk the egg yolks and sugar in a mixer until pale golden and fluffy. Heat the milk and vanilla in a heavy bottom pan until just boiling and leave to cool for 3 minutes. Add the cornflour and plain flour to the egg and sugar mix and continue whisking until fully incorporated. Turn on the mixer and pour half the hot milk into the egg mix slowly, gently whisking.

Whisk this mixture back into the saucepan with the remaining hot milk. Bring the mixture back to a simmer, stirring constantly with a flat spatula to ensure it doesn't catch on the bottom of the pan.

When the mixture is a thick consistency, decant to a large jug, allow to cool a little, whisking occasionally, and then pour the mixture into the pastry cases and leave to set in the fridge. Arrange the raspberries on top and brush with melted jam to glaze.

A lesson in juggling

It takes an energetic multi-tasker to run a sizeable smallholding and a restaurant with any degree of success. Ben Hutton, just 22 and not long out of university, appears to be managing just fine.

"I've always had an entrepreneurial mindset," says Ben who opened his eponymous restaurant in the medieval centre of Bury St Edmunds towards the end of 2014. "And I've always been interested in animals. I've helped my mother on the family smallholding since she started it six years ago as a way of providing good quality meat for the family – and now I run it myself alongside the restaurant." Like many a student, Ben helped finance his university years (he has a degree in zoology from Leeds) by waiting tables, and found that an interest in the world of hospitality grew alongside his love for and understanding of livestock.

The result? Bury has a new restaurant with a fresh approach. Most of the pork on the menu is sourced from the farm's herd of Oxford Sandy & Black, Kunekune and Large Black pigs, while the small flock of Jacob's sheep provides some of the lamb. Other ingredients are bought as locally as possible. Strictly for wool only are alpacas Pedro and Manuel, who trot round the paddock with the sheep, a couple of rheas and feisty geese, a Shetland pony named Poppy, several goats and busy crowds of runner ducks and hens.

Ben spends several hours a day on the farm, tending the animals and developing the plot, having made the conscious decision to only open the restaurant in the evenings on weekdays. There, Ben's girlfriend Rebecca Cooke runs much of the front of house operation but is to be found just as happily giving a coat of paint to the tables and chairs bought at auction as she is meeting and greeting guests or dipping into the kitchen to help Jim and his brigade on starters and puddings when things get busy.

The spacious L-shaped dining room is light-filled and light-hearted. Giant colourful paintings of cows are a backdrop to the counter while other walls are covered with quirky monochrome wallpaper with pigs and sheep and poultry, or painted in restful shades of heather and soft grey. Big mirrors and rows of filament lights illuminate the space and rustic pine tables and mismatched chairs are dressed with simple crockery and glassware.

Ben and Rebecca are proud of what they've achieved so young. "We're lucky. We have the outside life of the farm and the social counterpoint of the restaurant. It can be a juggling act, but we generally manage to keep all the balls in the air!"

Ben's Restaurant
43-45 Churchgate Street,
Bury St Edmunds IP33 1RG
T: 01284 762119
W: www.bensrestaurant.co.uk
/Ben's
@Bens_Restaurant

Accolades: *EADT* Suffolk Food & Drink Awards 2015 Field to Fork runner-up

Cost: Carte £30 average; set L Sat two courses £16 / three courses £20; wine from £18

Open: Tue – Fri 6-10pm; Sat 12-10pm; Sun 12-4pm. Closed Mon.

Details: Children welcome; wheelchair access

JIM ON HIS...

COOK'S CHEATS AND CHEF'S TIPS?

Never be fearful of buying live ingredients such as lobster, langoustine or freshwater crayfish. They are very simple to prepare and cook and once you have tasted the freshest flavour possible, you will never go back!

FAVOURITE CULINARY MOMENT?

Cooking for my non-food hero, David Attenborough. He was filming North Atlantic gannets on the Bass Rock just off North Berwick. It was when I had the deli in the town. The crew asked if I'd do two days of catering for the team – and of course I said yes. I made them breakfast rolls at 5am, and prepared lunch that they'd take out on the boat in a hotbox. Attenborough has called the Bass Rock the eighth wildlife wonder of the world apparently!

FOODIE NOSTALGIA?

Roast dinner at my grandparents' house. There was always the best meat there and freshly-made horseradish with beef. My mum followed in my grandmother's footsteps and I now take huge pride in my Sunday roasts too. I'd love Ben's to become known as the best place in Bury for a roast dinner.

FOOD HEROES?

Rick Stein for his combination of travel and food (I love his *Food Heroes* series and book in particular) and Heston of course for being such a groundbreaking chef. Hugh Fearnley-Whittingstall's rustic approach really appeals to me too – his mussels cooked in hay are fantastic!

MUSIC TO COOK TO AT HOME?

Reggae, something relaxing... I've always loved Bob Marley. During service I might have something a bit more energizing and upbeat to get everyone moving!

PERFECT DAY OFF?

I love family time really. My stepdaughter, Poppy, is just three and a half and I love just spending time with her and my partner Hayley so we often take a picnic to Thetford forest or the Kings Wood. Or I'll just pick up some delicious bread and cheese from Gastronome in Bury and some meats from Edi's or Rolfe's – on a sunny day that's perfect for me!

FAVOURITE TIME OF YEAR?

I love the summer for tasty greens and good shellfish, but also September to February for great tasting game birds. The kitchen is cooler too!

FAVOURITE SUFFOLK VIEW?

I like the view of the field out the back of where I live in Wattisfield with the horse enjoying the sun and my dog playing in the lake.

MEMORABLE CULINARY MOMENTS?

A chateaubriand at a restaurant on Guernsey. I can't remember its name but I took my mum there for her 50th. It's a fantastic spot high up on the cliffs overlooking the sea. I guess a combination of the place, the event and the family there all helped make it perfect – but the meat was fabulous! At the other end of the scale, I'll never forget cooking a leg of lamb in a pit fire with some mates in a friend's back garden in East Lothian. We lobbed in some jacket potatoes wrapped in foil and two and a half hours later it was the most delicious meat ever! Very Ray Mears!

ULTIMATE DINING DESTINATIONS?

I can't wait to go to Dinner by Heston Blumenthal for my birthday! The ideas and innovation behind his cooking are incredibly clever. I might take Hayley to the Fat Duck when it reopens to return the favour!

AMBITIONS?

I always wanted to be a chef though I did work as a motorbike courier for a while. I went back to the kitchen because I valued my life too much! I'd love to have my own modern European style bistro some day, but I'm very happy where I am for now.

JIM'S SIGNATURE DISHES

STARTERS

Smoked salmon and golden beetroot carpaccio, wasabi foam, pea shoots

Pan-seared breast of wood pigeon, smoked bacon, pea and parmesan risotto, white truffle and balsamic syrup

Confit rabbit, chilli and coriander spring rolls, cucumber lime and mint yoghurt, chilli jam, watercress

MAINS

Pan-roasted fillet of hake, polenta and saffron potato cake, buttered samphire, white wine, chorizo and tomato velouté

Local mixed game and juniper berry suet pudding, sautéed kale and pancetta, honey-crushed carrots, mulled wine jus

Lobster ravioli, fresh pea and Parma ham broth, horseradish cream, wilted spinach.

PUDDINGS

Balsamic strawberry and crème pâtissière tart, Pimms jelly, vanilla mascarpone

Poached rhubarb mille feuille, crystallised ginger, baby toffee apples

Chocolate and chilli brownie, strawberry sorbet, minted tuile biscuits

Foraging from land and sea: Nature's free larder

The Sail Loft has lowered canvas in Southwold's landscape of saltmarsh and dune

Robert Mace

THE SAIL LOFT ROBERT MACE

A huge leap of faith, the thrill of new discovery and the necessity of plentiful sage advice are not only the preserve of safely foraging the natural larder in Suffolk's verdant countryside but also the trepidatious realities of re-opening a much-loved yet abandoned restaurant in Southwold, affectionately dubbed 'Notting Hill-on-Sea'. Once a well-known celebrity eatery, the boarded-up 'Dutch Barn', in the lee of the dunes on Southwold's southern seafront, was bought by three local families in 2014, who set about directing it on a new phase of good fortune.

Step forward one Robert Mace to become Head Chef of the newly-opened Sail Loft. In 'Macey', the quintet of determined creative owners at the helm have made a wise investment and less of a culinary gamble. A very familiar face on the coastal restaurant scene, he has spent numerous years running the best kitchens around Southwold and working with the delicious ingredients of north-east Suffolk. While local producers and farmers on his doorstep and their delicious crops might be firm friends, it is in days spent foraging that Robert finds the perfect antidote to a hot kitchen, garnering a hard-won harvest from Mother Nature.

Wild fungi foraying is not for the faint-hearted nor the inexperienced, yet Jon Tyler of Wild About Woods, skilled bushcrafter and mycologist (mushroom hunter to you and me) would advocate the great British countryside as being there to be enjoyed by all. This culinary democracy extends to the wild harvest, albeit with a few key pointers and responsible foragers' code of conduct. This includes having a good reference guide, never taking more than a third of sustainable species to be found, keeping it legal, avoiding polluted areas and if in doubt, not consuming it. There is the aforementioned leap of faith in foraging and nothing beats learning from an expert. A distinctly green naturalist, Jon's trip to East Suffolk to meet Robert was heralded by the train arriving at nearby Darsham station, a demonstration of his eco-friendly outdoors lifestyle. He makes a convincing enthusiast for living off wild foods and in fact by sustainably harvesting and pruning, also helping our precious habitats and flora'n'fauna to flourish.

For Robert, himself a not-unaccomplished forager, this particular day was to be a distinct learning curve; in fact by the end of it, he would be cooking with a good half-dozen new edible discoveries. A bit of an enthusiast, Robert's chef – mentor when he headed up the Crown's kitchens in Southwold High Street was group executive chef of Adnams Hotels, Ian Howell. Robert and Ian would team up with the late great Peter Jordan, a prolific author on edible fungi and local authority, who shared the whole art of spotting your quarry,

usually hidden away under leaf litter and deep undergrowth, away from casual untrained gaze. With his parents living near Thetford Forest, Robert spent his childhood up trees and hiding in bramble bushes, leading to an appreciation of nature and rooting out edible goodies in the woods. The sandy and wooded coastal strip of Sole Bay gives lots of opportunities for him to slip out just after dawn to gather his own fresh delicious ingredients for that day's menu. "In terms of what I will confidently serve to our diners, I stick to a few easily identifiable mushroom species, the ceps of course, other edible boletes like bay, the iconic puffballs, parasol mushrooms and saffron milk caps. Keeping it straightforward, safe and of course delicious, is essential."

Our particular quest that day in May, was for a late spring rarity, the St George's mushroom, named not unsurprisingly after its timely appearance around our patron saint's day. Its distinctive mealy smell and white-creamy appearance at this time of year makes it a little easier to identify; the plethora of pale-capped mushrooms later in the autumn demand particular caution, there being some rather deadly cousins to watch out for. Over our few hours' foraying, we would visit four likely sites in the search for our tasty grail and not until near the end on the journey home would we stumble across our goal, a partial ring of these much-prized fungi nestled in the lush grass of a quiet country lane. But our earlier miles of trekking and searching were far from fruitless, the other varied handfuls of tasty shoots, flowers and green leaves we gathered gave great discussion for forager and chef and would create the spontaneity and sense of terroir for impromptu dishes back in the kitchen.

Talking to Robert as we wandered back with our haul of valuable mushrooms, I asked what he felt inspired to cook up with them. "Well there are so many possibilities, all these wild greens add so much depth to the mealy richness and lovely texture of the St George's, I could do a bit of a wild pesto to swirl through some pappardelle pasta ribbons with the mushrooms fried in garlic and flat-leaf parsley; maybe fricassée some in a cyder herb cream with spring vegetables alongside lemon-roasted Sutton Hoo chicken or fish; I love a frittata of local free range eggs, perhaps with some shredded hedgerow leaves and quickly fried St George's; and a great main course would be my favourite flat fish, turbot, simply pan-fried in garlic butter with some brilliant ceps and thyme-sauté potatoes."

Back in the kitchen there was excitement as Robert promised to rustle up a hedgerow risotto of sorts. "Obviously, rice is not a Suffolk speciality so how about a pearl barley orzotto, far more centred on what we do well here, combined with these fascinating unfamiliar wild greens and fabulous fungi?"

The array of foliage heading into the sauté pan and the creamy mixture was a foodie's fantasy, Jon took up the commentary as he handed them to Robert. "So for the St George's mushroom and barley orzotto we have hop shoots, have to have them in Southwold of course; sea beet tops like salty spinach; hedgerow garlic for the savoury base; nettle shoots, just be a bit cautious; wild radish flowers for a peppery rocket-like edge; fennel tops from the dunes for an aniseedy edge; and picked not 50 yards from the restaurant's front door, spring beauty leaves for a final freshness on the top."

Forager's pearl barley 'risotto' with St George's mushrooms and wild spring greens

Orzotto to give its now-adopted name, this lovely slow-cooked potage is a delicious alternative to the Italian rice classic. Cook the grains more than you would for al dente arborio. Desirable wild spring greens include sea beet, samphire, sea purslane, hop shoots, spring beauty, nettle tops, wild fennel fronds, hedgerow garlic and wild radish flowers. Obviously gather your harvest responsibly and safely, following the foragers code of practice and a reliable reference book. NB use gloves to handle the nettles! (serves 4)

Dressing

Large handful nettle tops, blanched and squeezed; 2 tbsp Marybelle crème fraîche; half a lemon, juiced

Make the dressing by blending the crème fraîche, blanched nettles, lemon juice and salt to taste.

Garnish

250g St. George's mushrooms, thickly sliced; 8 rashers smoked streaky Suffolk bacon, 4 shredded and 4 left whole; olive oil; butter; handful of soft tender wild greens

Before starting the risotto, prepare the garnishes. In a deep heavy frying pan over a medium heat, sauté the mushrooms and shredded bacon with a little oil and butter until just browning. Decant to a bowl and keep warm. Use the same pan to cook risotto. Grill the whole bacon rashers until crisp. Prepare soft greens into suitable sprigs or shredded, and set aside.

Risotto

650ml good chicken stock, plus more if needed; 1 medium onion, finely diced; 2 garlic cloves, crushed; 200g cooked pearl barley; 125ml dry Aspall cyder; unsalted butter; 2 handfuls sturdier wild greens

Bring the stock to a simmer in a separate saucepan.

Fry the onion and garlic in the frying pan without colouring until softened, approx. 5 mins.

Over a low-medium heat, add the barley and the cyder, bring to a good simmer, add a little salt and generous pepper with two good knobs of butter, stirring continuously with a spatula until almost dry.

Add a ladle of hot stock at a time, turn up and bring back to the boil, reduce heat to a gentle simmer and stir regularly, repeating with a ladle of stock as it is absorbed for 35 - 45 minutes, until the grains are swollen and tender. Warm soup plates.

Add the sturdier greens, shredded, into the risotto with two more knobs of butter. Cover and leave to wilt. Check consistency and taste, adjusting with more hot stock or seasoning if needed.

To serve with the garnishes, stir in the mushroom and bacon mixture. Spoon risotto onto warm plates, top with the crisp bacon, drizzle with generous dressing and garnish with the softer greens.

Baked east coast crab

Always an indulgent favourite, perfect for alfresco summer afternoons. Serve with chunky chips and a simple green salad.

2 dressed crabs; 1 long shallot, finely diced; ½ tsp Dijon-style mustard; ½ tsp tomato purée; 1 tbsp chopped wild fennel tops; 100ml Marybelle double cream; lemon halves for squeezing; 50g breadcrumbs; 25g parmesan, finely grated

Pre-heat oven to 190c. Remove crabmeat from the shells and reserve both. Combine crab with next five ingredients. Add lemon juice to taste plus light salt and generous pepper, mix well and adjust.

Combine crumbs and cheese. Spoon crab mix back into shells and top with crumble. Bake for 15-20 minutes until golden and bubbling.

Roast Wrentham asparagus, fried duck egg, hedgerow garlic and hazelnut pesto

A quick light lunch. Asparagus, eggs and bruschetta need preparing together. (serves 4)

100g roast hazelnuts; large handful hedgerow garlic leaves; small bunch flat leaf parsley; 30g parmesan, finely grated; 1 bunch asparagus, trimmed; Hillfarm local rapeseed oil; 4 duck eggs; unsalted butter; thick cut sourdough or granary bread; garlic clove, halved; lemon wedges, flesh-side charred, to serve

Heat your char-grill pan. Pre-heat the oven to 200c. Place nuts, herbs, parmesan and a little salt in a pestle and mortar and roughly grind. Add oil to just loosen the mixture to a pesto texture. Taste and adjust seasoning. Snap woody ends off the asparagus spears, toss in a little oil, season, then roast on a hot baking sheet for 5 mins until just tender.

In a frying pan over a low-medium heat, heat up a little oil and lots of unsalted butter before lightly frying duck eggs without browning. Rub the bread with garlic, then lightly oil and season the bread. Char-grill until golden on both sides.

Serve up the asparagus onto warm plates, top with an egg, drizzle with the pesto, and serve with a wedge of charred lemon.

Lemon posset with Suffolk raspberries

A simple easy dessert, which goes down so well. A good crunchy accompaniment like a shortbread or oat biscuit gives texture.

250ml Marybelle double cream; 70g caster sugar; 1 lemon, zested and juiced; sweet ripe local raspberries

Place the cream, sugar and zest in a heavy pan over a gentle heat, simmer for 3-4 mins until the sugar is dissolved. Mix in the juice then remove from heat.

Pour into ramekins or glasses. Cool and refrigerate for 2-3 hours until completely set. Serve garnished with fresh Suffolk raspberries.

Relaxed coastal dining

Belying 600 years of history on its footprint, the latest exciting incarnation of this iconic property as The Sail Loft into an all-new distinctive beachside café-bar-restaurant aptly fits its unique location between the town and Southwold harbour.

The freshness of the design – in off-beat unique furnishings, interesting art, a sense of the artisan – versus the historical permanence – in a distinctive landscape backdrop and an atmospheric setting of a reworked old net shed and sailmaker's works dating back to 1840 – mirrors the sensitive blend of Robert's modern food, a twist on the comfort classics, exploiting local, seasonal, delicious ingredients from field and sea to fork, but giving them a touch of adventure on the plate. Dining from little kids to big and the flexibility of all-day ordering gives a feel of laid-back family feasting, perfect for a seaside bolthole.

Southwold's coastal chic culture, the saltmarsh-beachside setting and those big blue skies above, combine into a compelling pitch for this modernist foodie destination, topped as it is by the excellence of the eating and drinking. Roaring log fires in winter, beautiful sunsets and alfresco lawns in summer, plus crossing the road for paddling, sandcastles and hearty walks along the dunes, all add to the relaxed year-round appeal.

The Sail Loft
53 Ferry Road, Southwold IP18 6HQ
T: 01502 725713
www.sailloftsouthwold.uk
/thesailloftsw
@thesailloftsw

Cost: Carte £25 average; wine from £16.95

Open: All day and evening; food orders 8am-9pm

Details: Blackboard daily specials; bar drinks; take-away coffees and beach picnic hampers; car parking

ROBERT ON HIS...

LUCKY DAY OFF?

Hopefully but unlikely, I'd get to lie in from the kids until 9am, straight down to Southwold beach for sandcastles, bit of a paddle and finishing with a cheap Mr Whippy '99'; back home for a barbecue, whole grilled sea bass, my veg patch salad, buttered new potatoes, ripe strawberries with vanilla ice cream and a Crunchie honeycomb bar, smashed up with one of my expensive saucepans on the patio, the family love that! Oh and a couple of cold beers of course. Happy lazy day.

TOOLS OF THE TRADE?

An expensive freebie from a chef's demo, I stepped in to demonstrate American All-Clad cookware at the Adnams Cellar & Kitchen store in Saffron Walden and was given this great non-stick frying pan, love it to bits, as good as new eight years on.

MIDNIGHT FEAST?

Plain crisp and salad cream sandwiches, thanks Grandma! And those childhood teas, corned beef salad smothered in the yellow stuff, addictive, so different from mayo.

CHILDHOOD AMBITIONS?

An eager schoolboy cadet, I would have been a soldier otherwise, probably in the infantry. But apparently aged 3, I said I wanted to be like "them men in white coats", parents thought I meant a doctor until I said "those with the tall hats"!

CULINARY HEROES?

Chef-restaurateur Mark Hix, his style is so similar to mine, natural ingredient-led food; Hugh Fearnley-Whittingstall got me into foraging and wild foods; Fergus Henderson at London's St. John, that whole 'nose-to-tail' eating; and personally Ian Howell, head chef and mentor for 8 or 9 years at Adnams Hotels.

FAVOURITE PLACES TO SHOP?

To shop – love talking cheese at Nutters in East St, Southwold, their range and enthusiasm is lovely, go in for one thing and come out with three; the Thickitt's Emmerdale Farm Shop at Darsham, near Yoxford, especially for its butchery; and Wangford Farm Shop for its home-grown veggies, such as great greens and fun Halloween pumpkins.

FOODIE NOSTALGIA?

Salad cream from grandma; Cornish pasties from Dad's love of his beloved Cornwall and going on holiday there as a kid – remember eating a huge one aged about 8, rolled home and didn't eat much the rest of that week!

BEST DISHES EVER EATEN?

Lunch in Gascony, south-west France on a duck farm, skewers of duck heart and livers, griddled on an open fire, just with green salad and vinaigrette; on my stag do, bit of a gastronomic treat, exquisite back-to-back Three Michelin-starred meals at The Fat Duck and The Waterside Inn, both in Bray, Berkshire, the hard-to-choose highlight would have to be Alain Roux's halibut poached in seawater with sea vegetables, after champagne in the celeb-reserved summerhouse on the jetty.

FOODIE DISCOVERIES?

Always fascinated by foraging and not knowing what will turn up. Jon showed me something new fifty yards from the Sail Loft's door, amazing delicate green called Spring Beauty or Winter Purslane, a peppery pea-flavoured spinach type leaf, lovely and juicy.

WELL-THUMBED COOKBOOK?

Marco Pierre White's *Wild Food from Land and Sea* for its delicacy and simplicity, I remember when aged 17 trying to cook his vichysoisse with oysters and caviar but used cheap lumpfish roe from the cornershop, pretty dire results.

INSPIRING SUFFOLK VIEW?

Has to be here out over the dunes from upstairs or from the kitchen window back across the saltmarshes. What a view that is for a chef, we don't normally get to see daylight...!

ROBERT'S SIGNATURE DISHES

STARTERS

Potted Blythburgh pork, pickled fennel, treacle and rye bread

Sour dough, n'duja, wild fennel and mozzarella pizza

Salt-baked carrots, Sail Loft ricotta and honeycomb salad

MAINS

Anchor Smokehouse mackerel kedgeree, fried duck egg

Pan-fried gnocchi, red onion, spinach, Fielding Cottage goat's cheese, hazelnuts

Char-grilled Red Poll rib eye, beef dripping chips, house steak butter, Norman's salad leaves

PUDDINGS

Sail Loft 'PBJ' Alaska

Neal's Yard cheese, ale chutney, walnut bread

Dark chocolate brownie, burnt marshmallow, honeycombe

THE PACKHORSE INN, MOULTON
PHIL SKINNER

Berried treasures: Jewel colours and fragrant sweetness

Phil Skinner's pudding menu
at The Packhorse Inn is a true treat
for all the senses

L - R: Paul Williamson, Phil Skinner.

THE PACKHORSE INN PHIL SKINNER

If ever a fruit evoked a season, it is the strawberry. That little heart-shaped, ruby-red, sweetly-juiced mouthful holds the promise of everything most delicious about an English summer. It captures heady warmth, time off and pleasure; it's a fruit that can transport like no other.

Paul Williamson, who grows strawberries in 10 acres of polytunnels on the family fruit farm just outside Bury St Edmunds, sees things from a slightly more prosaic angle. On a hot day in late June, he's concerned about maintaining a constant temperature around the fruit (25c is ideal) and keeping the crop fed and watered – strawberries are high-maintenance, needing a thirsty five minutes of watering and nutrients every hour and a half in warm weather. They also need dry air to prevent mildew, so on the day of our visit the sides of the polytunnels have been lifted. "It's a careful balancing act," Paul explains as we walk along the 100m rows of traditional Elsanta and the newer varieties, Sonata and Malling Centenary. The berries cascade, mostly large and red but some yet to ripen, over the edges of raised gutters packed with the coir matting that provides a disease-resistant growing medium. "The temperature inside the tunnels can be 10c higher than outside when the sides are down. The fruit needs this warmth to ripen but it mustn't get too hot, and we have to make sure the right amount of moisture is reaching the roots and that there's a flow of dry air through the plants."

Pickers – they work in the cool of the early morning or late afternoon – are due to arrive soon to pack punnets of ripe fruit that will be safely cold-stored ready to be sent on to the Williamsons' retail and wholesale customers.

Phil Skinner is one of these customers. Head chef at The Packhorse Inn, Moulton, he has a soft spot for the strawberries which pepper his summer pudding menu. "Customers love them," he says, a berry poised for tasting, "and for me to be able to say they are picked from a grower just a few miles from the pub is fantastic. They really are delicious." He's glad too, he adds, to have the chance to visit the farm and see first hand the care that goes into producing the fruit. "As a chef, I love being close to ingredients. I want to know where the food I cook and serve has come from, how it's been reared or grown. Customers ask about it a lot nowadays."

Phil has worked at The Packhorse Inn since the newly-refurbished pub-restaurant with rooms opened in October 2013 as the flagship Chestnut Group property. His partner Tecora Smith, also at The Packhorse Inn from the start, is their pastry chef and together the pair work hard to create inventive ways of showing seasonal fruit

at its best. "We talk about food and discuss ideas all the time, and even though T (everyone calls her that!) is really the one with the pastry skills, I love working with soft fruit too. It's about the colour, the taste, the fact that local strawberries really do have a season, and that they can be used in so many different ways." At The Packhorse Inn, this ranges from the simple bowl of berries offered at breakfast to more elaborate tartlets, mousses, ice creams and sorbets on the lunch and dinner menus.

A strawberry consommé, for example, lifts a simple dish of fresh berries and mascarpone beautifully. "It's a way of using some riper fruit," Phil explains. "I just mix the fruit with icing sugar and leave it to macerate above the stove, then pass it off through a sieve. It's then poured at the table. So simple and so delicious." Elsewhere, a scoop of zingy berry sorbet cuts perfectly through the richness of a peanut butter parfait or indulgent chocolate brownie, while his Bakewell tart with its strawberry sorbet-filled cannelloni [*see recipe*] shows a degree of inventiveness and originality that he happily admits to be the influence of long-time chef colleague, Chris Lee.

Phil's chef skills were initially honed at the Suffolk College, Ipswich. During his student days he gained experience at the Galley, Woodbridge, and once qualified he worked at The Bildeston Crown as a commis under Chris. He moved to The Packhorse Inn in October 2014 as sous chef and was promoted to head chef the following summer. "It's a fabulous place to work. Boss Philip Turner gives us a lot of latitude in terms of menu creation and we have a busy kitchen with a great team. It's definitely hard work, but I'd say there are four really good moments for every difficult one! It's exciting to be involved in such a fast-growing business, and to contribute to its success."

Although Phil loves playfulness on the menu, he also embraces what he calls an 'old school' style, particularly when cooking fish, an ingredient he enjoys using. "I will always pan-sear a fillet of fish, for example, rather than use sous vide techniques which for me make the texture a bit spongy."

He buys through Marrfish and Direct Seafood both of which sell fish landed on the East Anglian coast or fished in cold Scottish waters. "I think once you've cooked one steak you've cooked a thousand. But with fish, you have to think carefully every single time. It's a challenge to get the skin crisp and the flesh perfectly flaky for every plate and I take real pride in achieving that." On the menu when we meet is trout with a carrot and cardamom purée, baby artichokes and truffle gnocchi [*see recipe*], but it might equally be a piece of sole with brown shrimps and baby vegetables, lobster simply grilled and served with buttery, lemony juices, or an abundant bouillabaisse with crusty bread and a garlicky rouille.

For meat lovers, Phil sticks to local suppliers too. Lamb is from Semer and might appear as a sharing dish of rump and shepherd's pie with wild mushrooms, peas, celeriac and broad beans, while Fordham pork is popular served as a loin and shoulder with pear, spring onion and pomme purée.

As we leave the Williamsons, Phil smiles, glad to have had time with a supplier like Paul and glad to have a few punnets of berries in the back of his car, food for creative thought no doubt on the drive home later with Tecora.

Strawberry Bakewell tart, yoghurt mousse and strawberry sorbet

A comforting but stylish rendition of this traditional favourite with lots of textures and flavours to glam' it up.

For the pastry case, 500g ready-made quality pastry will fit the required size perfectly, lined with parchment and baking beans, before cooking until light-golden in a medium-hot oven. We serve the sorbet in a strawberry 'fruit leather' cannelloni and garnish the dish with fresh strawberries, dried strawberry pieces, baby basil leaves and strawberry purée. If you want to serve the tart simply, a good vanilla ice cream and a strawberry compôte would work well too.

Bakewell tart

250g butter unsalted, softened; 250g sugar;
5 eggs; 125g ground almonds; 125g flour;
23cm/9 inch sweet pastry case, blind baked;
good strawberry jam

Pre-heat the oven to 180c. Start with the frangipan by beating the butter and sugar together until light and fluffy. Add the eggs, one by one, whisking well in between, then mix in the almonds and sieved flour. Spread the tart case generously with strawberry jam; then layer on the frangipan on top and bake at 180c for 30 minutes until golden-brown and cooked through. Allow to cool and remove to a wire rack. Cut and reheat before serving as required. A dusting of icing sugar looks good.

Sorbet

1 litre of trimmed strawberries, puréed;
350g sugar; 250g water

Bring the ingredients to a good simmer, stir until melted, pass through a fine sieve or muslin and cool down for an hour in a wide container. Churn the sorbet in an ice cream machine until sorbet texture and then freeze until required.

Yoghurt mousse

500g natural yoghurt; 75g caster sugar;
13 gelatine leaves, softened in cold water;
1 lemon, juice only; 20g egg whites;
15g caster sugar; 500ml double cream

Whisk the natural yoghurt and the 75g of sugar together. Warm the lemon juice and whisk in the strained gelatine before adding this to the yoghurt mix. Whisk the egg whites, add the 15g amount of sugar and continue until stiff peaks; fold this into the yoghurt mix. Whisk the double cream to soft peaks and mix with the yoghurt mix. Decant into a suitable plastic lidded container and refrigerate until set.

Pâté de fruits

15g pectin; 70g caster sugar;
750g strawberry purée; 780g caster sugar;
185g glucose; 15g citric acid

Mix and warm together the pectin, 70g sugar and the fruit purée until dissolved and bring to a simmer. Stir in the 780g sugar and the glucose and then continue to heat up to 105c, measured on a cooking thermometer. Remove from the heat and whisk in the citric acid. Pass through a sieve and pour into a deep wide plastic tray. Cool and refrigerate, before cutting when set.

Woodpigeon breast, confit leg and baby beets

A smart starter with beetroot purée and red vein sorrel (serves 4)

2 woodpigeons, legs and breasts; duck fat; 4 baby beets; 50ml white wine vinegar; 50ml olive oil; pinch of salt and caster sugar; vegetable oil; 100g flour; 2 eggs, beaten; 200g breadcrumbs

In a small saucepan, cover the pigeon legs with duck fat and bring to the gentlest simmer, cover and cook for two hours until tender. Allow to cool, remove legs, reserve fat and pick off meat. Mix meat with a little of the duck fat, season, roll in cling film to a cylinder shape and chill for 2 hours.

Simmer beets until just al dente, cool slightly and peel. In a snug pan, boil up the vinegar, oil, 50ml of hot water, the pinch of salt and caster sugar. Pour over the beetroot, cover and leave somewhere warm. Pre-heat your deep fat fryer to 180c.

Meanwhile in a hot frying pan, pan fry the oiled and seasoned pigeon breasts until pink. Rest for a few minutes. Slice leg meat thickly. Place flour, egg and breadcrumbs in separate soup plates. Dip slices in flour, then egg, then crumbs, pressing firmly. Gently knock off excess and deep fry carefully until cooked. Keep warm before serving with the carved breast meat and beets.

Loin and shoulder of pork, pear, spring onion

A hearty main course enjoyed with cabbage and pomme purée (serves 4)

1 shoulder of pork; 500g mirepoix (carrot, celery, onion and leek roughly cut); 75g tomato purée; 1 bottle of red wine; 2 litres of good quality beef stock; 4 baby pears, peeled, cooked, halved, seeds removed; caster sugar; 4 spring onions; unsalted butter; 4 x 100g pork loin portions; rapeseed oil

Pre-heat your oven to 140c. In a very hot pan, seal the oiled and seasoned shoulder on all sides until browned; remove from pan. In a large ovenproof lidded casserole dish, brown the mirepoix, add the purée and red wine, reducing liquor down to a quarter volume. Return the shoulder and pour over stock. Bake for 5 hours or until falling off the bone. Reserve the liquor and cool joint, Remove the meat, discarding unsavoury parts. Just cover with liquor and refrigerate.

Caramelise pears in a hot pan with some sugar until browning. Keep warm. Blanch spring onion in salted water and colour in some foaming butter and seasoning. Keep warm. In a hot pan over a high heat, fry the oiled and seasoned loins until all sides are coloured; bake for 3-4 mins. Allow to rest and keep warm. Reheat the shoulder before serving together.

Fillet of trout, carrot purée and baby artichokes

Serve with potato gnocchi, sautéed spinach, red endive leaves and blanched baby carrots. (serves 4)

500g carrots, finely-sliced; 2 crushed cardamom pods; 250ml chicken stock; 4 baby artichokes; lemon juice; 75ml olive oil; 50g carrot, 50g celeriac, both diced; 2 garlic cloves; pinch of salt and sugar; 200ml dry white wine; 4 trout fillets, skin-on; 50g butter

For the purée: sweat the carrot and cardamom in butter until soft but with no colour; add 50ml of the stock and cook until the carrots are breaking down. Blitz and pass through a fine sieve. Keep warm.

For the artichokes, peel the stalk and remove all outer leaves; reserve in water with lemon juice. In a hot pan over a high heat with the oil, sauté carrot and celeriac for 1 min; add the artichokes and cook for a further 2 mins; then the garlic, salt and sugar. Add white wine and reduce to almost no liquid. Add the 200ml of chicken stock and simmer until the stalk of the artichoke is soft. Keep warm.

For the trout: pan-fry the oiled and seasoned fillets, skin side down in a hot pan. After 2 mins, add the butter and when foaming, turn the fish over and cook for a further minute or longer, depending on size. Serve together.

Country chic

Is it a pub? Is it a hotel? Is it a restaurant? Philip Turner, owner of The Chestnut Group is happy for his flagship property to defy categorisation.

"We want The Packhorse Inn to be a blend of what's best about a pub, a restaurant, and a hotel," he explains. "We aim to provide fabulous food, a convivial relaxed atmosphere at the heart of the local community, and a glamorous bed for the night." It seems straightforward enough, but of course it's taken monumental effort to realise the vision.

The Packhorse Inn, tucked up against the medieval bridge over the river Kennett and just a couple of miles from Newmarket, reopened under new ownership in October 2013. Fully refurbished with a large dining and bar area at its heart and a polished-country feel, The Packhorse Inn is unrecognizable from the tired, unloved pub that once occupied this space. It now caters for a mix of local residents, is popular with the Newmarket racing fraternity, with business guests who use the private Club Room for meetings, and with overnight visitors from further afield drawn no doubt by the slew of awards and recommendations the place has garnered since opening.

Philip's wife, Amanda, has put her stylish eye to work on the interiors. Throughout, the look is classily rural, with old pictures on the walls, enveloping shades of deep plum and mushroom, reclaimed furniture and an open fire. Quirky details such as a boar's head and a stone sculpture of a horse mix with the more conventional high-end pub-restaurant notions of waxed oak floors, comfortable seating, sumptuous fabrics and gleaming tableware. Upstairs, and in an adjacent 'coach house', are eight individually-designed en suite bedrooms where vast beds, Egyptian cotton sheets, huge mirrors, luxurious throws and indulgent bathroom products will tempt visitors to linger.

Amanda has done a similar job at the group's second property, The Rupert Brooke in Grantchester, and as this book goes to press is turning her attention to the latest projects in the Chestnut Group portfolio.

And while all things Suffolk find pride of place in the kitchen, the bar offer is far more eclectic. "Of course we sell Adnams ale but there's a place here for Fuller's London Pride and Norfolk Woodforde's Wherry too," says Philip, who works closely with his sister, Louisa, managing director of Wymondham-based wine merchants, Peter Graham Wines, to put together a bespoke wine list. The list scours the old and new world to offer everything from crowd-pleasing pinot grigios and sauvignon blancs to a fabulous 2010 Puligny-Montrachet and some big-hitting classics from the Bordeaux vineyards of St Emilion, St Julien and Margaux.

The Packhorse Inn
Bridge Street, Moulton,
nr Newmarket CB8 8SP
T: 01638 751818
W: www.thepackhorseinn.com
/packhorseinn
@moultopackhorse

Accolades: Three AA Rosettes 2015, *The Publican Morning Advertiser* Best Food Pub East Midlands & East Anglia 2014, *Alastair Sawday's*; *Michelin Eating Out in Pubs*; *Waitrose Good Food Guide* 2015 score 3; AA 5-star accommodation

Cost: Carte £34 average; set L (Mon - Thu) two courses £18 / three courses £24; wine from £16.95

Open: All year 8am-11pm

Details: Children welcome; wheelchair access; dogs welcome (£10 charge overnight); bar drinks and snacks; sandwiches and light lunches; car parking

PHIL ON HIS...

FAVOURITE BIT OF KITCHEN EQUIPMENT?

A really good, high-powered jug blender, it's essential for making smooth purées and soups. I've got a great Enpee in the kitchen at The Packhorse Inn.

FAVOURITE LOCAL FOODIE PLACES

Aqua Eight, Ipswich – one of my all time favourites! I always order something different and it's always delicious, tasty, original. I think I like it because it is so totally different from what we cook at The Packhorse Inn, not a type of cooking I ever do.
The Butt and Oyster, Pin Mill – a great place to have a bite to eat and catch up with friends. It's a lovely spot to sit, chill and chat; I could stay at that pub for ages!
Hollow Trees Farm Shop, Semer – I love taking my nephew and nieces there; we'll have a walk, go to the shop, have something at the café.

IF NOT A CHEF?

I'd be involved in the family business. My dad and uncle run a haulage company in Ipswich called Green and Skinner. I was thinking of getting involved but in the end I chose cooking.

MIDNIGHT SNACK?

It's a bowl of cereal every time – and it's got to be Sultana Bran, not sure why, but it hits the spot after a hard day's cooking. Maybe I've had enough of good food by midnight!

INSPIRING SUFFOLK VIEW?

Landguard Point, Felixstowe – especially watching the boats come and go and the general view across the estuary to the Shotley Peninsula.

COOK'S CHEATS AND CHEF'S TIPS?

Soak garlic in warm tap water for a while before peeling. The skin comes off easily and you don't get that sticky residue on your fingers.

BEST DISHES EVER EATEN?

It has to be the Le Gavroche signature classic Soufflé Suissesse. Nothing can beat it.

LUCKY DAY OFF?

Time with my girlfriend Tecora is very precious and when we manage to get the same day off, we'll make the most of it, maybe going to Aldeburgh for fish and chips with Tecora's mum's cockapoo, Jude, who loves a walk on the beach. Otherwise, the boating lake at Thorpeness is great fun and often we just love going to the cinema.

ULTIMATE DINING DESTINATIONS?

Tecora and I will splash out on a lush meal once a year. Last time we went to Midsummer House in Cambridge and it was amazing, a real eye-opener, a way of seeing what is possible with food. Daniel Clifford is a massive talent. We'd love to get to Tom Kerridge's Hand and Flowers in Marlow but the waiting list is about six months!

CULINARY HEROES?

I guess I wanted to become a chef after seeing them on TV – people like Jamie Oliver, such a huge inspiration to so many people, or Sat Bains, Tom Kerridge and Daniel Clifford.

WELL-THUMBED COOKBOOKS?

I'd love to build up a library of cookbooks in time but to be honest for now the Internet does a perfectly good job when I'm looking for recipes!

MUSIC TO COOK TO AT HOME?

Ed Sheeran, anything acoustic. I do most of the cooking at home and I like to create a calm environment.

PHIL'S SIGNATURE DISHES

STARTERS

Seared scallops, black pudding, cauliflower florets, apple purée

Duck liver parfait, toasted brioche, melon chutney

Truffled goat's cheese with quince, fig and hazelnuts

MAINS

Fillet of stone bass, brown shrimp tortellini, parsley pearl barley

Wild garlic risotto, morels, girolles, asparagus

Char-grilled rib of Suffolk beef to share with chips, wild mushrooms, French beans, béarnaise sauce

PUDDINGS

Chocolate fondant with vanilla ice cream

Pear and almond frangipan, Amaretto ice cream

Local cheeseboard, including Suffolk Gold, Baron Bigod and Suffolk Blue, served with port jelly and biscuits

Taking the plunge: boarding a lobster boat on the river Ore

For self-made chef-restaurateur Paul Yaxley, hard work and passion has been rewarding

L-R: Bill Pinney, Paul Yaxley.

BOSS

It all seemed so simple on the phone. Paul Yaxley loves his lobster as do the foodie guests in this north Suffolk oasis, who can't seem to get enough of this luxurious meaty crustacean. Now not saying it's entirely a culinary desert around here but this chef has got his finger on the pulse of what suits his diners and they drive from far and wide. The appeal of this prime shellfish is clear, dominating the specials board of The Fox And Goose and announcing its local origin.

"So let's visit Bill over in Orford, he's our man, no-one knows more about lobsters around here," was Paul's affirmation in our planning. That's Bill, one of the Pinneys, a Suffolk surname synonymous with fine smoked fish and seafood and famed for all that is delicious from the beautiful East coast; he is The Fox And Goose's seafood supplier.

The family's good achievements are thanks, in no small part, to 70 years of tradition and his father Richard Pinney's original ingenuity in the post-war years to restore the tradition of oyster farming in Butley Creek. Like many successful food-business dynasties in Suffolk, they have been pioneering, not just in the way they left the slump of post-war London in the 1940s to seek their fortune, but in how they have expanded from those first oyster beds. The business now boasts a smokehouse, a village seafood café – The Butley-Orford Oysterage in the Market Square, two commercial fishing boats and a seafood shop on the Quay.

As we head to the Creek and Pinney's farmstead fishery through the private lanes of Gedgrave Estate, we drop down between the arable fringes and the saltmarsh through gameshoot coverts to a hidden world in the lee of the river wall. Here stands the Pinneys' home, a charming redbrick family house, where a smoky fragrance fills the air from the adjoining smokery.

Walking down to the fishing sheds, Paul and Bill start chatting and it's easy to see a kindred spirit in these two entrepreneurial characters, shaped by their respective tradition, the classic cookery of fine dining for the former and a fisherman's long-standing craft for the latter. A shared sense of valuing the history and integrity of their respective businesses is clear; in the Fox and Goose a 16th century Guildhall-turned-historical inn next to the village church at the heart of community life; and in Pinney's not just three generations of a fishing family business but also protecting a centuries-long heritage of Suffolk coastal shellfish-farming. And it is apparent from both of them how respect for the past is pivotal to present success but also how considered evolution, rather than wanton revolution is shaping the future.

On this sunny day, the beautiful riverscape and wildlife-rich habitat couldn't fail to stir the soul. The fine weather did not hide the rawness of the fishermen's toil and discomfort, especially in the cold and wet in the obvious exposure to the elements. Bringing in seafood delights for diners and chefs is not a career choice for the faint-hearted.

Hilarity ensued as we broached the marram-grassed riverbank and realised Bill's gentle ribbing about inappropriate land-lubbers garb and footwear (some of us had not even brought wellies, ahem!) and his comedic quip, "well we will have to use the van to get you out there then on the big boat," was serious. Now an old Ford Transit with no doors to the rear and little memory of better days didn't entirely inspire, though clearly it was an old faithful carthorse ferrying delicious cargo for the family's fishing vessels. Our visions of driving submarine out to the 'Southern Cross' a few hundred metres downstream were clearly outlandish. Bill swiftly returned under power from his super-fast row out with the tide, now steering a small engined skiff. We were swiftly instructed to climb into the 'Tranny' and hold on tight. Full of mirth and trepidation, we were gently reversed into the water to jump cautiously aboard. A few minutes under propeller motored us out to our berth for some hard pot-hauling, but our embarkation acrobatics were not yet over as we inelegantly clambered aboard, flopping over the sides.

As Bill set about checking the day's catch, there was a distinct dawning for Paul; that unbridled enthusiasm a true chef has for his raw materials as he got up close and warily personal, a need to know what makes his prized ingredient so tasty and understand more about it for his diners' enjoyment. A little nip for an old hand like Bill was a rare lapse and showed another discomfort his crews deal with to get our precious lobster treats.

Back on dry land later, disembarkation a lot less daunting, we toured the holding pens at the fishery, where tidal flow twice-daily replenishes the harvested lobsters to keep them in prime condition with nutrient-rich sea water.

Paul was keen to talk about the sustainability of lobsters and it was very evident how controlled Bill's fishing techniques are, both as a responsible skipper but also with tight government control. At the Fox and Goose, they like to serve lobster in style, buying the big juicy specimens so they can thickly carve the tail meat; it was reassuring to hear that this actually helps the younger more effective breeding-stock to get a claw-hold on territory and reproduce faster.

On the way back to Fressingfield to get to grips with the catch, Paul spoke fondly of the first taste, "Pinney's seafood just blew my previous supplier out of the water, the lobsters' quality and freshness of course, alongside the family's integrity and the local provenance story."

Nothing goes to waste from this premium ingredient; shells are roasted to infuse vinaigrettes and ground down for shellfish bisque soups. Paul's favourite ways to serve it usually starts with the same signature technique. After a quick humane despatch, they are poached and cooled in a fragrant lemon, herbed and spiced courtbouillon, before the shelled meat heads into ravioli; a warm chorizo and red pepper salad; being grilled with wild garlic and mint alongside spring vegetables and new season potatoes; the choices and popular dishes here are endless.

Orford lobster, samphire, sweetcorn pannacotta, tomatoes, herbs and almonds

A light but indulgent alfesco starter perfect for a sunny dinner party. Prepare the pannacotta, lobster and tomatoes ahead. (serves 6)

Sweetcorn pannacotta

300g sweetcorn,cooked in water, reserving 50ml cooking liquor; 75g milk; 100g cream; 1 tsp sea salt; 1½ leaves gelatine, soaked in cold water

Place all ingredients except the gelatine into a heavy saucepan over a medium heat, bring to the boil, simmer for a minute. Cool and carefully blend with the strained gelatine. Once smooth, pass through a fine sieve into a large jug. Pour into 6 small oiled dariole moulds (about 120ml size) up to three-quarters full and refrigerate until set.

Lobsters

A few star anise; large pinch of coriander seed; 1 bay leaf; zest of 1 orange; 2 local East Coast lobsters, 1kg approx each

Add flavourings to a large pan of boiling water. Humanely despatch the lobsters and carefully drop in. Simmer well for about 8 minutes and remove to a tray. Once cool enough to handle, twist off the head from the tail, crack open the claws, remove meat and repeat for the tails. Ensure shells are reserved for the dressing. Store both in the fridge.

Dressing

Shells from two lobsters; 100ml rapeseed oil; 2 long shallots, half a carrot, half a leek, half a fennel bulb and 2 celery sticks, all thinly sliced; 1 garlic clove, crushed; ½ tsp coriander seeds and fennel seeds; 2 star anise; 1 dsp tomato purée; 150ml apple juice; ½ bunch basil leaves, finely sliced; good fish stock

In a deep large frying pan, heat the oil over a medium-high setting and add the shells carefully. Move around gently and cook for a few minutes, add in the vegetables and spices and cook for another 5 minutes. Add in the tomato purée and apple juice. Reduce until almost evaporated, cover the shells with fish stock and bring to the boil, simmering for 30 minutes. Turn off the heat for 10 minutes, then strain through a fine sieve into a similar clean saucepan. Boil to reduce by a good half to roughly 200ml and strongly tasting of lobster. Once cooled, add the basil and whisk in 100ml of rapeseed oil. Whisk together and adjust seasoning.

Garnishes

Samphire sprigs, washed, trimmed and blanched to al dente, kept warm; soft herb leaves eg lemon balm, coriander cress, basil cress, watercress; 12 cherry tomatoes, halved, baked in a low oven with a sprinkle of icing sugar, sea salt, black pepper and thyme leaves until semi-dried; flaked almonds, toasted

To serve

Carve lobster meat into chunks. Release the pannacotta from the mould by running under warm water and place in the centre of four chilled plates. Scatter around with lobster, dot around the tomatoes, followed by the samphire, lobster dressing and herb salad, finishing with a flourish of almonds.

Shipcord Suffolk cheese and truffle rarebit

Alternatives to topping beef fillet include grilling it on griddled chicken or baked cod. You could substitute half the cheese for Suffolk Blue or parmesan or other hard cheese. (makes plenty)

350g Shipcord cheese; 100g milk; 1 tsp English mustard powder; 50g breadcrumbs; 25g plain flour; 1 egg; 2 yolks; 1 tbsp strong black truffle oil;

In a pan on a low heat melt the cheese and milk together until smooth but avoid boiling. Add the mustard powder, breadcrumbs and flour. Cook on a low-medium heat for 2 mins or until it starts to thicken. Cool for a few minutes in a bowl.

Pour the mixture into a food processor, seasoning with light salt and generous pepper to taste. Add the eggs and truffle oil. Purée until smooth, approx. 1 min. Transfer to a plastic container and refrigerate until firm.

Pre-heat your grill on high before using. Take out a golf ball-sized piece of rarebit mix and flatten out between clingfilm in your hands. Peel off and place on your chosen cooked ingredients. Grill until coloured golden.

Potted shrimp butter sauce

We serve this over lovely East coast fish such as wild sea bass and local vegetables, perhaps new season asparagus or samphire. This makes a lovely starter in itself, set into small jars, then warmed to a hot room temperature before serving with toast and tomato chutney. And if you don't like shrimps, try making it with crab, salmon or prawns. Store in fridge and use within three days. (it makes plenty – reduce quantities if needed)

250g butter, at room temperature; half a nutmeg, grated; 1 tsp cayenne pepper; zest and juice of 1 lemon; 1 garlic clove, peeled and finely chopped; 2 long shallots, peeled and finely diced; 1 dsp each of tarragon, flat leaf parsley and basil, finely chopped; 400g freshly-cooked brown shrimps, peeled

Place butter, nutmeg, cayenne, zest, juice and garlic into a food processor and blend for about 2 minutes until incorporated. Transfer to a mixing bowl. Add the shallots, herbs and shrimps. Mix well. Refrigerate in a plastic container, covered.

Tip the solid mixture out of the tub and cut off as much as required. Warm through in a small saucepan and serve.

Local ripe strawberries with gooseberry-elderflower gel

Other seasonal fruit works well such as raspberries, loganberries and tropical imports. The gel is also delicious with griddled mackerel fillets or pork steaks. We serve this with red chilli dust and basil meringues for crunch. (serve 4)

250g gooseberries; 250g water; 125g elderflower cordial; 50g sugar; 1tbsp agar agar

Place all the ingredients in a pan except the agar agar and bring to the boil, simmer for 2 minutes and remove. Decant to a bowl, cool until warm. Purée in a food processor and pass through a sieve into a clean pan. Bring to a simmer and whisk in the agar agar, continue cooking for a minute or until the mixture thickens slightly, pour into a container, cool and chill in the fridge until firm. Place into a food processor and blend until smooth, adding a little more elderflower cordial if needs be to loosen the mix. Return to the fridge.

To serve

2 large handfuls ripe strawberries, de-hulled and sliced; vanilla sugar

Place a few dots of the gel on cold plates and top with strawberries, dusted in vanilla sugar. Place on your chosen garnishes.

Never grim(m) with fairytale food

The fable has the geese endlessly praying whilst Mr Fox patiently waits to select the fattest bird; how apt for a restaurant renowned for leaving its guests well-fed and satiated... What's more, the sidegate in the Fox and Goose's carpark might just come in handy if Paul Yaxley's soul-satisfying food hasn't entirely done the trick leading as it does to the beautiful 14th century church next door or for a post-prandial constitutional in its quite charming graveyard. In fact, you dine seated on Church Estates property as this old Guildhall is also on ecclesiastical grounds.

The 'F & G', as it is known, is all about indulgence. There is no pretence to healthy eating or quick business lunches here, this is about proper relaxation and a little dining escapism. Prior ownership saw high and lows for this quaint hostelry and restaurant, most notably in the skilled hands of '*The Hotel Inspector*' Ruth Watson, and her husband David, for much of the Nineties. But what a difference a few years had made; when Paul arrived to snap it up in 2002, he found it forlorn and bedraggled, unbefitting of one of Suffolk's previously best restaurants.

With trademark enthusiasm and unstinting determination, Paul and his supportive wife Sarah set about restoring the F & G's culinary reputation as a relaxed destination restaurant and country pub. With a well-stocked bar and two atmospheric neighbouring dining rooms downstairs with beams and fireplaces a-plenty there is space and comfort for all, plus more with a refined restaurant for evening dining above and atmospheric alfresco eating on the quaint pondside terrace. Paul similarly offers something for everyone on his menus too, from fixed price fine dining, pub specials à la carte, simple classics, not forgetting an eight course taster and Sunday lunch. And naturally, the wine selection gets the same characteristic Yaxley relish.

A humble Broads boy made good, catering college encouraged Paul on to great things and gave him training opportunities to learn his hard graft and be inspired (The Norfolk Mead, Stower Grange and the Old Ram at Tivetshall) before he found himself co-owning his own local restaurant, Taps in Horning, aged just 21, a good testbed to perfect his management skills and culinary technique. The hard graft hasn't stopped since.

The Fox & Goose
Church Road, Fressingfield,
nr Harleston IP21 5PB
T: 01379 586247
W: www.foxandgoose.net
/foxandgoose1609
@foxygossip

Accolades: 2 AA Rosettes 2015; *Hardens* and *Michelin* listings

Cost: Restaurant set L two courses £15.95 / three courses £20.95 & set D two courses £27 / £34; tasting menu 8 courses £50 and optional wine flight £25; Set Sunday L two courses £20 / three courses £25; carte £25 average in pub; wine from £15.95

Open: 12-3.30pm / 7-11pm; food served Tue – Fri 12-2pm / 7-8.30pm, Sat 12-1.45pm / 7-8.30pm, Sunday 12-2pm / 6.30- 8.15pm

Details: Bar drinks; alfresco dining; terrace; private dining; disabled facilities; event catering; car parking

PAUL ON HIS...

SOCIAL MEDIA?

I'm a bit of a tweeter, my hashtag on Twitter is @foxygossip. I follow Great British Chefs and Staff Canteen among other foodie sites.

LAST SUPPER?

On the menu: Suffolk lobster of course, with wild garlic and mint butter; wild game probably partridge or mallard, wild mushrooms and roasted roots; peach tarte tatin with lemon grass-basil ripple ice cream; Vacherin cheese and a good bottle of port. On the invite list: Rik Mayall; Cookie Monster; Richard Branson; Lee Mack; Stephen Fry to keep Sarah, my wife and better half, entertained; and my three year-old daughter, Lily.

FOODIE DISCOVERIES?

Now getting into sous vide vacuum cooking in a water bath, great for control and consistency and of course, labour-saving, perfect way to cook fish and game birds, keeping them moist and tender, for example.

Starting to use more clever gastronomy products, to help with flavour, texture and presentation. Things like maltodextrin, a dried starch, turns oil into a powder, which is fascinating. Love using gels in my food too. With all the modern techniques, they need to be used sparingly and thoughtfully.

CHILDHOOD AMBITIONS?

Definitely wanted to be a footballer, a midfielder, for the Canaries of course, being a Norfolk lad. Did actually trial for them, was pretty good, but a bad leg break scuppered my chances in the beautiful game, medically 'retired' they call it.

COOK'S CHEATS AND CHEF'S TIPS?

To make zesting easy, push greaseproof over the rough side of the grater before tackling your citrus fruits; to get more juice out of them, gently roll them well on the kitchen unit then microwave until warm; any spare prepared fruit always goes well blended into purées for coulis and other dishes

MIDNIGHT FEAST?

Pizza from the freezer straight in the oven, nothing special, add on the deli leftovers from the fridge; or a good old bacon sarnie, smoked Suffolk streaky, fried egg, toasted bread, definitely no sauce. And at work, has to be the boys' home-made bread, love grabbing a quick roll, no time to even butter it.

TOOLS OF THE TRADE?

Disposable gloves are must-haves for handling fish and meat; clingfilm is always being used on everything; and of course, a sharp knife is essential.

BEST DISHES EATEN?

London is king for me when dining – still remember my first top restaurant experience, with Michel Roux Jr. at Le Gavroche, I was amazed by the artichoke heart with truffles, chicken mousse and truffle jus; since then, so many others, perhaps Philip Howard at The Square and Brett Graham at The Ledbury.

LUCKY DAY OFF?

Has to involve sailing on the river or out to sea. Often on Mum and Dad's boat, a sailing cruiser, getting under sail from its mooring on the Broads. Always take a picnic Fox and Goose-style, usually exotic leftovers! Prosecco to get the day started and good crisp Kiwi Sauvignon Blanc to follow. And if I am lucky, cheese and port to fall asleep with.

INSPIRING SUFFOLK VIEW?

Bit of escapism from work of course, so it would be on the Suffolk coast with my wife, Sarah and Lily, just getting away from it all, Southwold, Walberswick, Aldeburgh, somewhere with beach, water and lots of fresh air.

ULTIMATE DINING DESTINATIONS?

I tend to head to London to be spoilt outrageously but if not, maybe Midsummer House in Cambridge or Sat Bains up in Nottingham.

PAUL'S SIGNATURE DISHES

STARTERS

Caramelised mackerel, gooseberry-elderflower purée, ginger apples, lemon balm, almonds

Rillettes of duck, liver bavarois, raisins, fennel, walnuts and crackling

Ham hock terrine with apples, mustard, parsnip crisps, quails' eggs and crispy pig's ears

MAINS

Trio of Suffolk pork: belly, fillet, cheek with peach-almond chutney, sprouting broccoli, butternut squash purée and mille feuille potatoes

Hake fillet with roast cauliflower, gem lettuce, tarragon gnocchi, marinated grapes and potted prawn butter

Partridge with pears, roast parsnips, chestnut foam, potato fondant and thyme jus

PUDDINGS

Rhubarb parfait, with mandarin sorbet, poached rhubarb, pistachio cake and mandarin jelly

Warm summer fruit tart with elderflower chiboust

Chocolate and peanut butter mousse with popcorn, salted caramel and caramelised white chocolate sorbet.

1921, BURY ST EDMUNDS
ZACK DEAKINS

Single estate: Denham Castle lamb takes centre stage at 1921

Zack Deakins puts a confident, fine-tuned spin on first-rate seasonal ingredients

L - R: Neil Clarke, Zack Deakins.

1921 ZACK DEAKINS

Neil Clarke shoulders a sack of feed as if it were feather-light, strides to the middle of the field, and slashes it open. His flock comes running, bleating hungrily, eager to reach the pellets that he shakes out in a semicircle.

"I didn't feed them this morning because I thought we'd do this," he laughs. Phil captures the moment on camera quickly before the animals disperse, pellets eaten, and go back to grazing the picture-perfect fields of the Denham Estate.

Back in the farm truck, Neil, who looks after all the livestock with one other member of staff and a "sort of sheepdog", rattles off numbers.

A thousand of the estate's 1,500 acres is given over to arable, most of the rest left for Fallow deer and a breeding flock of 320 or so rare breed ewes, Soay and Wiltshire Horn. These ewes are crossed with a Southdown or Hampshire ram to create the Denham Castle lamb – about 600 of them are born a year – that is unique to the estate.

The breed is the result of research by the late Michael Gliksten who bought the farm – originally several hundred acres of top fruit – in 1979, quickly grubbing up the unprofitable apples and pears in favour of rearing livestock alongside the crops. Now, Michael's widow Cecilia runs the operation, overseeing everything from breeding to the on-site butchery and the all-important relationships with chef customers around the UK.

And so, one day last year, Cecilia picked up the phone to Zack Deakins. He was settling in at the stove of his new Bury St Edmunds restaurant, 1921, and welcomed the approach. "I wasn't familiar with Denham Estate, but Cecilia sent me some samples and I loved the taste straightaway. The lamb is a bit gamey, has a real flavour, not the insipid taste that you sometimes get. I've had it – and the Denham Estate venison – on my menu right from day one. It was a no-brainer."

The ethical and environmental aspect of the Denham Estate approach appeals to Zack too, "The fact that the sheep are raised on native grasses, clover and wild herbs makes for incredible flavour and tenderness, even in the fat. And the whole family story and careful farming practices give me peace of mind in what I'm buying."
He pauses, looking round the lambing pens, empty, bar a couple of ewes yet to lamb, and three nuzzled up in deeply-strawed pens with their still-wobbly offspring, born just hours earlier. The lambs stay with the mother before being weaned at 12 weeks and are finished slowly outside for about a year. The presence of an on-site abattoir means stress to animals is kept to a minimum. "So often I've had to send meat back because there'll be blood spots in it caused by stress at slaughter, but that never happens with either the Denham lamb or venison," says Zack.

At 1921, lamb appears in a variety of guises during spring and summer. "It's such a versatile meat; there are so many cuts that can be used, each with their own flavour and texture," Zack says.
"I particularly like using saddle [see main recipe] but I might do rump with peas, broad beans and gnocchi, a classic French navarin, or slow-cooked shanks. Confit belly is popular and I use the sweetbreads to make croquettes for our canapé menu. I could use lamb year-round but I think it has a particular affinity with spring flavours so I tend to keep it to that time of year – it's delicious with wild garlic."

At home he'll keep things simpler. "Customers expect a certain level of cooking and presentation – I love being creative plating up – but at home I'll simply braise a shoulder and eat it with mash and sprouting broccoli. Cooking the meat slowly really intensifies the richness of the flavour and softness of the texture; it also means you can make cheaper cuts like shoulder or neck taste incredible."

Zack's menu at 1921 is rooted in the classic French tradition. Intense flavours abound – this is a place to eat pan-fried veal sweetbreads, meaty brill with braised pork belly and sea-salty palourde clams, or in autumn hearty confit rabbit with salsify and girolles, or an indulgent crème brûlée. Zack is an unashamed cream- and butter-lover ("I adore Lescure in particular"), and is fond of adding a shaving of truffle to give earthily-decadent depth to dishes such as Ardleigh asparagus with truffle croquettes, shimeji mushrooms, hazelnuts; or autumn truffle arancini with trompette de la mort, Braeburn apple, salt-baked celeriac.

"I think eating out at 1921 should be something special. You're not going to do it every day so what's wrong with giving your tastebuds a treat once in a while?" The treat does admittedly come from the finest ingredients sourced from around the world (ceps are South African, ham is often artisanal Ibérico, and he likes to use Morteau sausage, smoked traditionally over juniper and conifer by small producers in the heart of France), but Zack is supportive of locally-produced ingredients whenever they are the best. "That's one of the reasons I love spring and summer – asparagus from Lawford, strawberries from Lindsey, wild garlic which my assistant manager Jess and her partner Jiri (my chef de partie!) pick locally."

Zack's approach has been honed over years observing, cooking, learning, leading in a variety of kitchens, from food-led pubs to fine dining destination restaurants. He's worked hard – 17 hours a day is not uncommon, especially now as he establishes 1921 – but he wouldn't have it any other way. "Working hard comes with the job of being a chef, and, yes, getting some sort of work-life balance can be hard," he says. "If you want to succeed, you need to start young and aspire to being like the people above you. It's about drive, determination and desire, and that never changes even when you have your own place."

Now that he does have his own place, thanks to a business partnership with Paul Bailey, Zack is exactly where he wants to be. He sits relaxed in the comfortable bar area of 1921, taking a brief moment out of the kitchen to chat, "I've always wanted my own place – what chef doesn't? And I love the fact that I can bring everything I've learnt over the years together in one place and offer food that I like and that I think people want to eat."

Roasted saddle of Denham Estate lamb with braised shoulder and wild garlic purée

At 1921 we serve this duo of lamb alongside baby artichokes hearts. Ask your butcher for two trimmed loins plus caul fat crépinette; lardo is smoked cured pork fat. Braise the shoulder the day before; reheat alongside the garlic purée whilst resting the loin parcels. (serves 4)

Saddle of Suffolk lamb

1 slice good white bread (crusts removed); 1 garlic clove, finely chopped; 1 rosemary sprig, leaves finely chopped; large pinch of sel rose (available from delis); two whole lamb loins; 250g minced lamb; 200g thinly-sliced pork lardo or pancetta; 100g crépinette; rapeseed or olive oil; unsalted butter

Break the bread into a food processor, add the garlic, rosemary and salt, pulsing to a fine crumb texture. Mix well with the minced lamb in a bowl. Split and roll into two long sausage shapes, to fit the lamb loins and sit on top, wrapping in the lardo to cover. Place each cylinder onto a sheet of crépinette to generously wrap it up. Secure well with clean butchers' string.

When ready to cook, pre-heat your oven to 185c fan. In a frying pan brown the unwrapped parcels in a splash of oil and a few knobs of butter when hot and foaming. Cook until even gold on all sides. Place on an ovenproof tray and bake for approximately ten minutes. Remove, keep warm and rest for ten minutes before carving.

Braised shoulder

Good lamb or beef stock; 300g lamb shoulder; rapeseed or olive oil; 1 carrot; 2 sticks of celery; 1 onion, all coarsely chopped; 2 cloves of garlic, peeled and chopped; 250ml red wine; 1 sprig of rosemary

Pre-heat the oven to 130c. In a large saucepan, bring sufficient stock to cover the lamb and vegetables to a simmer. Meanwhile heat up a heavy-based deep sauté pan, lightly oil and brown the shoulder until golden and remove. Using the same hot pan, fry the carrot, celery, onion and garlic until they start to colour. Add the red wine and reduce on a high heat until the liquid evaporates to a few tablespoons.

Transfer the vegetables, juices and lamb to a covered large casserole with the hot stock and rosemary. Bake for approximately four hours (or until the meat is tender and falling apart) and remove. Carefully transfer the lamb to a plate, removing any vegetables from it. Sieve the stock into a clean large saucepan. Discard the strained vegetables. Over a high heat, reduce the stock until thick and sticky. Decant to a clean bowl and allow to cool for an hour, covered.

Pick the bones, fat and sinew out of the lamb while warm and shred the meat. Transfer to a clean bowl and allow to cool for 45 minutes, covered. Next add enough of the stock to bind it, before rolling the mixture in cling film to form a tight cylinder. Wrap well all over. Chill this in the fridge overnight plus the spare stock. Just before serving, cut into desired portion size and then place on a deep oven tray with the remaining reduced stock. Reheat in a hot oven for approximately six minutes, being sure to baste it when warming through. Remove cling film before serving.

Wild garlic purée

100g washed wild garlic or ramsons leaves (stems removed); 50g butter; approx 200ml hot chicken stock

Melt the butter in a wide heavy saucepan, allowing it to lightly foam without colouring over full heat. Working quickly, carefully add the wild garlic to the pan and wilt, not allowing it to colour, whilst moving the contents around with tongs or a carving fork. Pour in the hot chicken stock and cook whilst stirring occasionally on a high heat until the stock has evaporated. Transfer to a liquidizer and carefully blend until smooth before pushing it through a fine sieve. When required, gently reheat the purée in a saucepan, stirring all the time.

To serve

Begin with a swipe of the wild garlic purée on four warm plates. Carve each lamb loin into two, and place one piece with a portion of braised shoulder on the purée. Finish with your chosen garnish and vegetables.

Cured cod with soy jelly

A Japanese-Scandinavian fusion to start an oriental supper in style. (serves 4)

Cod

200g sugar; 200g coarse sea salt; zest of two lemons; juice of one lemon; 50ml Adnams Suffolk vodka; 5g fennel seeds; 5g coriander seeds; 5g black peppercorns; 500g thick fillet of good quality fresh cod

Combine all the ingredients well, except the fish. Spread approximately half of this mixture onto the bottom of a deep, lidded plastic container. Place the cod on top, and cover with the remaining mix. Seal and refrigerate for at least 24 hours. Wash off marinade and pat dry before cutting fish into desired small shapes.

Soy jelly

150ml soy sauce; 1 stick of lemon grass; juice of half a lemon; 25ml maple syrup; 2 gelatine leaves; 50ml water; half a red chilli

Begin by soaking the gelatine in cold water until softened. Combine all the other ingredients in a small saucepan and bring to a simmer. Remove from heat and set aside to infuse for ten minutes. Sieve the liquid into a bowl and whisk in strained gelatine. Transfer to a small container before refrigerating to set. Turn out and cut into small cubes.To serve, dress your cod with a jelly cube.

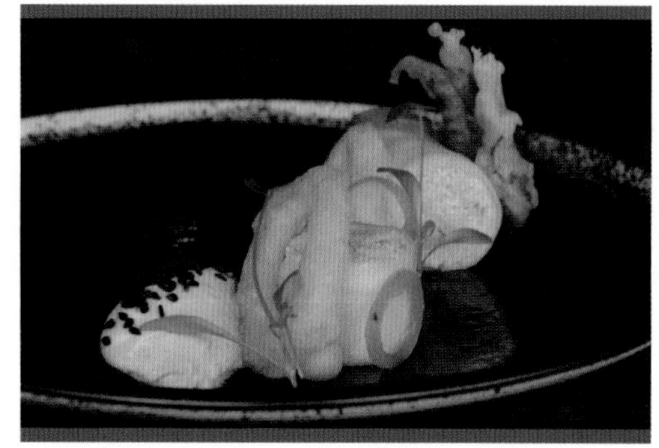

Crab, wasabi and mooli roll

East coast crab is some of the best. This recipe adds a little zing to its natural sweetness. We garnish it with avocado mousse, crispy squid tempura, pickled shallots and coriander leaf. (serves 4)

100ml each of olive oil, water and white wine vinegar; 10g wasabi paste; pinch each of salt and sugar; 250g picked white crabmeat; 1 small mooli, peeled; 2 tbsp good mayonnaise

Simmer the first six ingredients in a saucepan. Carefully mandolin the mooli very thinly and dry on a tea towel. Add to the saucepan, take off heat and allow to cool. Combine the crabmeat well with the mayonnaise in a bowl. Lay out the mooli strips on a large sheet of cling film, slightly overlapping each other to cover a 10cm by 20cm area with no gaps. Spoon the crab mixture along the middle of the mooli before rolling up, completely encasing the mix. Wrap the resulting cylinder in cling film and place in the fridge to set.

To serve, place sliced portions of the unwrapped crab roll, garnished on cold plates.

Lavender pannacotta with strawberry consommé

A smart elegant and light finish to a summery meal with fresh strawberries, meringue pieces and micro basil leaves. (serves 4)

Pannacotta

200ml double cream; 50ml whole milk; 60g sugar; 5g dried lavender flowers; 1 gelatine leaf, soaked in cold water

Bring all ingredients except the gelatine to a simmer in a saucepan. Remove from heat and infuse for five minutes. Whisk in the strained gelatine, sieve and decant into four oiled moulds. Refrigerate until set.

Strawberry consommé

1kg strawberries; 1 sliced orange 200g icing sugar

Roughly chop the strawberries and place into a bowl with the orange slices and icing sugar. Cover with cling film and leave in a warm place to macerate for 3 - 4 hours. Pass the liquid through muslin and chill in the fridge until serving.

To serve, dip the moulds in hot water carefully. Turn out the pannacotta into separate bowls and pour the consommé around.

Relax, it's just fine dining

For a new restaurant to make it in eatery-busy Bury St Edmunds, it has to offer something quite different.

Zack Deakins and business partner Paul Bailey kept this in the forefront of their minds as they nurtured the 1921 concept over the months leading up to its opening in September 2014. The result? A 50-cover fine dining restaurant that offers friendly, relaxed service, a quirky mix of modern and traditional – and exquisitely-prepared food.

The exposed brickwork and dark beams of the 17th century building just off Angel Hill are offset with light-coloured walls hung with the abstract art of Zack's mother, talented artist Marnie Deakins; there's glamour in the shape of a spectacular chandelier that sparkles at the back of the room; and retro charm in the form of the baby grand piano and deep leather seats in the canapé bar.

The bar area itself is a big draw. "We don't want people to feel they have to sign up for the full three-course experience," Zack explains. "I like the fact that people can come in for a drink and canapés, maybe before going to the theatre."

The canapé menu offers eight bites for £8, the stunning plates including the likes of scallop tartare with lime and tomato; cured cod, avocado and wasabi; and smoked Morteau sausage roll with piccalilli.

Zack's food is the result of an absolute dedication to his profession. Classroom training at Westminster College was followed by a job at Elisha Carter's Islington

restaurant Lola's, which, he says, opened his eyes to the creative possibilities in cooking. From there, three years at Martin Wishart's eponymous, Michelin-starred restaurant in Edinburgh, taught Zack discipline and extreme attention to detail. "Martin's was a completely driven kitchen, and even though by then I could cook OK, I needed that structure. I loved it, learnt every day and achieved things I was seriously proud of."

A step away from fine dining saw Zack back in East Anglia and cooking at the Fox pub in Bulmer. "We did some great food there and it was definitely more relaxed than in Scotland! I could also reconnect with family and friends and have something of a life again." Pub-style cooking clearly appealed and Zack then spent a happy four and a half years at the Bildeston Crown as sous chef to Chris Lee. "I loved working with Chris, I learnt a massive amount from him and he allowed me to be creative. Above all, he's a good friend."

Zack's first head chef position took him back to the world of fine dining and 18 months at Le Talbooth, before he returned briefly to head up the Bildeston Crown kitchen. When the opportunity to open his own place arose, he didn't hesitate. Lucky Bury.

1921
Angel Hill, Bury St Edmunds IP33 1UZ
T: 01284 704870
W: www.nineteen-twentyone.co.uk
/1921angelhill
@1921AH

Cost: Carte £35 average; set L two courses £15 / three courses £18; wine from £17.75

Open: Mon - Sat 12-2.30pm and 6-9.30pm.

Details: Piano bar; canapés; cocktails; children welcome; private dining

ZACK ON HIS...

IF NOT A CHEF?

Definitely a winemaker (or wine-taster!).

WHAT RECENT FOODIE DISCOVERY HAS EXCITED YOU?

Since opening my own place, I've had to start doing a lot more work on the pastry section, something I'd previously avoided! I'm finding it surprisingly enjoyable and have discovered lightly fermented, sweetened Vietnamese yoghurt as well as the surprisingly amazing combination of rhubarb, celery and ginger with goat's milk pannacotta. I also now know that cooking crème brûlées in a Thermomix gives them a beautiful even texture (but I suspect most pastry chefs already knew this!).

WELL-THUMBED COOKBOOKS?

Eleven Madison Park: the Cookbook has been out for two or three years but it's really good; *Food for Thought* by Alan Murchison has one of the first inspiring books I read; and Sat Bains' *Too Many Chiefs, Only One Indian* is amazing.

CULINARY HEROES?

All the chefs I've worked for have been inspiring. Anyone creative, they don't have to be famous, just proud of their product and good at making it. I admire creativity and dedication more than anything.

CHILDHOOD AMBITIONS?

I've known I wanted to be a chef since I was 13. Before that I wanted to be in the film industry, like my dad.

FOODIE NOSTALGIA?

Mum's spinach pie! It's spinach, feta, ricotta, parmesan, cheddar and pine nuts wrapped in filo pastry. Technically, it is spanakopita, but we always called it spinach pie.

MUSIC TO COOK TO AT HOME?

Muse, Chvrches, Dave Matthews Band right now – but it changes weekly!

MIDNIGHT FEAST?

Pizza, mayonnaise and a Budweiser.

BEST DISHES YOU HAVE EVER EATEN?

L'Enclume, 2012, where I had a venison tartare with extraordinary fennel pearls containing rich aniseed liquor; El Celler de Can Roca, 2013, where the highlight of a 27-course menu was langoustine tails served with a langoustine bisque and a sherry reduction; and a tapas bar I went to in 2013 where I had cep croquettes that were so good they inspired the mushroom croquettes that are on our canapé list.

COOK'S CHEATS AND CHEF'S TIPS?

Bake potatoes instead of boiling them for mash. They won't be as watery and you can add a lot more butter, cream or milk. And crack quail's eggs into cold water and white wine vinegar before placing them in boiling water. Perfectly shaped poached eggs every time!

INSPIRING SUFFOLK VIEW

There's a winding road between Bures and Sudbury that goes through Lamarsh and overlooks the valley. That typifies Suffolk for me. There's a bench at the top of a steep hill that's pretty much only accessible by car and you get the best view in the county.

ZACK'S SIGNATURE DISHES

STARTERS

Guinea fowl boudin, confit wing, roasted langoustine, beetroot and orange

Orkney scallop ceviche with tomato consommé, heirloom tomatoes, basil pannacotta

Denham Estate venison carpaccio, duck liver and cocoa roulade, butternut squash, glazed fig

MAINS

Monkfish wrapped in Parma ham, local baby vegetables, clam vinaigrette, lettuce purée

Loin of venison, bitter chocolate, cherry and fennel

Fillet of local beef, ox tongue, burnt onion purée, horseradish hash browns

PUDDINGS

Poached rhubarb with rhubarb sorbet and carpaccio, celery, goat's milk pannacotta, candied ginger

Coconut parfait, pineapple spring roll, passion fruit sorbet

Chocolate fondant with honeycomb, blood orange, thyme

Green is the new black:

All for one at Darsham Nurseries

For Lola Demille, the symbiosis of plantsman, gardener and chef is a fruitful start

L-R: Niamh Mullally, Lola Demille.

HIGHGROVE

"Well, we can walk from here, we're picking over there, my favourite producer has to be us!"

Home-grown crops planted from seed and plucked from soil to table in minutes are a delicious bounty for any passionate chef. For Lola, her kitchen door of the Café Restaurant at Darsham Nurseries, where she is head chef, leads out onto horticultural paradise at this bucolic mélange, which blends holistic avant-garde garden centre with plant library, lifestyle store and most importantly, kitchen garden.

We will let David Keleel, the charming camera-shy but determined American plantsman, whose green fingers and hard labours created this little piece of sensory heaven, take up the story: "The genesis of Darsham Nurseries occurred one evening in 1993 at the end of a busy day at a Californian nursery I managed. There wasn't any great reasoning, just a sudden dawning, an inspiration that I wanted my own plant nursery, but much more; a showcase for food we'd grow, a centre for gardening education, even a venue for fine art and performance. I thought it could be a good partnership: gardens, horticulture, food of course, and music. We've not quite got there yet, but it's the next big push.

Eight hard years here (and a two decade career in ornamental gardening and design on both sides of the Atlantic) have created this emergent Narnian-like world of botanical bliss from the dejected spent wilderness of a long-abandoned Seventies-nursery. The Nurseries' wooden gates allude to Lucy's fantastical trip through those wardrobe doors on every visit. A labour of love, David's patience has now been rewarded, the grounds maturing into this garden designer's original vision, a life's work for a modern incarnation of the worldly Victorian plant hunter. But he would rebuff this 'unnecessary hyperbole', rather attributing much of its success to all the team around him, who till the soil and toil in the business; particularly for Lola and kitchen gardener Niamh Mullally, their pivotal three-point relationship being the essential nutrient on which the Nurseries thrive. "This triangulation is tricky. We never quite know from one day to the next who is really, truly in charge," says David. "In terms of the Café, the natural priority is to grow what Lola needs. We love her input, to give her what she wants to create fabulous food alongside Tom, her sous chef and partner, and to a degree with Nature's help, we can arrange it. Seeing her joy at harvest-time, when she likes what we've grown and how it cooks up, I am then deeply pleased and not a little relieved. Her knowledge, enthusiasm and standards are all a wonderful and necessary incentive. Niamh as grower is a force of nature. No-one here, and few anywhere, could match and keep up with her drive and ambition. I believe we have two rare finds, truly-gifted and instinctive

artists in their respective crafts." But the skill perhaps was in David creating an environment to attract them originally. He provides constant stimulus in his fruitful far-away discoveries from globe-trotting trips in the name of research (perhaps a little 'R & R' too), bringing back the excitement of unfamiliar seeds from far-off places: "I often think of myself as a food tourist. Wherever I travel I research and seek where the best, the most representative, the most unique cuisine will be. Next I befriend the locals into telling me where to eat off the beaten track, to go and find the food their grandmothers would have made. From there I endeavour to link the culinary to the horticultural in the local context by visiting plant nurseries. This year we've experimented with famous Vidalia onions from the American south, rare French radishes, a strange orange aubergine from Turkey, tomatillos from South America, a beautiful purple kohlrabi, and many more. I don't know if we do, but we try to grow the most delicious food through knowing every cell of its provenance."

It was David's earliest family memories which influenced him in kitchen gardening and particularly growing for the table, "I would watch my immigrant grandparents grow so much delicious food in their very small suburban Detroit garden; for months every year the produce we ate on our Sunday vists had been harvested in their own vegetable patch. So now, what excites me most in the growing world is my 'outdoor laboratory', the kitchen garden. It's a place to grow what we know and love and to grow any number of things just to see how they'll do and what they'll taste like. It's all about having fun and learning from our myriad mistakes in the gardens and exhilarating successes in the kitchen."

It is clear that in Lola, the Nurseries have found their very own Yotam Ottolenghi. Her background has been in cooking around the daily markets and the street food vibe of simple flavour-driven dishes, pared back to showcase ingredients and provenance. She loves putting far-from-humble vegetables and grains centre stage; her evident love affair, shared with Tom, a great chef and food blogger in his own right, is for all things culinary from the Middle East and Southern Mediterranean. Their cuisine here reverses the western emphasis on carnivorous platefuls, though proper kind farmyard meats remain a key, if small, part of her distinctly omnivorous approach; this continues with a shared feasting style of dining, encouraging tables to explore their signature small plates, a Suffolk mezze approach.

Wandering with these three botanical musketeers around the huge covered greenhouses, the kitchen garden with its beds (or what David calls the potager), the multi-hued, scented, textured borders of mixed vegetable and floral, it is fascinating seeing them chat avidly about how crops are developing, how not just the leaves and the flowers but the whole plant could be cooked; and how the growing might be tweaked next season. But it is in the tactility, the sharing of something to taste, the snapping of a pod, the nipping out of a shoot, the ripping of a salad leaf, the smelling of a herb, in the shared laughter, the sheer joy and the resonant pleasure of this communal passion, that the interaction bears fruit. Back to David for a few last apt words, "We grow so much - both in the spirit of exploration, and in the spirit of just being greedy and having fun."

Grilled asparagus spears, broad bean pods and flowers, home-made curds, fried Amalfi lemons

Ideally grow your own broad beans or discover a local kitchen garden. We use the tender immature pods whole (no longer than your ring finger) as you would runner beans. The tender plant tops and the flowers are also very delicious. Gardeners usually nip out the tops to deter blackfly, don't compost them, eat them! (serves 4).

Curd cheese

Rennet is available easily online or alternatively find a good cheesemaker and buy a fresh curd cheese.

1litre good milk; 1 tsp fine salt; 1 tsp liquid rennet

In a saucepan, heat the milk gently to around 38°C. If you don't have a thermometer, this is blood temperature, measure with a clean little finger (it should feel neither hot nor cold). Stir in the salt and rennet, cover with a lid or a thick cloth, and set aside for fifteen minutes. It should thicken into a wobbly mass. Pour this into a colander, lined with cheesecloth, muslin or a thin clean tea towel, bring the corners together and tie into a bag, leaving to drain for three hours or so. Turn into a bowl and put in the fridge.

Preserved lemons

You'll need to make these at least a day in advance. This recipe makes more than you need but they keep well and are delicious.

4 Amalfi lemons, ends removed; 4 tbsp coarse sea salt

Halve the lemons lengthways then cut into thin slices. In a large bowl, gently rub the salt into the lemon slices, leave for half an hour or so, then pack the lot into a Kilner (or similar) jar. Seal and leave somewhere warmish overnight. The lemons will be immersed in a weird savoury syrup and have taken on a real tang. You can leave to pickle for longer if you like. Refrigerate until required.

To serve

Grill the asparagus as you fry the bean pods.

Olive oil; preserved lemons, 16 slices; rice flour; 1 bunch British medium asparagus spears, trimmed; 2 handfuls of baby broad bean pods, halved lengthways; curd cheese, lightly cut through; broad bean flowers and tops, or herby alternatives

Put a deep frying pan on a high heat, add 1cm of oil and heat up. Toss the lemon slices in rice flour and knock off excess gently. Fry until crispy and golden. Remove with a slotted spoon and drain on kitchen paper. Keep warm.

Pre-heat your char-grill. Oil and season the asparagus and griddle, turning occasionally until browned and just soft to the point of a knife. Meanwhile in a hot frying pan, add a glug of oil and sauté the bean pods with seasoning. They should go a nice bright green and catch in places – this is all good.

Pile the asparagus onto plates along with the pods, then scatter over (in no particular order) the crispy lemon slices, a few tablespoons of the curds, bean flowers and tops.

Roast cauliflower, herb yoghurt, saffron butter & pinenuts

Pan-roasting really brings out the nutty flavours of brassicas, asparagus and other vegetables.

Small handful of mint and parsley leaves, finely chopped; 1 tbsp sumac plus more; 500g Greek yoghurt; good olive oil; 100ml white wine vinegar; 1 tbsp caster sugar; pinch saffron; 100g cold butter, cubed plus more; 150g pine nuts, toasted; 1 large cauliflower in florets; herbs to garnish (we use flat leaf parsley, amaranth and purple basil)

Preheat the oven to 200c. Mix the herbs, sumac and yoghurt into a dressing with seasoning and a splash of oil; then set aside. For the saffron butter, bring vinegar, sugar and saffron to a boil in a heavy saucepan, bubbling it away to a bright orange syrup. Whisk butter piece-by-piece until glossy. Fold in the pine nuts and keep warm.

Add a layer of oil to a snug ovenproof frying pan (accommodating the cauliflower in a single layer) and heat up on a high setting. Add the florets and brown on both sides. Bake in the oven to finish cooking, approx. 5 minutes or so, until stalks yield to a knife point. Toss with the butter sauce and parsley before sitting on a pool of yoghurt. Garnish with herbs and sumac.

Wild rabbit ragoût

We serve this with soft buttered polenta, herb-pickled celery and foraged alexanders. We brine our rabbit overnight to ensure it is tender but young rabbits will be fine. Use the loins for a warm salad. Start the day before. (serves 4)

1 onion, carrot, celery stick, leek; 2 rabbits, legs only; 3 pig's trotters, blanched; hot chicken stock

Pre-heat the oven to 160c. Cut the veggies into chunks and use as a bed in a deep roasting tin; add the rabbit legs and trotters. Cover with hot stock and braise gently for several hours, until the meat is falling off the bone. Gently remove the legs, leave to cool. Strain off the liquor and reduce by boiling down to a thick gravy. Cool in a container, add in the legs and refrigerate overnight.

1 large onion, carrot, celery stick, all finely diced; extra virgin olive oil; zest of 1 lemon; 2 thyme sprigs, leaves only; 2 tbsp tomato purée; 100ml milk; 50ml white balsamic vinegar

To serve, shred the rabbit meat from the bones and set aside. Soften the vegetables in medium-hot oil, add zest and thyme. Cook for one minute, add purée and fry over a hot heat for two minutes. Add milk, bring to low simmer, evaporate, pour in the vinegar and bring to a simmer. Add meat and simmer together. Serve in warm soup plates.

Buckwheat hazelnut brownies

This makes two small trays. Unusually, our recipe is best eaten cold, perhaps just with crème fraîche. NB If in doubt about under-cooked eggs, best not to consume.

400g good dark chocolate, chopped; 300g cold butter, cubed; 5 eggs; 500g light muscovado sugar; pinch of fine sea salt; 300g hazelnuts, roasted and skinned; 100g buckwheat flour

Pre-heat the oven to 180c. Line two small rectangular baking tins with parchment. Melt the chocolate and butter in a bain-marie. Lightly whisk the eggs and sugar together with the salt. Pulse the nuts with the flour to a crumble texture. Whisk the chocolate mix into the eggs gently until just combined and fold in the nut mixture. Pour into trays. Bake for 25 minutes or until just crisp and setting on top, it should be slightly under-done in the middle. Cool before slicing.

Café culture and chic retreat

Darsham Nurseries exudes what the French would call its terroir, a sense of place, in landscape, climate, geology, flora and fauna, and an evolution in keeping with its natural character. But it is clearly shaped by human endeavour and a particular soul-satisfying style, which threads through the gardens, retail and eating areas.

If the Nurseries' character as an emotive botanical-culinary movement expresses the plantsman-grower-chef corporate as it were, the enterprise is most influenced by David Keleel's love of design and form "I've always admired the great art museums that are made up of a single sensibility. Like their collections, I grow and stock plants that I've always loved or which provide us with scent, visual pleasure, or something delicious to eat. The shop sells things that, for the most part, I'd be happy to own, and the Café serves food that I love and deeply enjoy eating. I'm certainly not comparing myself in any way to people like Peggy Guggenheim, but that singularity of vision has always inspired me."

This is really the good life, the gardens soon will provide the Café during the harvesting season with nearly half of its self-sufficient needs in vegetables, salads, fruits and herbs, increasing each year as the grounds mature and new land is cultivated.

Full of a relaxed, slightly bohemian style, the beautifully nonchalant natural design of smart salvaged textures and clever touches instantly gratifies. As a light, airy, colourful space, it brings the outside in, while the huge terrace doors lead diners out to graze and relax at courtyard tables. A botanical showcase of edibles and ornamentals, the terrace is surrounded by raised beds of espalier apple trees and eclectic planting; a meeting point of garden and kitchen. Don't be surprised to see Lola and Tom, secateurs in hand, raiding the borders to forage ingredients for their cooking – how much more fresh, local and seasonal could one want?

Darsham Nurseries
Main Road, Darsham,
near Yoxford IP17 3PW
T: 01728 667022
W: www.darshamnurseries.co.uk
/DarshamNurseries
@DarshamNurserie

Cost: Carte £25 average; wine from £21.50

Open: Breakfast from 8.30am; lunch from 12-3pm; Sun brunch 10am-3.30pm; summer Fri evenings 6-9.30pm

Details: Alfresco dining; private parties; car parking

LOLA ON HER...

FOODIE DISCOVERIES?

Every day here is a culinary journey from garden to chopping board. I am amazed by Niamh's skill and David's discoveries – we harvest so many varieties, 34 of tomatoes, 42 of salad greens, 20 of radishes, 12 of beans and 8 of courgette. Things like stripy Peppermint Pink chard, delicious and beautiful; red-stemmed spring onions, called 'Reddy'; all those tasty colourful heirloom tomatoes, ones like 'Black Cherry' and 'Berkeley Tie-Dye'; Kalettes, a brassica cross between kale and brussels sprouts and the traditional Welsh Onions, both edible and ornamental for their cut flowers. Happy days...

SOCIAL MEDIA?

We all tweet, @lolademille @thomeagle and @darshamnurserie (the 's' wouldn't fit...). Tom's foodie blog, "In Search Of Lost Thyme" is brilliant, head to the Darsham Nurseries website to find it.

CULINARY HEROES?

All of these have made the Middle East and the Southern Med. so accessible: Claudia Roden was the legend that started it all off; Yotam Ottolenghi has revolutionised how people perceive vegetables, spices and the region generally; Sam and Sam Clark are doing similar with Moorish cooking.

LUCKY DAY OFF?

Start with a Bloody Mary and a full Turkish deli-style breakfast, off to the beach round here, Walberswick or Covehithe; dog walking, paddling, walking to Southwold's BlackShore Harbour to eat seafood; back for some gardening and picking supper, Negroni cocktails, light the barbecue and chill to Talking Heads.

WELL-THUMBED COOKBOOKS?

Honey & Co: Food From The Middle East, written by the fab' London diner team of the same name; Diana Henry, all her books are just great; *Istanbul: Recipes From The Heart Of Turkey* by Rebecca Seal, the food, life and the heartbeat of the city.

FAVOURITE PLACES TO EAT?

To eat – Mains in Yoxford just down the road, owner-run, dependable and well-done classic food; Enzo's in Southwold's High St. for authentic stone-baked Neapolitan pizza; Butley-Orford Oysterage, really simple seafood platters and smoked eel for Tom.

UNFULFILLED DREAM JOB?

Something practical and outdoors and hands-on, working with animals or wood. Possibly a guinea pig breeder, don't ask!

MIDNIGHT FEAST?

Generally a scotch egg from a late night garage if the fridge is bare; quick Asian 'pot noodles' home-style with kimchi pickles, lots of chillies and tom yum paste; and those cheap supermarket crème caramels.

ULTIMATE DINING DESTINATIONS?

Istanbul every time, go back to my old haunts and the latest new eateries; must visit Berber & Q in Dalston, East London, a middle eastern-inspired barbecue joint; and The Sportsman in Seasalter, Kent, totally about local provenance, they also make their own butter and even sea salt!

TOOLS OF THE TRADE?

At work, a mandolin for creating textures with vegetables; at home my well-seasoned cast-iron skillet frying pan. "I was once told if you can't 'kill' someone with a piece of kitchen equipment, it isn't heavy enough or up to the job". I am not violent though!

LAST SUPPER?

On the menu – big barbecue and mezze affair, lots of Turkish breads, mechoui Moroccan slow-baked spiced lamb in a wood oven, seafood, salads, more of the same until we expire... On the invite list – all my friends and family, David Bowie for music and conversation.

LOLA'S SIGNATURE DISHES

STARTERS

House-cured Anatolian pastirma beef, tarator and pickled walnuts

Harissa-grilled mackerel, fennel and blood oranges

Marinated courgettes, goat's curd and mint

MAINS

Monkfish cheek, blood cake and piquillo peppers

Porchetta pork belly, kohlrabi 'slaw

Spring lamb stew with baby artichokes, broad beans and peas

PUDDINGS

Salted sourdough chocolate mousse, crème fraîche

Halva ice-cream and almond biscuits

Pistachio baklava with rose labneh

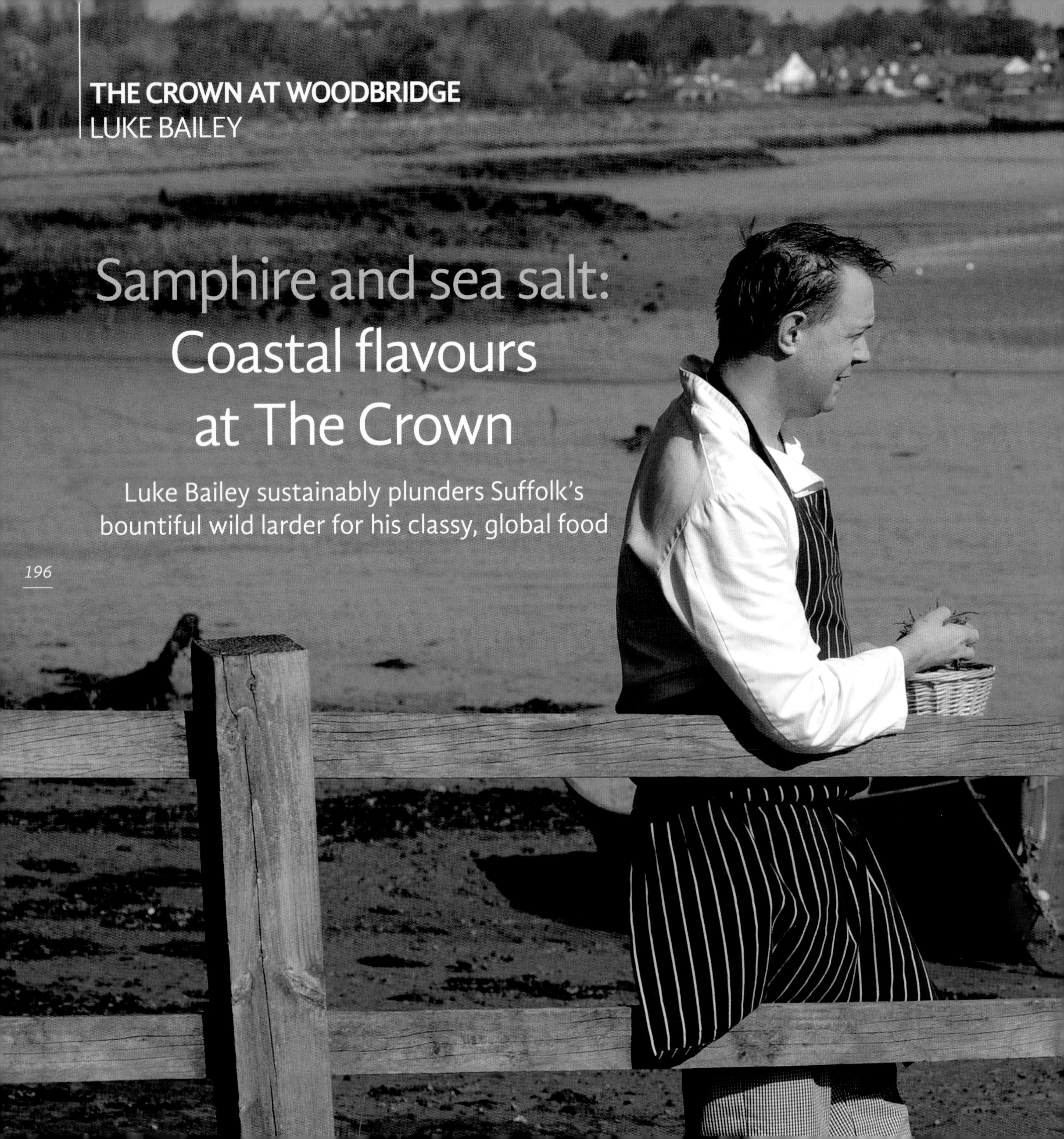

Samphire and sea salt: Coastal flavours at The Crown

Luke Bailey sustainably plunders Suffolk's bountiful wild larder for his classy, global food

L-R: Luke Bailey, Garth Wray.

THE CROWN AT WOODBRIDGE LUKE BAILEY

Wicker basket in hand, perhaps full of samphire sprigs or delicate mauve sea aster flowers, that chef you often see down by the river or on the sand dunes, could well be Luke Bailey. He'll be gathering delicious natural provender for his earthy cooking at The Crown, a 16th century former coaching inn in Woodbridge.

"I have a passion for foraging," he says. "I was brought up here around Woodbridge and the Deben estuary was my playground. It was all very *Swallows and Amazons*, messing about in boats sometimes up to my neck in mud, crabbing, swimming, fishing. I still love nothing more than being by the water and of course foraging which I've been doing properly for the last 10 years."

Luke's interest was sparked by reading Alys Fowler's book, *The Thrifty Forager*, and at the same time discovering Hugh Fearnley-Whittingstall's River Cottage television series, and he wasted little time in following their lead. "I used to go out foraging with the late great Peter Jordan, a fungi expert and author of *The Complete Book of Mushrooms*. One summer's day we came back laden with St George's mushrooms, a delicious treat and a new ingredient for me. He took me to his secret cep spot – there aren't many places in east Suffolk where the porcini, or pennybun as it's also known, grows in abundance. It was unbelievably exciting!"

Though Luke still enjoys a good fungi foray, he's more likely to be found collecting wild coastal vegetables such as sea-beet, sea-purslane or sea-kale. "I love getting out in the open air, it's a great antidote to the kitchen stresses. Carefully harvesting plants helps them flourish too (one never uproots the whole plant, so effectively this is pruning). These vegetables are also far healthier than any cultivated plant as no fertilisers or pesticides have been used. They are just the essence of the sea, a great partner to any fish or seafood, and as the character is in their salty flavour and texture, a chef doesn't need to do too much with them."

The 'less is more' theory is one Luke follows at The Crown. "I pick over the leaves to remove old, woody bits, rinse them several times, and then blanch until al dente, usually for just a minute, before I plunge them into iced water to keep the colour and then drain well. To reheat, I simply whisk up a reduction of dry white wine and butter, drop in the greens, and cook briefly until warmed through. They can then be used as a garnish on a seafood dish just as you would spinach – it really is that easy!"

To put the greens centre-stage, Luke recommends tempura, the Japanese method of crisp-frying in batter made with self-raising and cornflour whisked up with ice-cold light beer such as Adnams Regatta or Spindrift. "I make a tempura duo with Deben oysters and sea greens, a natural local combination, which I serve with either a hot wasabi horseradish mayonnaise or a lime and chilli-spiked soy dipping sauce."

The Crown menu of course goes well beyond wild brassicas, reading in fact like a who's who of Suffolk produce – Sutton Hoo

chicken, Gressingham duck, Marybelle Dairy, Simpers Deben shellfish, Blythburgh pork and Darsham-reared Red Poll beef all feature. "We've always had a long menu, a 'something for everyone' approach, but because we are so busy, the turnover of ingredients is very quick and fresh ingredients are coming through the kitchen door, morning and afternoon. I love nothing better than working with Tony, my very able and long-standing South African sous chef, to get the best out of fantastic seasonal ingredients."

"Culinary pretensions have no place here" Luke insists, describing his food as "elegant but earthy. With this amazing local produce, the skill in being a good chef is knowing when to stop to show it off at its best. We deliberately don't want our dishes to be like grandma used to cook or something you can easily do at home. We like to excite the palate, however we won't be clever for the sake of it and we always want to satisfy hearty appetites."

Luke, a local boy who trained at Suffolk College, Ipswich, worked closely for five years with Stephen David in relaunching The Crown as a boutique inn-restaurant back in 2009. He cites Stephen as possibly the biggest influence on his career to date, and says he's happy to continue to build on the solid foundation he inherited here: "I love Stephen's 'local gone global' philosophy. Our menu dips into many cuisines, though it's definitely not fusion because each dish remains distinct and true to its culinary origin."

"We put our spin on classic British or French dishes but the globe-trotting also takes in Scandinavian house-cured fish, a bit of Mediterranean for colour, the warming rich spices of North Africa, and zingy middle eastern and south-east Asian flavours."

Luke has done his fair share of actual globe-trotting, always with a culinary emphasis: "One of my biggest professional highlights was spending time in the kitchens of Noma, Copenhagen, repeatedly named the best restaurant in the world. René Redzepi is a culinary force and what was so rewarding was to see how he uses humble, often foraged, local foods from his Nordic countryside to create stunning gastronomic masterpieces."

"I've also been lucky enough to go to Morocco to learn about North African cuisine. Up in the Atlas mountains, Berbers taught me to make proper tagine with kid goat. Getting nibbled by inquisitive kids who rushed to welcome us as we entered their paddocks and then being butted out of them by the protective male billies was an experience – I know chefs have to get familiar with the origins of their food but that brought new meaning to getting hands-on with the ingredient!"

"The real McCoy of any native dish, especially tagine, prepared by a local is totally different from the sanitised recipes we see here! Goat is a perfect substitute in all lamb recipes and for many ethnic dishes it's far more genuine. On my return to Suffolk, I bought great kid meat from a local Boer goat herd at Stowmarket to serve up proper tagine for The Crown's menu here. In fact it was so popular, I really must put it on again soon."

Crisp Asian Orford crab cakes with Deben samphire

A flexible easy recipe, the uncooked cakes, once coated, can be made ahead and chilled. I like to serve the dish garnished with an oriental-style fresh cucumber pickle and a simple red chilli syrup.

Crab cake mix

300g dressed crab meat, brown and white separated; 150g warm mashed potato; 2 heaped tsp root ginger, peeled and grated; 1 heaped tsp garlic, peeled and grated; 1 medium red chilli, deseeded and finely chopped; 1 tbsp coriander leaves, shredded; 2 spring onions, trimmed and finely chopped; 1 tbsp nam pla (Thai fish sauce); finely-grated zest and juice of half a lime; pinch of ground white pepper and sea salt

Mix the brown crabmeat thoroughly into the other ingredients with seasoning, before lightly folding in the white meat until the mix holds together. Chill for two hours or until required. Before coating, divide and roll the crabcake mixture into 8 or 12 balls to suit. Flatten into thick patties.

Coating

4 tbsp seasoned plain flour; 3 large eggs, beaten; half loaf of two day-old white bread as fine crumbs; sunflower or rapeseed oil for deep frying

Taking three soup plates, put the flour, eggs and crumbs separately into each. Warm up the oil in your deep fryer on a medium-hot heat. Dip each crab patty alternately into the flour, then the egg (draining well) and repeat both stages again, finally coat in the crumbs. Ensure each cake is properly covered, pressing in the coating gently all over. Chill for at least one hour or until ready to cook. Remove from the fridge and uncover for 30 minutes before frying.

Pickled cucumber

1 deseeded cucumber in long ribbons, marinated for an hour in a seasoned dressing, whisked together, from 1 tbsp mirin, 1 tbsp white rice vinegar, 1 tsp salt, 1 tsp caster sugar, 1 tsp root ginger, peeled and grated and 1 tsp sesame oil

Red chilli syrup

1 medium red chilli, finely sliced (seeds left in for heat) and stirred carefully into a hot syrup of 100ml water and 100g golden caster sugar before cooling

Buttered samphire

2 large handfuls of samphire, washed and trimmed; a large knob of butter; black peppermill and sea salt

Blanch the samphire in boiling water for less than a minute until still al dente. Drain well and toss with seasoning and butter to coat. Keep warm.

To serve

Place the room temperature crabcakes in your fryer basket a few at a time and lower very carefully into the oil, frying until golden. Drain on kitchen paper and keep warm, until all are cooked. Divide the samphire onto four warm starter plates. Top with the hot crisp crab cakes. Top with a tangle of cucumber ribbons and a drizzle of the red chilli syrup.

Crispy Blythburgh pig's cheek

Try on a warm salad or with curried parsnip purée and minty yoghurt

4 pig's cheeks, trimmed; seasoned flour; good local rapeseed oil; 2 bay leaves; few sprigs of fresh thyme; 3 garlic cloves, peeled and crushed; Small glass of dry white vermouth; Rich chicken stock; flour, beaten eggs and breadcrumbs

Pre-heat your oven to 140c. Flour the cheeks and fry until brown in a hot pan with a glug of oil. Transfer to a snug, lidded casserole with the bay, thyme and garlic. Add the vermouth to the frying pan and heat, then add to the pork, and repeat with enough simmering stock to cover the meat. Bake for 4 hours until tender. Remove from stock and cool. Press with a tray and a heavy weight in the fridge. When required, pull into mouth-sized pieces. Pre-heat your deep fat fryer to its hottest setting. Coat the pork alternately in seasoned flour, egg and breadcrumbs. Fry until golden, remove with slotted spoon and allow to drain on kitchen paper. Season lightly and serve.

Herb-crusted Suffolk lamb cutlets

A smart alternative to roast leg or slow-baked shoulder for a dinner party, enjoy with seasonal vegetables and fondant or dauphinoise potato.

2 lamb racks, French-trimmed; good local rapeseed oil; 50g dry white breadcrumbs; handful of chopped soft green herbs; 25g hard cheese, such as parmesan, finely grated; Dijon-style mustard

Pre-heat your oven to 200c fan. Lightly oil the lamb and lay fat-side down in a medium-hot pan until well-browned. Next seal the ends of the meat. Remove to a plate. In a food processor, blend up the crumbs with the herbs and seasoning. Mix through the cheese and then drizzle in the oil. Check the mixture clumps up when you pinch it, if not, add more oil.

Brush the fat side of the lamb with mustard and pack on the herb crust neatly, pressing down firmly. Place on a hot tray, crumbs uppermost and lightly drizzle with oil. Bake for 20 - 25 minutes until golden and still pink inside. Allow to rest for 8 minutes.

Carve down slowly through the bones to keep the crust intact before plating.

Baked strawberry cheesecake

This makes a whole dessert for slicing to serve six or more. Alternatively use small individual moulds as pictured and then perhaps glam the dish up with Pimms jelly, red chilli syrup and a minted berry salsa.

250g ginger biscuits in crumbs; 80g butter, melted; 150g hulled strawberries; 4 eggs, beaten; 175g caster sugar; grated zest of 1 lime; 1 tbsp honey; 2 tsp vanilla extract; 500g mascarpone; 200g crème fraîche; more strawberries to decorate

Mix the biscuits and butter well together. Press into a buttered 18cm spring-form tin. Refrigerate until set. Finely dice the strawberries and drain in a sieve. Pre-heat oven to 170c fan. Whisk together the remaining ingredients until smooth and then gently fold in the diced strawberries. Spoon the mixture into the tin. Bake for 45 minutes until just golden. Cover with a tea towel to cool and then refrigerate in the tin.

To serve, run a hot knife around the edge and unclip. Slice up the remaining strawberries and decorate.

Riverside elegance

The Crown at Woodbridge provides a stylish setting for the robust flavours and dashing presentation of Luke Bailey's food. "A townhouse inn for the 21st century" is how the owners of The Crown like to describe their revitalised historic property. The words 'cosseting', 'contemporary' and 'cosmopolitan' spring to mind too.

This is a place that digs deep into its location by the stunning river Deben to offer a menu that's earthily close to its roots – think pig's cheeks from pork raised just minutes away, steamed Deben mussels harvested a chug up the creek via the Simpers' traditional bawleys, not to mention Luke Bailey's enthusiasm for foraged sea greens – but which puts a modern and stylish spin on dishes.

The glass-roofed, granite-topped bar, nautically complete with a skiff suspended from the ceiling, is a relaxed space where locals are welcomed as much as visiting weekenders. From behind the bar come local Adnams Southwold ales, draught Aspalls cyders and Calvors lager, all brewed within an hour's drive of The Crown. The reach becomes global with a smart wine list and cocktails shaken with Londonesque panache. It was not always so. The then chef-patron Stephen David (The Crown is now steered by general manager Garth Wray) took on a tired and unloved 17th century former coaching inn back in 2008. That rough diamond in the hands of Chelsea designer David Bentheim became the polished gem of a smart coastal bolthole and dining destination it now is.

The Crown's interiors whisk you to Nantucket with river-inspired cool lines and soft blue, grey, green tones, warmed up by quirky, interesting art. Overnight guests choose from ten stylish but unfussy, big-bedded rooms with The Crown's relaxed signature vibe. Woodbridge is now firmly on discerning travellers' radar as an upmarket haunt and the gateway to the Heritage Coast jewels of Southwold, Aldeburgh and more. The Crown is owned by T A Hotel Collection, a five-strong East Anglian group, which includes fashionable Aldeburgh's Brudenell and White Lion as well as the iconic Swan Hotel at Lavenham.

The Crown at Woodbridge
Thoroughfare, Woodbridge,
Suffolk IP12 1AD
T: 01394 384242
W: www.thecrownatwoodbridge.co.uk
/crownatwoodbridge
@woodbridgecrown

Accolades: Two AA Rosettes, *Michelin Guide*, *Alastair Sawday's* UK Pub with Rooms award, *The Independent* Top 50 UK Gastro Pubs and UK Top 50 Sunday Roasts

Cost: Carte £28 average / midweek set £15-20 / Sun lunch £25; wine from £18

Open: All year 7am-11pm

Details: Bar drinks; wheelchair access via front door; children welcome; dogs allowed in bar; 10 bedrooms; car parking

LUKE ON HIS...

ULTIMATE DINING DESTINATIONS?

Can't wait to visit San Sebastián, north of Barcelona, for its amazing restaurant scene, especially the three Michelin-starred El Celler de Can Roca for its creative take on traditional Catalan cooking and local produce. I must get down to River Cottage in Dorset to do a foraging course with John Wright, hopefully meet the main man, Hugh [Fearnley-Whittingstall] and absorb that whole earthy-hippy vibe! As mentioned, Marco's cutting edge recipes were inspirational, so I would love to have eaten at Harvey's in London back in the late Eighties.

TAKE FIVE RECIPE?

A warm smoked eel salad. Roast some beetroot wedges or buy pre-cooked, crisp some smoked streaky lardons, gently heat up a favourite salad dressing (try Scarlett and Mustard's creamy cider tarragon), toss with some mixed leaves and flake over Pinney's smoked eel.

BEST DISHES EVER EATEN?

René Redzepi's reindeer moss, cep mushrooms, crème fraîche and toasted juniper at Noma, Copenhagen; ox cheek ravioli at Restaurant Gordon Ramsay, London; the goat tagine with prunes and salted lemons, cooked by the Berbers for me in Morocco.

MUSIC TO COOK TO AT HOME?

Always rock & roll, the Stones, The Who, Oasis – anything loud!

LUCKY DAY OFF?

Has to be by a river, probably the Deben, a bit of foraging, boat trip to a good pub, cyder and a barbecue as the sun sets – bliss!

FAVOURITE CULINARY MOMENTS?

Cooking with one of my food heroes, TV chef Val Warner of *What To Eat Now* fame, for a VIP lunch at the Aldeburgh Food and Drink Festival was a real joy. Spending a week in Morocco was very memorable too learning about authentic Maroc cuisine such as their earthy tagines.

FAVOURITE PLACES TO EAT LOCALLY?

Aqua Eight, Ipswich such a variety of pan Asian cooking, I love their chicken gyoza, followed by seafood curry.
Elveden Inn, near Thetford my chef mate, Matt Hearn, runs this lovely pub-restaurant. We worked together at Seckford Hall.
Darsham Nurseries, near Yoxford so glad it's re-opened, great for a lunchtime treat on a day off.

WELL-THUMBED COOKBOOKS?

White Heat by Marco Pierre White. All of Keith Floyd's books, so entertaining and politically incorrect!

LUKE'S SIGNATURE DISHES

STARTERS

Seared king scallops, crisp pig's cheek, jalapeño gribiche, smoked bacon caramel

Ramsholt venison rillettes, pickled walnuts, sloe gin jelly, toasted Tide Mill soda bread

Chargrilled Simpers' asparagus, soft-boiled pheasant egg, pan-fried St George's mushrooms, mustard dressing

MAINS

Moroccan spiced Gressingham duck, roasted breast, braised leg & date pastilla, crispy hearts, smoked aubergine and pine nut purée

Rolled Blythburgh pork herb porchetta minted spring vegetable 'vignole' stew

Pinney's Orford smoked haddock, bubble 'n' squeak, poached hen's egg, aged cheddar and leek cream

PUDDINGS

Caramelised High House conference pear tarte tatin, honeycomb ice cream, Aspall cyder butterscotch sauce

New season forced rhubarb & blood orange jelly, ginger pannacotta, spiced rhubarb sorbet, toasted almonds

Suffolk Blue cheese beignets, The Crown's apple and Adnams Broadside chutney, dressed leaves

Estuary life: Nautical heaven at The Bell

Nick Attfield's coastal inns naturally centre around the sea

L-R: Jonathan Simper, Nick Attfield.

A love of seafood is to be expected when you own two seaside pub-restaurants and Nick is no exception.

Raking for mussels down at low tide in the rich silt of the river Deben at Ramsholt may not exactly look like a natural activity for this spreadsheet-loving businessman cum accidental chef-restaurateur but Nick's passion for Simpers of Suffolk shellfish is definitely enthusing. His pristine Hunter wellies might look perhaps more used to gracing elegant boats at Southwold quayside but his foodie determination to get hands-on more than makes up for his slight discomfort on the muddy foreshore.

Divested of his now properly mucky boots, and back up at the Simpers' family farm in their purification plant, Nick is more in his element, examining the rows of gurgling tanks filtering this precious piscine harvest before delivery out to kitchens across the region. Along with his two Adnams-tied tenancy properties, The Fish Hut is also a very familiar sight at food festivals and swish events, Nick's cheery beach-themed pop-up take-away on wheels, specialising in, you've guessed it, seafood (either his trademark cones of fish and chips or these Deben mussels, steamed marinière-style with a Suffolk cyder twist). Regaling shared tales of how to cook and serve up these purply-blue pearlescent bivalves demonstrates the shared obsession for Nick and fish farmer Jonathan.

Moules-frites and obligatory mayonnaise may be the national dish of Belgium but we Brits are now keen consumers of mussels; as Suffolk's only producer, the three generations of Simpers have timely resurrected a centuries-old tradition of shellfish-farming in the rich clean waters of the Deben estuary, downstream from Woodbridge. Some of the best habitat in the UK, our local chefs would agree wholeheartedly with the delicious end results (quality-wise). And very importantly for Nick, he can be assured of the green credentials of hand-production in this low impact manner and the relatively minimal food miles in delivery. Especially as his chefs have to sustainably purchase huge quantities of seafood to satisfy the hordes of seafood-loving customers with their regular fishy fix.

Sailors talk of the sea being their mistress and she is a similar force for Nick in his maritime-centred trio of businesses on the shores of another Suffolk river estuary, the Blyth to the north. The watery setting has a big impact in Walberswick and at Nick's other place, The Harbour Inn in Southwold over the water, where flooding is no laughing matter; consistently subject to the elemental invasion of inescapable spring tides once or twice a year, gushing up inside from beneath The Harbour Inn's floor. You only have to look outside at the wall plaque, denoting the 1953 tideline to realise the charm of its natural vulnerability "If as I do, you accept the huge benefit of being in such iconic East Anglian coastal settings amidst her prettiest seascapes, the sacrifice of occasional watery intrusion and subsequent loss of business is well worth that effort!" Nick says. "And after five years, we've got it sorted; and there's always a silver PR lining when we flood!" Nick indeed cuts a familiar stoic figure on local media commenting on the state of the Suffolk floods, usually pictured calf-deep in his aforementioned wellies amid the ripples inside the pub. "It's all about the planning, our salvage plan is down to a fine art, we get the warning, it's all hands to the deck, everything out with a swift removal, and the pumps go on. Once the tide recedes, we do a deep clean to remove Mother Nature and carry on pretty much as if nothing ever happened!"

And the Blyth estuary with its imposing temperamental water meadow is a very familiar scene for Nick as he drives between both pubs, across the sound at Blythburgh, dominated by the 'Cathedral of The Marshes' and the A12 passing through, the conduit for this tourist mecca. Indeed such is the time commuting in his car that it has become somewhat of an in-joke with friends, who think his life is spent just driving between the two. Fortunately, a penchant for fast luxury motors has created his surrogate family, he jokes. There is no time for encumbrances such as regular vacations, holiday homes or children when you are this busy and passionate about what you do.

Yet his appreciation for a few of the finer things is perhaps understandable when you hear the background of this business-obsessed restaurateur. It was more the extra-curricular activity as President of the Wine Society at Durham University than studying for his Economics degree which opened his eyes to the 'high life'. One of Nick's housemates, Liz had already gained a retail graduate placement at Harrods, and luxury department stores were a mesmerising proposition. Trademark enthusiasm and not insubstantial smooth-talking would see this 'grape aficionado' join one of the largest businesses in the world of wine. Not just limited to 26 on-site restaurants and drinking spots in this 'little Knightsbridge corner shop' plus the wine merchants in the famous Food Halls, his 'oenophile playground' would include the whole Harrods airport boutique and hamper empire worldwide, plus stocking the family's private cellars. All in all, well over ten million pounds' worth of wine on sale at any one time, not bad for a Wenhaston schoolboy whose one trip to the store previously was for the Willy Wonka-esque Toy and Sweet Depts. After five hard-grafting but halcyon years as Assistant Wine Buyer, number two in managing the whole Harrods liquor operations, Nick hankered for the joys of home and the Suffolk coast. He took with him that foodie grounding which he credits with his success as a restaurateur, perhaps 'only a self-taught cook rather than chef' as he puts it; yet it was the exposure to the world's greatest ingredients, which taught him hugely about food and obviously drink). The best caviar, foie gras, truffles, pata negra ham, (these weren't even on Nick's radar in Suffolk), tea with the Indian ambassador, working with the world's best chefs and producers, all of this rubbed off on him and gave him an enviable, appreciative insight.

On a rare trip back to the family, Nick would pop into their favourite pub, The Bell of course, and the rest is pretty much history. A few years as manager there and then he would take on his first Adnams tenancy at The Golden Key in desirable Snape. Earning his spurs as a landlord and the brewery's quick respect, he would in 2010 at the age of 33, be given the keys to one of their busiest flagships, The Harbour Inn in Southwold Harbour, combined just four months later with a second set of keys back at The Bell. Passion brings its own reward.

Deben mussels steamed with Aspall Suffolk cyder, leeks, Marybelle cream and parsley

Our Suffolk version of the classic Gallic marinière style. Serve with lots of warm crusty bread. Chunky chips and a good dressed salad are optional for a heartier lunch.

To prepare your mussels

Remember the mussels have been purified by the farm, so do not keep them under tap water, which will add new impurities for the live mussels to start filtering!

Keep the mussels chilled and tightly bundled and they will happily live for 2-3 days after leaving the purification tanks of the farm. Do not store in water, they will die.

Just prior to cooking check through all the individual mussels. Any that are open and do not close with a simple tap to their base should be discarded as dead.

Any barnacles growing on the shells can be easily dislodged with the back of an old knife.

The final preparation is to remove the "beard", a fibrous tassel from the mussel, which comes away easily with a gentle tug. Once this is done, you must cook the mussels as soon as possible.

Fish stock

Ask your fishmonger for the bones and heads of non-oily fish. Wash off any blood and remove any innards.

Place in a big enough pan with a covering of water and a good-sized glass of drinkable dry white wine. Add roughly-chopped carrot, celery and fennel bulb together with a bay leaf and herb stalks – flat leaf parsley, dill, fennel, chives, for example. Add some lemon segments to the broth and simmer gently for approximately 25 minutes, skimming the surface of any foamy impurities. Pass through a sieve, cool and refrigerate until required. Clingfilm when cold.

To serve

1 leek, cleaned and finely shredded; unsalted butter; 250ml dry Aspall cyder; 125ml good fish stock; 125ml Marybelle double cream; pinch of saffron; sea salt and white peppermill; 2kg live closed Deben mussels, cleaned; large handful of soft herbs (flat-leaf parsley, dill, fennel, chives etc), finely shredded; 1 lemon, halved for squeezing

In a deep frying pan over a low-medium heat, soften the leeks in a good knob of butter until soft.

Pour in 125ml cyder and the fish stock, boil and reduce down by half. Add double cream, a pinch of saffron, and salt and white pepper to taste.

Bring to a simmer. Taste and adjust seasoning.

In a separate heavy lidded saucepan, bring remaining cyder to the boil and add mussels.

Stir in well, put lid on, bring back to a boil, stir again, cover again and simmer hard for 4-5 minutes. Check nearly all shells are open.

Drain the mussels, discarding any closed ones. Add to the sauce, along with soft herbs and the lemon juice to taste.

Ham hock terrine

A lovely spring starter with asparagus, poached eggs and dressed leaves. (serve 4+)

**I smoked Suffolk ham hock;
2 sticks celery, I large carrot, I onion, all chopped; 1 bay leaf; pinch of peppercorns; few herb stalks, eg thyme and parsley; small handful flat leaf parsley leaves, shredded; sea salt and black peppermill; tsp wholegrain mustard; 4 cornichons, finely chopped; softened gelatine leaves**

In a lidded saucepan, cover the hock and the next six ingredients with water. Simmer gently until very tender, for about 3 hours. Remove the ham hock and put aside to cool. Strain the pan, reserving the liquor, cool and refrigerate but discard the solids.

Line a loaf tin with plenty of cling film to wrap the terrine tight later. Shred the now-cooled ham hock meat into a bowl (discarding unsavoury bits). Mix with flat leaf parsley and black pepper, plus a little whole-grain mustard and cornichons if you like. Taste and adjust seasoning. Pack the mixture into the tin, firmly down evenly.

Measure and warm liquor with sufficient softened gelatine leaves. Pour over terrine to cover and allow to soak in, topping up after five minutes. Tuck in the clingfilm overhang on top. Seal with loose foil and weigh down the top and refrigerate overnight.

Fish & chips, The Bell Inn-style

Fresh local North Sea cod is key as are mushy peas, home-made tartare sauce, Aspall malt vinegar and Stokes tomato ketchup! Cook this in batches. (serves 6)

**568ml chilled Suffolk lager; 568ml cold water; 500g plain flour; 1 tsp Bird's custard powder (or saffron);
12 medium potatoes, peeled and cut into 1cm equal chips; sea salt and black peppermill; rapeseed oil for deep-frying; 6 x 150g cod fillets**

Mix the lager and water in a large bowl, and whisk in flour and custard powder. Leave to rest in the fridge for 30 minutes.

Prepare a large container of iced water. Blanch chips in boiling water until they are just softening. Carefully scoop out into iced water. Drain well and sit in a colander. Tip onto clean tea towels and pat dry. Heat your fryer to 180c. Carefully fry chips until crisp and golden. Remove from the oil, drain for a minute and then tip out on to plenty of kitchen paper. Keep them warm.

Next fry the fish. Pat the fish fillets dry with kitchen paper, then dip into the batter. Carefully lower into the deep-fat fryer, heated to 180c, one or two at a time and fry for 3-4 minutes until golden-brown. Drain on kitchen paper and keep warm, repeating with the remaining cod portions. Salt the chips and plate up with the fish.

Sticky toffee pudding

This is a delicious dessert and also fun for afternoon tea. Always best served warm, a microwave does a good job of reheating it. We serve it with hot butterscotch sauce and something dairy and cool. (serves 8)

**180g chopped dates; 200ml water;
75g butter; 175g muscovado sugar;
2 large eggs; 1 tsp bicarbonate of soda
175g self raising flour; good dash of vanilla extract**

Preheat the oven to 180c. Grease and line a regular deep roasting tray. Place the dates and water in a pan and bring to a good simmer. Meanwhile cream the butter and sugar in a mixer using a beater and then slowly add the eggs. Once the dates have been brought to the boil, take off the heat and rest for 5 minutes; then whisk in the bicarbonate of soda. Gently fold the flour into the butter mixture and then finally mix in the dates and vanilla. Evenly spread the mixture out in the tin. Bake for 25-30 minutes until the centre of the pudding is firm but springy. Leave to cool and cut into approx. 8 portions.

Ap-peal-ing to all

The Bell Inn, one of Suffolk's best-known and busiest, and with 600 years of history behind it, was particularly well-established when Nick Attfield took it on back in 2011. But this was not new territory, in fact an old friend, as he had both run it with the previous landlords in the early Noughties and before that, as a student during holidays, living in nearby Wenhaston. One of the key challenges for Nick has always been preserving all that is so good and well-loved by staff and long-standing regulars but trusting his instinct and insight with careful improvement.

One of two flagship properties he runs within Adnams' tied tenancy estate, The Bell benefits from Nick's passions for both catering and business; he fortunately adores food, beer and wine, plus a day off is a rare thing for this dynamo. With such a buoyant trade and a keenly-priced menu, he keeps a close eye on the finances (as an economics graduate, you would expect nothing less). And boring things like margins and spreadsheets become essential when sunny highdays and holidays see his places thronged from noon to dusk; the Heritage Coast becoming tourist heaven as it does.

While seafood is naturally the mainstay of The Bell's enticing menu of proper pub classics and delicious daily specials, it's not just fruits of the sea which dominate proceedings. Nick's team of in-house trained chefs trawl not just the sea but also the land in their search for the tastiest produce from local producers on their doorstep.

And getting to know where their ingredients come from is important research, that has featured them longlining on a Lowestoft fishing boat, spending a day pig farming with the Butlers at Blythburgh Free Range Pork, herding up sheep and a bit too 'hands-on' lambing, learning cydermaking with Aspall; this is an entertaining list of Nick getting 'close to the coalface'. This local produce cooked simply and carefully sums up what The Bell Inn is all about. The kind of busy place where you know the long menu will all be super-fresh ingredients and you are hard-pressed to make a decision about what to choose. Fortunately, Southwold's finest beer is very well-kept so another pint while you decide is never a hardship...

The Bell Inn
Ferry Road, Walberswick IP18 6TN
T: 01502 723109
W: www.bellinnwalberswick.co.uk
/bellinnwalberswick
@walberswickbell

Accolades: Adnams Pub Business of The Year 2013; *The Publican Morning Advertiser* Best Business Innovation and Highly Commended in Best Fish and Chips National Pub Food Challenge 2013; Best Main Dish The British Street Food Awards 2012 and 2010; *The Good Pub Guide*; main entries *Alastair Sawday's* and *The Good Pub Guide*

Cost: Carte £24 average; wine from £16.50

Open: All year daily 11am-11pm; food served 12-2:30pm & 6-9pm

Details: Bar drinks; wheelchair access; children welcome; dogs in bar; six bedrooms; car parking

NICK ON HIS...

FOODIE NOSTALGIA?

Angel Delight remains a long-standing childhood treat, butterscotch flavour, although I haven't had it for years, must pick up a packet from the supermarket! Similarly with Maynard wine gums every Christmas morning.

FAVOURITE PLACES LOCALLY?

To eat – Well I don't get out much! Jonny is doing a great job with The Bell At Sax' in Saxmundham. To shop – one of my local haunts is Mills & Sons butchery in Southwold Market Place. Back in the day at The Golden Key in Snape, Friday Street Farm Shop was a bit of a foodie treasure trove.To drink – I love the Two Magpies bakery, especially for a sausage roll or a pain au chocolat with great coffee.

ULTIMATE DINING DESTINATIONS?

Has to be the River Café in Hammersmith at its peak in the early Noughties. The Fat Duck before Heston got famous – I have indeed discussed the merits of butterscotch Angel Delight with the demi-god of molecular gastronomy.

Another special place in London was when New Zealand chef Peter Gordon opened The Providores, fusion food so ahead of its time.

And a final mention for Marco Pierre White's Parisian Chop House and his steak tartare prepared at the table in front of you, guéridon theatre at its best.

COOK'S CHEATS?

At the pub, we serve an awful lot of cherry tomatoes. To cut them swiftly, put a single layer between two plastic lids and cut horizontally carefully with a serrated bread knife whilst holding them down lightly. Easy peasy!

SOCIAL MEDIA?

I love the evolution of food and dining out, so tend to follow those at the vanguard of cuisine, modern digital foodies like Jay Rayner, Giles Coren, Jamie Oliver, Rick Stein; and lots of people in street food, they are the really interesting ones to watch for what will be the next big thing.

INSPIRING SUFFOLK VIEW?

Well obviously the stunning iconic views I am privileged to enjoy at Southwold harbour and at Walberswick near the dunes. But apart from those, big decision-making time has always taken me to the river Alde at Snape or Burrow Hill at Butley.

BEST DISHES EVER EATEN?

Perfect risotto in Italy, I have yet to dine anywhere on a risotto of the calibre I experienced learning how to cook in northern Tuscany on a wine-buying trip while working for Harrods. Perhaps not-so-stylish but no less gastronomic, eating very fresh, split langoustines straight from the pan, on top of a bin for the shells with the Brittany fishermen who caught them. So authentic, so delicious.

IF NOT A CHEF?

Probably would have had my own smallholding or possibly food programming on TV, behind the scenes working on the creative visuals, not in front of the camera!

MIDNIGHT FEAST?

Has to be a sausage sandwich, real butchers' bangers, thick white bread, salted butter, and absolutely no sauce!

FOODIE DISCOVERIES?

Street food is so important to me and the future of British cooking. Suffolk can be stuck in a bit of a time warp, so being part of this slightly bohemian, very contemporary London-centric world keeps me in the foodie loop.

CHILDHOOD AMBITIONS?

I was fascinated by medicine, the science bit as the responsibility for welfare of patients freaked me, hence me not pursuing it. (Un)fortunately a careers teacher was a great francophile and got me interested in wine.

NICK'S SIGNATURE DISHES

STARTERS

Wild mushrooms in a white wine cream, sourdough toast and dressed rocket

Smoked ham hock and black pudding fritters, home-made piccalilli

Suffolk smokies cheese gratin with granary toast

MAINS

Lamb shank, apricot and aubergine tagine with pomegranate, pistachio and coriander couscous

The Bell's fish pie

Vegetarian 'fish and chips' – marinated halloumi in a chilli, ginger and coriander batter, minted mushy peas and tartare

PUDDINGS

Chocolate and walnut brownie with cinnamon ice-cream

Baked Alaska-style lemon meringue pie

Raspberry and pistachio Bakewell tart

SUFFOLK FEAST: 20 OF OUR FAVOURITE PLACES

We don't claim that our 20 dining pubs and restaurants are the *only* places in Suffolk to enjoy the bounty of the county – far from it – but every one of them will prepare you a meal with care and flair using local ingredients. Go for an exceptional fine dining destination where the linen is as crisp as the friendly service is polished, or stretch out in a pretty pub garden deep in the Suffolk countryside; maybe you'd rather eat in a buzzy, contemporary town-centre restaurant, or share your (triple-cooked) chips with a daring seagull in outstanding coastal eateries. You choose.

Pea Porridge
28-29 Cannon Street,
Bury St Edmunds IP33 1JR
01284 700200
www.peaporridge.co.uk

The Brudenell Hotel
The Parade,
Aldeburgh IP15 5BU
01728 452071
www.brudenellhotel.co.uk

The Great House
Market Place,
Lavenham CO10 9QZ
01787 247431
www.greathouse.co.uk

The Crown At Southwold
90 High St, Southwold IP18 6DP
01502 722275
www.adnams.co.uk/
hotels/the-crown

The Duke's Head
Slugs Lane, Somerleyton,
Lowestoft NR32 5QR
01502 730281
www.somerleyton.co.uk

The Leaping Hare
Wyken Vineyards, Stanton,
Bury St Edmunds IP31 2DW
01359 250287
www.wykenvineyards.co.uk

The Anchor At Walberswick
The Street,
Walberswick IP18 6UA
01502 722112
www.anchoratwalberswick.com

The Angel Hotel
Angel Hill,
Bury St Edmunds IP33 1LT
01284 714000
www.theangel.co.uk

The Bell At Sax'
31 High St,
Saxmundham IP17 1AF
01728 602331
www.thebellatsax.co.uk

Tuddenham Mill
High Street, Tuddenham,
nr Newmarket IP28 6SQ
01638 713552
www.tuddenhammill.co.uk

Buxhall Coach House
Buxhall Vale,
Stowmarket IP14 3DH
honortownsend@btinternet.com
www.honorsflavours.com

The Swan At Lavenham
High Street,
Lavenham CO10 9QA
01787 247477
www.theswanatlavenham.co.uk

Ben's Restaurant
43-45 Churchgate Street,
Bury St Edmunds IP33 1RG
01284 762119
www.bensrestaurant.co.uk

The Sail Loft
53 Ferry Road,
Southwold IP18 6HQ
01502 725713
www.sailloftsouthwold.uk

The Packhorse Inn
Bridge Street, Moulton,
nr Newmarket CB8 8SP
01638 751818
www.thepackhorseinn.com

The Fox & Goose
Church Road, Fressingfield,
nr Harleston IP21 5PB
01379 586247
www.foxandgoose.net

1921
Angel Hill,
Bury St Edmunds IP33 1UZ
01284 704870
www.nineteen-twentyone.co.uk

Darsham Nurseries
Main Road, Darsham,
nr Yoxford IP17 3PW
01728 667022
www.darshamnurseries.co.uk

The Crown At Woodbridge
Thoroughfare,
Woodbridge IP12 1AD
01394 384242
www.thecrownatwoodbridge.co.uk

The Bell Inn
Ferry Road,
Walberswick IP18 6TN
01502 723109
www.bellinnwalberswick.co.uk

Richard's Relish
LAWSON'S
DELICATESSEN
ALDEBURGH
01728 454052

menu

SUFFOLK FEAST

FOOD LOVERS' GUIDE

Read on to discover some of Suffolk's tastiest treats in our 'little black book' of all that is delicious about our county. Whether you have lived here for decades, just moved in or are a welcome visitor, we hope you enjoy exploring the familiar and perhaps not-so-familiar foodie places listed on the following pages; indeed there are some spots that locals would really rather keep secret!

It's quite possible that places and things that you love may be missing; omissions made either by oversight or because we just don't know about them. Why not share the knowledge with us by emailing suffolkguide@feastpublishing.co.uk

OTB signifies just over the Suffolk border and worth showing your passport for!

ALCOHOLIC DRINKS

BREWERIES

Centuries of brewing tradition and modern techniques mean Suffolk's beers and ales need little introduction. From notable brands to small microbreweries, we get the best of grain.

Adnams Brewery
Sole Bay Brewery, East Green,
Southwold IP18 6JW
T: 01502 727200
W: www.adnams.co.uk/beers

Bartrams Brewery
T: 01449 737655
W: www.bartramsbrewery.co.uk

Calvors Suffolk Lagers and Ales
T: 01449 711055
W: www.calvors.co.uk

Green Jack Brewery
T: 01502 562863
W: www.green-jack.com

Old Cannon Street Brewery
86 Cannon Street, Bury St Edmunds
IP33 1JR
T: 01284 768769
W: www.oldcannonbrewery.co.uk

St Peter's Brewery
St Peter's Hall, St Peter South Elmham,
nr Bungay NR35 1NQ
T: 01986 782322
W: www.stpetersbrewery.co.uk

Hoxne Brewery
T: 07515 003503
W: www.hoxnebrewery.co.uk

Nethergate Brewery
T: 01787 283220
W: www.nethergate.co.uk

St. Jude's Tavern and Microbrewery
(beers only sold at Tavern)
69 St. Matthew's Street, Ipswich IP13EW
T: 07879 360879
W: www.stjudestavern.com

Mauldon's Brewery
T: 01787 311055
W: www.mauldons.co.uk

Greene King
T: 01284 763222
W: www.greeneking.co.uk

VINEYARDS

East Anglia produces award-winning English wines, taking more trophies than any other region of the UK. They are building a following, so why not help fly the flag for our great grapes.

Giffords Hall Vineyard
Shimpling Road, Hartest IP29 4EX
T: 01284 830799
W: www.giffordshall.co.uk

Wyken Vineyards
Wyken Road, Stanton IP31 2DW
T: 01359 250287
W: www.wykenvineyards.co.uk

Shawsgate Vineyard
Badingham Rd (B1120), Brabling Green,
nr Framlingham IP13 9HZ
T: 01728 724060
W: www.shawsgate.co.uk

Wissett Wines at Valley Farm Vineyards
Rumburgh Road, Wissett,
nr Halesworth IP19 0JJ
T: 07867 009967
W: www.valleyfarmvineyards.co.uk

CIDERHOUSES

Perhaps more familiar to the West Country, our few cidermakers more than make up for their rarity with the quality of their produce.

Aspall Cyder
T: 01728 86050
W: www.aspall.co.uk

Castlings Heath Cottage Cider
T: 01787 211118
W: millgreenbrewery.co.uk/our-cider

DISTILLERIES

An extension of the brewing expertise, the art of distillation has thrown up a real artisan flair.

Adnams Distillery
Sole Bay Brewery, East Green, Southwold IP18 6JW
T: 01502 727200
W: www.adnams.co.uk/spirits

WINE MERCHANTS AND WINES

For most, good food would be missing a link without a good vintage – a fine vintner is essential in helping you find the right bottle.

Adnams Stores *(Southwold and other places)*
Victoria Street, Southwold IP18 6GB
T: 01502 725612
W: www.cellarandkitchen.adnams.co.uk

Richard Kihl Fine Wines
140-144 High Street
Aldeburgh IP15 5AQ
T: 01728 454455
W: www.richardkihl.ltd.uk

DJ Wines *fruit wine and liqueurs*
T: 07882 649833
W: www.dj-wines.com

T & W Wines
5 Station Way, Brandon IP27 0BH
T: 01842 814414
W: www.tw-wines.com

NON-ALCOHOLIC DRINKS

HOT DRINKS

Morning coffee is a great British tradition. These expert roasters bring Suffolk passion and good taste into their delicious brews.

Paddy and Scott's Coffees
The Bean Barn, Moat Park, Framlingham Road,
Earl Soham IP13 7SR
T: 08444 778586
W: www.paddyandscotts.co.uk

The Suffolk Coffee Company
T: 01728 660744
W: thesuffolkcoffeecompany.co.uk

Thistledown Cottage Coffee
T: 07818 813028
W: www.thistledowncottagecoffee.co.uk

Deepmills Coffee
T: 07549 999481
W: www.deepmills.co.uk

COLD DRINKS

Our fertile earth and history of mixed farming make orchards and soft fruit plantations a familiar part of our horticultural landscape.

Maynard House Orchards
T: 01284 388680
W: www.applejuice.uk.com

High House Fruit Farm
T: 01394 450263
W: www.high-house.co.uk

James White Drinks
T: 01473 890111
W: www.jameswhite.co.uk

Hedgerow Cordials
T: 07950 248263
W: www.hedgerowcordials.co.uk

Edward's Cordials
T: 07731 351892
W: www.edwardscordial.co.uk

Impressions Drinks
T: 07792 911396
W: www.impressionsdrinks.co.uk

Stoke Farm Orchards
T: 01449 774944
W: www.tastesofanglia.org.uk

FOODS

MEAT

Native heritage breeds, home-grown feed and bedding, generations of livestock farming and modern selective techniques make Suffolk meat some of the best.

Blythburgh Free Range Pork
T: 01986 873298
W: www.freerangepork.co.uk

Kenton Hall Estate *Longhorn beef*
T: 01728 862062
W: www.kentonhallestate.co.uk

Alde Valley Lamb *via Salter & King, Aldeburgh*
T: 01728 452758
W: www.salterandking.co.uk

Musks Newmarket Sausages
T: 01638 662626
W: www.musks.com

Powters Newmarket Sausages
T: 01638 662418
W: www.powters.co.uk

Peakhill Farm *Grass-fed beef*
T: 01728 602248
W: www.peakhillfarm.co.uk

The Culford Flock
Jacob lamb and Highland/Angus beef
T: 07846 862037
W: www.club-noticeboard.co.uk/culfordflock

Cratfield Beef *Traditional breed beef*
T: 01986 798099
W: www.cratfieldbeef.co.uk

Hundred River Farm *Hereford beef*
T: 01502 476063
W: www.hundredriverfarm.co.uk

Denham Estate *Lamb*
T: 01284 810231
W: www.denhamestate.co.uk

Red Poll Meats *Heritage free range meats*
T: 01728 687627
W: www.redpollmeats.co.uk

Procter's Sausages
T: 01473 281191
W: www.procters-sausages.co.uk

POULTRY

Farmed poultry is another prime agricultural harvest in the county. That old-fashioned flavour of yesteryear comes from the right breeding, slow maturing and the best grain feeds.

Sutton Hoo Chicken
T: 01394 386797
W: www.suttonhoochicken.co.uk

Gressingham Duck
T: 01473 735456
W: www.gressinghamduck.co.uk

PA Mobbs and Sons
Turkeys and guinea fowl
T: 01986 798340
W: www.pamobbsandsons.co.uk

WILD GAME

Shooting helps create an inescapable part of the Suffolk farming landscape of field, hedgerow and wood, ensuring habitat for our precious flora'n'fauna and of course tasty great value meat from fur and feather.

The Wild Meat Company *Oven ready game*
T: 01728 687627
W: www.wildmeat.co.uk

Truly Traceable *Game pies and savouries*
W: www.twitter.com/trulytraceable

Long Melford and Lavenham Game
T: 07812 580765
W: www.gametoeat.co.uk

Denham Estate Venison
T: 01284 810231
W: www.denhamestate.co.uk

Bluebell Woods *Wild Venison and Deer Control*
T: 01502 733501
W: www.wildvenison.co.uk

Discover Venison
T: 07545 477693
W: www.discovervenison.co.uk

FISH AND SHELLFISH

see Places to Shop – Fishmongers and Seafood

MEAT PRODUCTS

Superb quality farmyard meats as raw materials, and additions like home-grown flour for pastry, make for a proper Suffolk ploughman's lunch, and high tea!

Truly Traceable *Game pies and savouries*
W: www.twitter.com/trulytraceable

The Pie Kitchen
T: 07846953340
W: www.the-pie-kitchen.co.uk

Suffolk Pâté Company
T: 01449 760629
W: www.thesuffolkpatecompany.co.uk

The Gamekeeper's Daughter *OTB Game and Foraged Dishes*
W: www.gamekeepers-daughter.co.uk
T: 01206 298089

SMOKED PRODUCE

Going back only a few generations, come autumn most households in the country would be smoking the legs and belly of their hog to last through the cooler months.

Stour Valley Smokehouse
T: 07720 524800
W: www.suffolkmarketevents.co.uk

Suffolk Smokehouse and Deli
T: 01728 768263
W: www.suffolksmokehouse.net

Artisan Smokehouse
T: 01394 270609
W: www.artisansmokehouse.co.uk

VEGETABLES, SALADS AND HERBS

Smallholdings and market gardeners exploit the fertile soils and sunny climate for the flavours and texture of their leafy harvests. Earthy roots, crisp brassicas, sweet legumes and funky new-wave v eggies are profitable crops for clever farmers and food-lovers alike.

Trimley Herbs
T: 07807 658689
W: www.trimleyherbs.co.uk

Langham Herbs
Open to visit and veg box deliveries locally
T: 07772 457063
W: www.langhamherbs.co.uk

Waveney Mushrooms
T: 01986 782571
W: www.waveneymushrooms.co.uk

The Chilli Company
Chilli plants and products
Norwich Road, Mendlesham IP14 5NQ
T: 01449 766677
W: www.chillicompany.com

BAKERY AND CAKES

The best of grain gives bakers and cakemakers the finest raw ingredient in flour combined with our staple British beet sugar (Silver Spoon), rich dairy and free range eggs.

Pump Street Bakery *Artisan breads*
T: 01394 459829
W: www.pumpstreetbakery.com

Rattla Cottage Bakery *Artisan breads*
T: 01728 830770
W: www.rattlacottagebakery.co.uk

Simply Home Bake *Cakes and sponges*
T: 01473 829348
W: www.suffolkmarketevents.co.uk

Farmhouse Cooking *Cakes and savouries*
T: 01728 746344
W: www.farmhousecooking.co.uk

Harrisons Bakery *Cakes*
T: 01502 572510
W: www.harrisonsbakery.com

The Penny Ben Bakehouse *Artisan breads*
T: 07737 537880
W: www.thepennybunbakehouse.co.uk

The Cake Shop Bakery *Breads and cakes*
T: 01394 382515
W: www.cakeshopbakery.co.uk

The Dotty Bakers *Cake mixes*
T: 07534 554665
W: www.thedottybakers.co.uk

Bardwell Mill Bakery *Breads*
T: 07821 361153
W: www.facebook.com/bardwellmillbakery

Pakenham Water Mill Flour
Mill Road, Pakenham,
Bury St Edmunds IP31 2NB
T: 01359 230275
W: www.pakenhamwatermill.org.uk

The Friendly Loaf Bakery *Breads and quiches*
T: 01284 754252
W: www.thefriendlyloaf.co.uk

The Wheaten Mill *Cakes*
T: 01473 827010
W: www.wheatenmill.co.uk

Two Magpies Bakery *Breads and cakes*
88 High Street, Southwold IP18 6DP
T: 01502 726120
W: www.twomagpiesbakery.co.uk

Woodbridge Tide Mill *Stone-ground flour*
Tide Mill Way, Woodbridge IP12 1BY
T: 01394 385295
W: www.woodbridgetidemill.org.uk

Tudor Bakehouse *Breads and cakes*
11 Broad Street, Eye IP23 7AF
T: 01379 870974
W: www.tudorbakehouse.co.uk

Earsham Street Café *Cakes*
11-13 Earsham Street, Bungay NR35 1AE
T: 01986 893103
W: www.earshamstreetcafe.co.uk

Cakes To Celebrate
T: 01986 781382
W: www.cakes-to-celebrate.co.uk

Suffolk Cupcake Company
W: www.suffolkcupcakes.co.uk

Marriage's Millers *OTB Flours*
T: 01245 354455
W: www.flour.co.uk

CHARCUTERIE

With a great heritage in all things piggy and a historic seafaring tradition, curing and preserving pork and other meats has always been an artisan skill par excellence in Suffolk.

Lane Farm Country Foods
T: 01379 384593
W: www.lanefarm.co.uk

Suffolk Salami Co.
T: 01379 384593
W: www.suffolksalami.co.uk

Grangeworth Foods
Hams and bacon using Blythburgh Free Range Pork
T: 01728 628229
W: www.grangeworthfoods.co.uk

Marsh Pig *OTB*
Using Blythburgh Free Range Pork
T: 01508 480560
W: www.marshpig.co.uk

CHEESE

Whilst we don't milk the local Red Poll any longer commercially, dairy farming is still key, not least for a new wave of rich tasty cheeses and passionate cheesemakers.

Suffolk Farmhouse Cheeses
Suffolk Gold & Suffolk Blue
T: 01449 710458
W: www.suffolkcheese.co.uk

Rodwell Farm Dairy *Shipcord and Hawkston*
T: 01473 830192
W: www.rodwellfarmdairy.co.uk

Fen Farm Dairy *Baron Bigod brie*
T: 01986 897128
W: www.fenfarmdairy.co.uk

Hamish Johnston Fine Cheeses
T: 01394 388127
W: www.hamishjohnston.com

Mrs H's Cheese Stall
T: 07557 028234
W: www.mrs-h-cheesestall.co.uk

DAIRY AND ICE CREAM

With lush pasture making rich cream and butterfat, it is no surprise we have superb dairy products such as crème fraîche, frozen desserts and butter.

Marybelle Dairy and Suffolk Meadow Ice Cream
T: 01986 784658
W: www.marybelle.co.uk

Alder Tree Fruit Cream Ices
T: 01449 721220
W: www.alder-tree.co.uk

Parravanis Ice Creams
T: 01502 715970
W: www.parravanis.co.uk

Fen Farm Dairy *Raw milk and dairy produce*
T: 01986 897128
W: www.fenfarmdairy.co.uk

Hundred River Farm
Ice cream and dairy produce
T: 01502 476063
W: www.hundredriverfarm.co.uk

DESSERTS

The perfect 'afters' for any Suffolk feast, most of us love something to indulge our sweet tooth, whether it be the best of ripe local fruits or other decadent delights.

Love Meringues
W: www.twitter.com/lovemeringues

Henrietta Inman Pâtisserie
T: 01728 663238
W: www.henriettainman.co.uk

Vanilla Pâtisserie
T: 01728 768010
W: www.vanillapatisserie.co.uk

PRESERVES

The best fresh produce is that picked at the right time; pickled crisp vegetables and sweet jarred fruit showcase this perfectly.

Mrs Bennett's Pickles
T: 01473 822650
W: www.mrsbennetts.co.uk

Mr Bees Honey
T: 07503 773630
W: www.mrbees.co.uk

The Apple Butter Company
T: 07985 411289
W: www.applebuttercompany.co.uk

Bee House Honey Company
T: 07975 591617
W: www.beehousehoneycompany.co.uk

Fruits of Suffolk
T: 01449 760397
W: www.fruitsofsuffolk.co.uk

Jules and Sharpie *Hot chilli preservaments*
T: 01621 814529
W: www.julesandsharpie.co.uk

CONFECTIONERY

Over coffee or any time of the day, an energy boost or simple luxury, sticky sweet meats and fine chocolates hit the spot.

Ailsa's Country Cream Fudge
T: 01502 740365
W: www.aldeburghfoodanddrink.co.uk

B Chocolates
T: 01728 687967
W: www.bchocolates.co.uk

Petite and Sweet *Chocolates and wedding favours*
T: 07908 200179
W: www.petiteandsweet.co.uk

Raw Nibbles
T: 0844 3755 914
W: www.rawnibbles.co.uk

Artistry in Cocoa
T: 01638 660503
W: www.artistryincocoa.co.uk

FOOD LOVERS' GUIDE

Your deliciously indispensable companion to enjoying Suffolk, edible and otherwise

CONDIMENTS AND OILS

The great meats, cured and smoked charcuterie, creamy cheeses and seafood call for something good on the side. Our preserving expertise extends to all manner of superb saucery.

Scarlett and Mustard *Dressings*
T: 01728 685210
W: www.scarlettandmustard.co.uk

Stokes Sauces *Table sauces*
T: 01394 462150
W: www.stokessauces.co.uk

Hillfarm *Virgin rapeseed oil and mayonnaises*
T: 01986 798660
W: www.hillfarmoils.com

Salubrious Sauce Company
T: 01394 446028
W: www.salubrioussauceco.co.uk

East Coast Chilli Company *Chilli sauces*
T: 07563 360703
W: www.eastcoastchillicompany.co.uk

Norfolk & Suffolk Speciality Foods
T: 01986 780902
W: www.nssfoods.co.uk

Sym's Pantry
T: 07933 710185
W: www.symspantry.com

Jules and Sharpie *Hot chilli preservaments*
T: 01621 814529
W: www.julesandsharpie.co.uk

LARDER STAPLES

The simple things in the kitchen are often taken for granted. But without them, much of our fabulous cooking wouldn't be the same.

Aspall *Vinegars*
T: 01728 86050
W: www.aspall.co.uk

Hodmedods *Dried and canned peas and beans*
T: 01986 467567
W: www.hodmedods.co.uk

SPECIALIST DIETARY PRODUCTS

Special diet choices and sensitivity should not preclude enjoyment and indulgence. These expert suppliers produce tasty results on the plate.

Food By Lizzi *Vegetarian & vegan foods*
T: 07724 004171
W: www.foodbylizzi.com

Glorious Fodder *Gluten-free foods*
T: 07795 388190
W: www.gloriousfodder.co.uk

GLOBAL SPECIALITIES

Sometimes home cooking with local ingredients just needs a lift; zingy flavours and warm spices bring back nostalgic holiday memories from around the world.

Red Chilli Kitchen *Vietnamese spice products*
T: 07854 923200
W: www.redchillikitchen.co.uk

Red Hot Chilli Fella *Chilli Products*
T: 07807 555570
W: www.redhotchillifella.co.uk

SNACKS

Busy lives and eating something on the run or just nibbling over drinks, why not seek out something with a taste of Suffolk?

Munchy Seeds
T: 01728 833004
W: www.munchyseeds.co.uk

Raw Nibbles
T: 0844 3755 914
W: www.rawnibbles.co.uk

Hodmedods *Snack peas and beans*
T: 01986 467567
W: www.hodmedods.co.uk

Newlands Cheese Straws
T: 07850 072061
W: www.newlandscheesestraws.com

CHARCOAL

Our beautiful wooded landscape is well-managed and sustainably-cropped, producing great charcoal for low 'fire miles'.

Barbecube
T: 01449 721220
W: www.barbecube.co.uk

CountryCare Charcoal
T: 01728 747474
W: www.countrycare.co.uk

GOURMET PET TREATS

Even our canine companions, cooks' best friends, deserve to be spoilt occasionally with local food.

Barkers of Suffolk
T: 01473 597598
W: www.barkersofsuffolk.co.uk

PLACES TO EAT

CAFÉS AND EATING PLACES

Smaller or simpler eating places are often some of the most appealing foodie destinations where we comfortably escape to for a wholesome delicious light bite.

Café Bencotto, Felixstowe
128 Hamilton Road, Felixstowe IP11 7AB
T: 01394 276745
W: www.cafebencotto.co.uk

Jimmy's Farm, Wherstead
Pannington Hall Lane, Wherstead,
nr Ipswich IP9 2AR
T: 01473 604206
W: www.jimmysfarm.com

Farm Café and Shop, Marlesford
Main Road, Marlesford,
nr Wickham Market IP13 0AG
T: 01728 747717
W: www.farmcafe.co.uk

The Aldeburgh Market
170-172 High St, Aldeburgh IP15 5AQ
T: 01728 452520
W: www.thealdeburghmarket.co.uk

Simply Delicious, Leiston
70 High St, Leiston IP16 4BZ
T: 01728 833078
W: www.simplydelicioussuffolk.co.uk

Munchies, Aldeburgh
163 - 165 High Street, Aldeburgh IP15 5AN
T: 01728 454566
W: www.aldeburghmunchies.co.uk

Butley-Orford Oysterage, Orford
Market Hill, Orford IP12 2LH
T: 01394 450277
W: www.pinneysoforford.co.uk

Pump Street Bakery Café, Orford
1 Pump Street Orford IP12 2LZ
T: 01394 459829
W: www.pumpstreetbakery.com

Lizzy's Coffee Shop, Risby
Risby Barn, South Street, Risby,
nr Bury St Edmunds IP28 6QU
T: 01284 810022
W: www.risbybarn.co.uk

Suffolk Food Hall, Wherstead
Wherstead, nr Ipswich IP9 2AB
T: 01473 786616
W: www.suffolkfoodhall.co.uk

Two Magpies Bakery Café, Southwold
88 High Street, Southwold IP18 6DP
T: 01502 726120
W: www.twomagpiesbakery.co.uk

Bloomsberries Café and Deli, Lakenheath
Christmas Hill Farm, Station Road,
Lakenheath IP27 9AB
T: 01842 861144
W: www.christmashill.co.uk

Paddy and Scott's Cafés
12 Abbeygate Street, Bury St Edmunds IP33 1UN
T: 01284 760661
22a Well Close Square, Framlingham IP13 9DS
T: 01728 621246
High Street, Hadleigh IP7 5EF
T: 01473 823601
W: www.paddyandscotts.co.uk

Sole Bay Fish Co. Restaurant, Southwold
Shed 22e, Blackshore Harbour,
Southwold IP18 6ND
T: 01502 724241
W: www.solebayfishco.co.uk

Fornham Organic Café
Church Cottage, Fornham All Saints IP28 6JW
T: 01284 717175
W: www.theorganicshopltd.co.uk

Mr Allard's Farm Shop Café, Stowupland
Rendall Lane, Stowupland, nr Stowmarket IP14 4BD
T: 01449 615006
W: www.mrallardsfarmbutchery.com

The Chilli Company Café, Mendlesham
Norwich Road, Mendlesham IP14 5NQ
T: 01449 766677
W: www.chillicompany.com

The Dancing Goat, Framlingham
33 Market Hill, Framlingham IP13 9BA
T: 01449 766677
W: www.thedancinggoatframlingham.wordpress.com

The Common Room Café, Framlingham
22 Bridge St, Framlingham IP13 9AH
T: 01728 768238
W: www.thecommonroomfram.com

Cafe Kottani, Bury St Edmunds
30 Buttermarket, Bury St Edmunds IP33 1DW
T: 01284 766551
W: www.facebook.com/cafekottani

No 4 Hatter Street at Abbeygate Cinema, Bury
4 Hatter Street, Bury St Edmunds IP33 1LZ
T: 01284 754477
W: www.abbeygatecinema.co.uk/food-and-drink

Café Knit, Lavenham
46 High Street, Lavenham CO10 9PY
T: 01787 249865
W: www.cafeknit.com

TAKE-AWAYS

Seek out the better 'chippies' and you are in for a treat. Fryers like the much-missed John Bond (of Needham Market) keep this most delicious of British signatures alive.

Aldeburgh Fish and Chip Shop
226 High St, Aldeburgh IP15 5DB
T: 01728 452250
W: www.aldeburghfishandchips.co.uk

Bury Chippy
64a St Andrews Street South,
Bury St Edmunds IP33 1SD
T: 01284 754589

Mrs T's Fish and Chips, Southwold Harbour
BlackShore Harbour, Southwold IP18 6TA
T: 01502 724709

TEAROOMS

Tea is a great British institution, so whether it's a case of bone china, crusts off and pinkies raised or just a good slice of home-made fruitcake and a mug of builders' finest, do take time for tea.

Mill Tea Room at Pakenham Water Mill
Mill Road, Pakenham,
Bury St Edmunds IP31 2NB
T: 01359 230275
W: www.pakenhamwatermill.org.uk

Tilly's of Halesworth
10 Market Place, Halesworth IP19 8BA
T: 01986 835899
W: www.tillysofhalesworth.co.uk

Thorpeness Meare Shop and Tearooms
Thorpeness Meare, Thorpeness IP16 4NW
T: 01728 452156
W: www.meareshop.co.uk

Riverside Tearoom, Orford
Orford Quay, Orford IP12 2NU
T: 01394 459797
W: www.riversidetearoom.co.uk

Baileys 2 Coffee Shop and Tearooms, Bury
5 Whiting St, Bury St Edmunds IP33 1NX
T: 01284 706198
W: www.baileys2.co.uk

Harriets Café Tearooms, Bury St Edmunds
57 Cornhill Buildings, Bury St Edmunds IP33 1BT
T: 01284 756256
W: www.harrietscafetearooms.co.uk

Earsham Street Café, Bungay
11-13 Earsham Street, Bungay NR35 1AE
T: 01986 893103
W: www.earshamstreetcafe.co.uk

Really Rather Good, Bury St Edmunds
31A Abbeygate St,
Bury St Edmunds, Suffolk IP33 1LW
T: 01284 756181
W: www.rrgood.co.uk

The Secret Garden, Sudbury
21 Friars St, Sudbury, Suffolk CO10 2AA
T: 01787 372030
W: www.tsg.uk.net

PLACES TO DRINK

PUBS (qv INNS)

The great Suffolk pint is a natural expression of our grain farmers and maltsters, the skill of the brewer, and the art of keeping a good cellar, seek out some of our best hostelries and quaff in confidence.

St. Jude's Tavern and Microbrewery, Ipswich
69 St. Matthew's Street, Ipswich IP13EW
T: 07879 360879
W: www.stjudestavern.com

The Rampant Horse *Calvors brewery tap*
Coddenham Road, Needham Market IP6 8AU
T: 01449 722044
W: www.therampanthorse.co.uk

The Cadogan Arms, Ingham
The Street, Ingham, nr Bury St Edmunds IP31 1NG
T: 01284 728443
W: www.thecadogan.co.uk

The Lord Nelson, Southwold
42 East Street, Southwold IP18 6EJ
T: 01502 722079
W: www.thelordnelsonsouthwold.co.uk

The Bell Inn, Middleton
The Street, Middleton IP17 3NN
T: 01728 648286

The Five Bells, Wrentham
Southwold Road, Wrentham NR34 7JD
T: 01502 675249
W: www.five-bells.com

The Queens Head, Blyford
Southwold Road, Blyford IP19 9JY
T: 01502 478404
W: www.queensheadblyford.co.uk

The Ship, Levington
Church Lane, Levington IP10 0LQ
T: 01473 659573
W: www.theshipinnlevington.co.uk

The White Hart, Blythburgh
London Road, Blythburgh IP19 9LQ
T: 01502 478217
W: www.blythburgh-whitehart.co.uk

The White Horse, Westleton
Darsham Road, Westleton IP17 3AH
T: 01728 648222
W: www.westleton-whitehorse.co.uk

St. Peter's Hall, St. Peter South Elmham
St. Peter South Elmham, nr Bungay NR35 1NQ
T: 01986 782288
W: www.hallcatering.co.uk

The De La Pole Arms, Wingfield
Church Road, Wingfield, nr Diss IP21 5RA
T: 01379 384545
W: www.delapolearms.co.uk

The Black Tiles, Martlesham
Black Tiles Lane, Martlesham,
nr Woodbridge IP12 4SP
T: 01473 624038
W: www.blacktiles.co.uk

The Triangle Tavern, Lowestoft
St. Peter's Street, Lowestoft NR32 1QA
T: 01502 582711
W: www.green-jack.com

The Geldeston Locks Inn
Lock's Lane, Geldeston, nr Beccles NR34 0HS
T: 01508 518414
W: www.geldestonlocks.co.uk

The White Horse Inn, Sweffling
Low Road, Sweffling IP17 2BB
T: 01728 664178
W: www.swefflingwhitehorse.co.uk

The Kings Head (Low House), Laxfield
Gorams Mill Lane, Laxfield IP13 8DW
T: 01986 798395
W: www.laxfieldkingshead.co.uk

The Blaxhall Ship
School Road, Blaxhall IP12 2DY
T: 01728 688316
W: www.blaxhallshipinn.co.uk

The Wenhaston Star
Hall Road, Wenhaston nr Blythburgh IP19 9HF
T: 01502 478240
W: www.wenhastonstar.co.uk

The Froize Inn, Chillesford
Main Road, Chillesford IP12 3PU
T: 01394 450282
W: www.froize.co.uk

WINE BARS

Sometimes only a glass of something dry and chilled, or fruity and red will do...

The Alex, Felixstowe
123 Undercliff Road West, Felixstowe IP11 2AF
T: 01394 282958
W: www.alexcafebar.co.uk

Beccles Wine Vaults
2A Blyburgate, Beccles, Suffolk NR34 9TA
T: 01502 713381
W: www.beccleswinevaults.co.uk

PLACES TO STAY

INNS

Good food and drink are natural bedfellows, Suffolk inns express this admirably, the new wave of boutique establishments put plate and glass on an equal gastronomic footing.

The Anchor At Walberswick
The Street, Walberswick IP18 6UA
T: 01502 722112
W: www.anchoratwalberswick.com

The Bell At Walberswick
Ferry Rd, Walberswick IP18 6TN

T: 01502 723109
W: www.bellinnwalberswick.co.uk

The Bell At Sax', Saxmundham
31 High Street, Saxmundham IP17 1AF
T: 01728 602331
W: www.thebellatsax.co.uk

The Packhorse At Moulton
Bridge Street, Moulton,
nr Newmarket CB8 8SP
T: 01638 751818
W: www.thepackhorseinn.com

The Dolphin, Thorpeness
Peace Place, Thorpeness IP16 4NA
T: 01728 454994
W: www.thorpenessdolphin.com

The Randolph, Reydon
Wangford Road, Reydon,
nr Southwold IP18 6PZ
T: 01502 723603
W: www.therandolph.co.uk

The Blyth, Southwold
Station Road, Southwold IP18 6AY
T: 01502 722632
W: www.blythhotel.com

The Crown Inn, Snape
Bridge Road, Snape IP17 1SL
T: 01728 688324
W: www.snape-crown.co.uk

The Eels Foot, Eastbridge
Eastbridge, nr Leiston IP16 4SN
T: 01728 648286
W: www.theeelsfootinn.co.uk

The Castle Inn, Bungay
35 Earsham St, Bungay NR35 1AF
T: 01986 892283
W: www.thecastleinn.net

The Black Bull *OTB*
27 High Street, Balsham, Cambs CB21 4DJ
T: 01223 893844
W: www.blackbull-balsham.co.uk

The Fritton Arms *OTB*
Church Lane, Fritton, Norfolk NR31 9HA
T: 01493 484008
W: www.frittonarms.co.uk

HOTELS

Why not linger and stay a while in whichever of our destinations you choose. Spoil yourself over an extra glass and stay up feasting.

The Angel, Bury St Edmunds
3 Angel Hill, Bury St Edmunds IP33 1LT
T: 01284 714000
W: www.theangel.co.uk

The Great House Restaurant-with-Rooms
Market Place, Lavenham CO10 9QZ
T: 01787 247431
W: www.greathouse.co.uk

The Swan, Southwold
Market Place, Southwold IP18 6EG
T: 01502 722186
W: www.adnams.co.uk/hotels

The Crown, Southwold
90 High Street, Southwold IP18 6DP
T: 01502 722275
W: www.adnams.co.uk/hotels

The Salthouse Harbour, Ipswich
1 Neptune Quay, Ipswich IP4 1AX
T: 01473 226789
W: www.salthouseharbour.co.uk

Tuddenham Mill, Tuddenham
High Street, Tuddenham, nr Barton Mills IP28 6SQ
T: 01638 713552
W: www.tuddenhammill.co.uk

The Swan At Lavenham
High Street, Lavenham CO10 9QA
T: 01787 247477
W: www.theswanatlavenham.co.uk

The Crown At Woodbridge
Thoroughfare, Woodbridge IP12 1AD
T: 01394 384242
W: www.thecrownatwoodbridge.co.uk

The Brudenell, Aldeburgh
The Parade, Aldeburgh IP15 5BU
T: 01728 452071
W: www.brudenellhotel.co.uk

Thorpeness Hotel and Golf Course
Lakeside Avenue, Thorpeness IP16 4NH
T: 01728 452176
W: www.thorpeness.co.uk

The White Lion, Aldeburgh
Market Cross Place, Aldeburgh IP15 5BJ
T: 01728 452720
W: www.whitelion.co.uk

B&Bs/GUEST ACCOMMODATION

Whether the charm of a rural village, the buzz of a town or the peace of a farm, a comfortable bed and a hearty breakfast is one of the greatest simple pleasures.

Lucy Redman Garden B&B, Rushbrooke
6 The Village, Rushbrooke IP30 0ER
T: 01284 386250
W: www.lucyredman.co.uk

Flindor Cottage, Framsden
The Street, Framsden IP14 6HG
T: 01473 890058
W: www.flindorcottage.co.uk

Valley Farm, Middleton
Valley Farm House, Middleton,
nr Saxmundham IP17 3NA
T: 01728 648217
W: www.valley-farm.co.uk

Sandpit Farm, Bruisyard
Low Road, Bruisyard, nr Framlingham IP17 2EB
T: 01728 663445
W: www.aldevalleybreaks.co.uk

Rendham Hall
Rendham Hall, Rendham, Saxmundham IP17 2AW
T: 01728 663440
W: www.rendhamhall.co.uk

Sweffling Hall Farm
Sweffling IP17 2BT
T: 07999 403928
W: swefflinghallfarm.wordpress.com

Church Farm, Bradfield Combust
The Street, Bradfield Combust,
nr Bury St Edmunds IP30 0LW
T: 01284 386333
W: www.churchfarm-bandb.co.uk

The Boltons B&B, Badwell Ash
The Street, Badwell Ash IP31 3DH
T: 07805 626088
W: www.theboltonsbandb.co.uk

Haughley House
The Folly, Haughley IP14 3NS
T: 01449 673398
W: www.haughleyhouse.co.uk

The Old Rectory Country House, Gt Waldingfield
Rectory Road, Great Waldingfield CO10 0TL
T: 01787 372428
W: www.theoldrectorycountryhouse.co.uk

West Stow Hall
Icklingham Road, West Stow IP28 6EY
T: 01787 372428
W: www.weststowhall.com

Holly Tree House B&B, Wingfield
Bleach Green, Wingfield IP21 5RG
T: 01379 384854
W: www.hollytreehousebandb.co.uk

HOLIDAY LETS

Getting under the skin of Suffolk for a weekend or longer, staying as welcome guests in a local community, surrounded by family and friends is the stuff of happy life-long memories.

The Wash House Studio, Orford
7 Coastguard Cottages, Quay Street,
Orford IP12 2NX
T: 01394 450959
W: www.orfordwashhouse.co.uk

Woodfarm Barns, Stonham Aspal
Crowfield Road, Stonham Aspal IP6 9TH
T: 01449 710032
W: www.woodfarmbarns.com

The Brewer's House, Southwold
55 Victoria Street, Southwold IP18 6JQ
T: 01502 722186
W: www.adnams.co.uk/hotels

Pinkney's Lane, Southwold
6 Pinkney's Lane, Southwold IP18 6EW
T: 01502 722186
W: www.adnams.co.uk/hotels

High Lodge Luxury Holiday Lodges
Haw Wood, Hinton, Darsham IP17 3QT
T: 01986 784347
W: www.highlodge.co.uk

Ore Valley Cottages, Little Glemham
Sink Farm, Church Road,
Little Glemham IP13 0BJ
T: 01728 602783
W: www.holidaycottagessuffolk-orevalley.co.uk

Valley Farm Cottages, Sudbourne
Valley Farm School Road, Sudbourne IP12 2BH
T: 01394 450979
W: www.valleyfarmcottages.co.uk

GLAMPING AND CAMPING

Whether you bring your own or enjoy the luxury of having it pitched there ready for you, there is nothing quite like being at one with nature, out under the stars and in the open air.

Suffolk Yurt Holidays, Bredfield *(glamp)*
Oak Cottage, Ufford Road, Bredfield IP13 6AR
T: 07907 964890
W: www.suffolkyurtholidays.co.uk

Alde Garden, Sweffling *(glamp)*
The White Horse Inn, Low Road, Sweffling IP17 2BB
T: 01728 664178
W: www.aldegarden.co.uk

Newbourne Woodland Campsite *(glamp & camp)*
Virginia House, Jackson Road,
Newbourne IP12 4NR
T: 01473 736201
W: www.newbourne-campsite.co.uk

Secret Meadows Luxury Camping, Hasketon *(glamp)*
White House Farm Wildlife Site, Hasketon IP13 6JP
T: 01394 382992
W: www.secretmeadows.co.uk

Dawn Chorus Glamping - Yurts and Shepherds' Huts, Barsham *(glamp)*
The Pines, Hall Road, Barsham,
nr Beccles NR34 8JN
T: 01502 713152
W: www.dawnchorusholidays.com

Ling's Meadow, Hepworth *(glamp) OTB*
Stanton Road Farm, North Common,
Hepworth, Diss, Norfolk IP22 2PR
T: 01359 250594
W: www.lingsmeadow.co.uk

Wardley Hill Campsite, Kirby Cane *OTB (glamp & camp)*
Wardley Hill Rd, Kirby Cane, Norfolk NR35 2PQ
T: 07733 306543
W: www.wardleyhillcampsite.com

PLACES TO SHOP

FARMERS' MARKETS

Perhaps a true expression of our historic family farms and artisan food and drink production, the best of these continue to thrive as an essential part of our Suffolk food scene.

Wyken Vineyards Farmers' Market, Stanton
Every Saturday 9am - 1pm
Wyken Road, Stanton IP31 2DW
T: 01359 250287
W: www.wykenvineyards.co.uk

Woodbridge Farmers' Market
2nd & 4th Saturdays monthly - 9am to 12.30pm
Woodbridge Community Hall,
Station Road, Woodbridge IP12 4AU
T: 07549 999481
W: www.woodbridgefarmersmarket.co.uk

Lavenham Farmers' Market
4th Sunday monthly 10am - 1.30pm
Lavenham Village Hall, Church St,
Lavenham CO10 9QT
T: 07704 627973
W: www.suffolkmarketevents.co.uk

Sudbury Farmers' Market
Last Friday monthly 9.30am - 2pm
St. Peter's Sudbury, Market Hill,
Sudbury CO10 2EA
T: 07704 627973
W: www.suffolkmarketevents.co.uk

Nayland Farmers' Market
2nd Saturday monthly 9.30am - 1pm
Nayland Village Hall, Church Lane,
Nayland, CO6 4JH
T: 07704 627973
W: www.suffolkmarketevents.co.uk

Jimmy's Farm Farmers' Market, Wherstead
1st Saturday monthly 10am - 2pm
Pannington Hall Lane, Wherstead,
nr Ipswich IP9 2AR
T: 01473 604206
W: www.jimmysfarm.com

Snape Maltings Farmers' Market
1st Saturday monthly 9.30am - 1pm
Bridge Road, Snape IP17 1SR
T: 01728 688303
W: www.snapemaltings.co.uk

Beccles Farmers Market
1st and 3rd Saturday monthly 9am – 1pm
Ellough Airfield, Ellough, nr Beccles
T: 01502 476240
W: www.becclesfarmersmarket.co.uk

Bury Provisions Market
Wednesdays and Saturdays
Buttermarket, Bury St Edmunds IP33 1DA
T: 01284 764667 (tourist information)
W: www.visit-burystedmunds.co.uk

DELIS AND FOOD HALLS

While we love local fresh seasonal produce, we get ever more fascinated with globe-trotting cuisines and flavours to add interest to our food. Well-stocked knowledgeable purveyors are a joy to explore.

Lawsons Delicatessen, Aldeburgh
138 High Street, Aldeburgh IP15 5AQ
T: 01728 454052
W: www.lawsonsdelicatessen.co.uk

Suffolk Food Hall, Wherstead
Wherstead, nr Ipswich IP9 2AB
T: 01473 786610
W: www.suffolkfoodhall.co.uk

Leo's Deli, Framlingham
17 Market Hill, Framlingham IP13 9AN
T: 01728 724059
W: www.leosdeli.co.uk

Farm Café and Shop, Marlesford
Main Road A12, Marlesford,
nr Wickham Market IP13 0AG
T: 01728 747717
W: www.farmcafe.co.uk

Gastrono-Me, Bury St Edmunds
2 St John's St, Bury St Edmunds IP33 1SQ
T: 01284 718665
W: www.gastrono-me.co.uk

Earsham Street Delicatessen, Bungay
39A Earsham St, Bungay NR35 1AF
T: 01986 894754
W: www.earshamstreetdeli.co.uk

Chilli and Chives Deli-Café, Lavenham
16A High St, Lavenham CO10 9PT
T: 01787 249028
W: www.twitter.com/chilliandchives

Chilli and Chives Deli-Café, Hintlesham
George St, Hintlesham, nr Ipswich IP8 3NH
T: 01473 652020
W: www.twitter.com/chilliandchives

Seasonal Suffolk at Dedham Vale Vineyard *OTB*
Green Ln, Boxted, Essex CO4 5TS
T: 01206 273249
W: www.seasonalsuffolk.co.uk

FARM SHOPS

Agricultural diversification has become vital in recent years. Selling produce direct has saved many farmers and enabled communities to understand where their food comes from. Support your local farmer!

Hollow Trees Farm Shop, Semer
Semer, nr Hadleigh IP7 6HX
T: 01449 741247
W: www.hollowtrees.co.uk

Maple Farm Kelsale
Maple Farm, Kelsale,
nr Saxmundham IP17 2PL
T: 01728 652000
W: www.maplefarmkelsale.co.uk

Willow Tree Farm Shop, Glemsford
Lower Road, Glemsford, nr Long Melford C010 7QU
T: 01787 280341
W: www.willowtreefarmshop.co.uk

Friday Street Farm Shop
Friday Street, nr Snape IP17 1JX
T: 01728 602783
W: www.farmshopsuffolk.co.uk

Alder Carr Farm Shop, Creeting St. Mary
off St. Mary's Road, Creeting St. Mary,
nr Needham Market IP6 8LX
T: 01449 720820
W: www.aldercarrfarm.co.uk

Jimmy's Farm, Wherstead
Pannington Hall Lane, Wherstead,
nr Ipswich IP9 2AR
T: 01473 604206
W: www.jimmysfarm.com

Emmerdale Farm Shop, Darsham
Westleton Road, Darsham,
nr Yoxford IP17 3BP
T: 01728 668648
W: www.emmerdalefarmshop.co.uk

Wangford Farm Shop
Church Street, Wangford,
nr Southwold NR34 8AS
T: 01502 578246
W: www.wangfordfarmshop.co.uk

Railway Farm Shop, Benhall
Main Road, Benhall Green,
nr Saxmundham IP17 1HU
T: 01728 605793

Middleton Farm Shop
Reckford Farm, Middleton IP17 3NS
T: 01728 648936
W: www.middletonfarmshop.co.uk

Newbourne Farm Shop
Mill Road, Newbourne IP12 4NP
T: 01473 736407
W: www.newbournefarmshop.co.uk

Depden Farm Shop
Rookery Farm, Depden IP29 4BU
T: 01284 852525
W: www.depden.com

Wheldon's Fruit Farm Shop, Newton Leys
Joes Road, Newton Leys,
Sudbury CO10 0QE
T: 01787 374322
W: www.wheldonsfruitfarm.co.uk

Garnetts Gardens, Hacheston
The Street, Hacheston,
nr Woodbridge IP13 0DT
T: 01728 724589
W: www.garnettsgardens.co.uk

FOOD LOVERS' GUIDE

Your deliciously indispensable companion to enjoying Suffolk, edible and otherwise

Bloomsberries Café and Deli, Lakenheath
Christmas Hill Farm, Station Road,
Lakenheath IP27 9AB
T: 01842 861144
W: www.christmashill.co.uk

Mr Allard's Farm Shop and Butchery, Stowupland
Rendall Lane, Stowupland, nr Stowmarket IP14 4BD
T: 01449 615006
W: www.mrallardsfarmbutchery.com

The Chilli Co. Farm Shop and Café, Mendlesham
Norwich Road, Mendlesham IP14 5NQ
T: 01449 766677
W: www.chillicompany.com

La Hogue Farm Shop, Chippenham *OTB*
La Hogue Road, Chippenham,
nr Newmarket CB7 5PZ
T: 01638 751128
W: www.lahogue.co.uk

Hall Farm Shop & Café *OTB*
Hall Farm, Church Road, Stratford St Mary,
nr Colchester, Essex CO7 6LS
T: 01206 323176
W: www.hallfarmshop.com

BUTCHERS

Without doubt, well-bred, well-hung farmyard meats are what our foodie county is probably best known for. Befriend your local independent butcher.

Mills and Sons, Southwold
23 Market Place, Southwold IP18 6ED
T: 01502 722104
W: www. twitter.com/mills_and_sons

Rose House Butchery, Ipswich
5-7 St. Peter's Street, Ipswich IP1 1XF
T: 01473 213869
W: www.artisanbutcher.co.uk

John Hutton Butchers, Earl Soham
The Street, Earl Soham IP13 7SA
T: 01728 685259
W: www.johnhuttonbutcher.co.uk

Salter and King, Aldeburgh
107-109 High Street, Aldeburgh IP15 5AR
T: 01728 452758
W: www.salterandking.co.uk

E W Revett and Son Butcher, Wickham Market
81 High St, Wickham Market IP13 0RA
T: 01728 746263

Lavenham Butchers
1 High Street, Lavenham CO10 9PX
T: 01787 247226
W: www.lavenhambutchers.com

Eric Tennant Butchers, Newmarket
11 The Guineas Centre, Newmarket CB8 8EQ
T: 01638 661530
W: www.erictennantbutcher.co.uk

Ruse and Son Family Butchers, Long Melford
Hall Street, Long Melford CO10 9JF
T: 01787 378227
W: www.rusebutchers.co.uk

Elmswell Butchers
Station Road, Elmswell IP30 9HD
T: 01359 241181
W: www.christmashill.co.uk

Mr Allard's Farm Shop and Butchery, Stowupland
Rendall Lane, Stowupland,
nr Stowmarket IP14 4BD
T: 01449 615006
W: www.mrallardsfarmbutchery.com

Maisebrooke Farm Meats, Shipmeadow
Shipmeadow, nr Beccles NR34 8HJ
T: 01502 711018
W: www.maisebrookefarm.weebly.com

Neaves of Debenham
21 Cross Green, Debenham IP14 6RW
T: 01728 860240
W: www.neavesofdebenham.co.uk

Procter's Sausages, Ipswich
12, The Walk, Ipswich IP1 1EE
T: 01473 281191
W: www.procters-sausages.co.uk

Powters Butchers' and Newmarket Sausages
Wellington St, Newmarket CB8 0HT
T: 01638 662418
W: www.powters.co.uk

Clarke's of Bramfield
Low Road, Bramfield,
nr Halesworth, IP19 9JH
T: 01986 784244
W: www.kwclarke.co.uk

Creaseys of Peasenhall
The Causeway, Peasenhall, nr Yoxford IP17 2HU
T: 01728 660219

Emmerdale Farm Shop, Darsham
Westleton Road, Darsham, nr Yoxford IP17 3BP
T: 01728 668648
W: www.emmerdalefarmshop.co.uk

Rolfe's Butchers, Walsham le Willows
The Street, Walsham le Willows IP31 3AZ
T: 01359 259225
W: www.rolfesbutchers.co.uk

M & M Butchers
The Stores, Gipping Rd, Stowupland,
nr Stowmarket IP14 4AR
T: 01449 677720
W: www.stowupland.org/mm.html

BAKERS

Unsurprisingly in some of the UK's finest arable country, baking expertise is as strong as our farming skill. Check out the old familiar crusties to trendy slow-ferments.

Sparling and Faiers, Lavenham
11 Market Place, Lavenham CO10 9QZ
T: 01787 247297
W: www.discoverlavenham.co.uk

Tudor Bakehouse
Breads and cakes
11 Broad Street, Eye IP23 7AF
T: 01379 870974
W: www.tudorbakehouse.co.uk

COOKWARE

Good chefs, amateur or pro', need the best cooks' toys, both traditional tools and the latest kitchen wizardry.

Adnams Stores (Southwold and other places)
Victoria Street, Southwold IP18 6GB
T: 01502 725612
W: www.cellarandkitchen.adnams.co.uk

House and garden at Snape Maltings
Bridge Road, Snape IP17 1SR
T: 01728 688303
W: www.snapemaltings.co.uk

The Woodbridge Kitchen Company
7 Thoroughfare, Woodbridge IP12 1AA
T: 01394 382091
W: www.woodbridgekitchencompany.co.uk

The Steamer Trading Cook Shop, Bury St Edmunds
79 St John's St, Bury St Edmunds IP33 1SQ
T: 01284 705636
W: www.steamer.co.uk

The Galley Cookshop, Beccles
41-43 Smallgate, Beccles NR34 9AE
T: 01502 217075
W: www.thegalleycookshopbeccles.co.uk

FISHMONGERS AND SEAFOOD

With deep river estuaries and a long coastline, fresh fish continues to be a delicious treat, especially from our small in-shore day boats.

Pinneys of Orford Shellfish and Smoked Fish
The Old Warehouse, Quay St, Orford IP12 2NU
T: 01394 459183
W: www.pinneysoforford.co.uk

Maximus Fish at Friday Street Farm Shop
A1094 Friday Street, Saxmundham IP17 1JX
T: 01728 603854
W: www.maximusfish.co.uk

Simpers Deben *Shellfish and Wet Fish*
T: 01394 411025
W: www.simpersofsuffolk.co.uk

Dean Fryer's Fish Shed
opp. The White Lion, Market Cross Pl.,
Aldeburgh IP15 5BJ

Paul's Fishbox, Woodbridge
The Kiosk, Turban Centre, Hamblin Road,
Woodbridge IP12 1DE
T: 01394 384939
W: www.twitter.com/paulsfishbox

GARDEN CENTRES

There is nothing like growing your own, plucking the first crop as it shoots.

The Walled Garden, Benhall
Park Rd, Benhall, nr Saxmundham IP17 1JB
T: 01728 602510
W: www.thewalledgarden.co.uk

The Place for Plants, East Bergholt
Mill Road, East Bergholt CO7 6UP
T: 01206 299224
W: www.placeforplants.co.uk

Botanica
Chantry Farm, Campsea Ashe,
nr Woodbridge IP13 0PZ
T: 01728 747113
W: www.botanicaplantnursery.co.uk

Garnetts Gardens, Hacheston
The Street, Hacheston, nr Woodbridge IP13 0DT
T: 01728 724589
W: www.garnettsgardens.co.uk

Dogwood Garden Nursery, Risby
Risby Barn, South Street, Risby,
nr Bury St Edmunds IP28 6QU
T: 01284 811055
W: www.dogwood-gardencentre.co.uk

Harveys Garden Plants, Thurston
Harveys Garden Plants, Great Green, Thurston,
nr Bury St Edmunds IP31 3SJ
T: 01359 233363
W: www.harveysgardenplants.co.uk

Darsham Nurseries
Main Road, Darsham, nr Yoxford IP17 3PW
T: 01728 667022
W: www.darshamnurseries.co.uk

FUN STUFF

FOODIE EVENTS

Food festivals are a great advert for all that is good about our Suffolk food and drink scene.

Aldeburgh Food and Drink Festival
last weekend of September
Snape Maltings, Snape IP17 1SR
T: 01728 688303
W: www.aldeburghfoodanddrink.co.uk

Flavours At Henham Park Food Festival *early June*
Henham Park, nr Southwold NR34 8AN
T: 01394 275666
W: www.flavoursfoodfestivals.co.uk

Woodbridge Shuck Seafood Festival
first weekend of October
Woodbridge, Suffolk
T: 01394 383646
W: www.thewoodbridgeshuck.org.uk

Alde Valley Spring Festival *late April*
celebrating food, farming, landscape and the arts
White House Farm, off The Grove,
Great Glemham, nr Saxmundham IP17 1LS
T: 01728 663531
W: www.aldevalleyspringfestival.co.uk

The Big Onion Festival *early September*
The Courtyard, Elveden Estate, Elveden IP24 3TJ
T: 01842 898068
W: www.bigonionfestival.com

PettaFiesta *mid July*
Laffitts Hall, Framsden Rd, Pettaugh,
nr Stowmarket IP14 6DT
T: 07774 748476
W: www.pettafiesta.com

Bury St Edmunds Food & Drink Festival
last weekend of August
Buttermarket, Bury St Edmunds
T: 01284 766258
W: www.burystedmundsfestivals.com

Jimmy's Farm Sausage & Beer Festival
late July
Jimmy's Farm, Pannington Hall Lane,
Wherstead, nr Ipswich IP9 2AR
T: 01473 604206
W: www.jimmysfarm.com

FAMILY DAYS OUT

Not necessarily edible, just a few of our favourite leisure pursuits that help make our county so special for friends and family.

Iken Canoe
Iken Cliff, Iken IP12 2EN
T: 01728 688267
W: www.ikencanoe.co.uk

Southwold Maize Maze
Halesworth Road, Reydon, Southwold IP18 6SG
T: 01502 07801 065845
W: www.southwoldmaizemaze.co.uk

East Coast Mountain Bike Hire *(pre-booked)*
Snape County Store, Church Road, Snape IP17 1QE
T: 07706 479965 (text only)
W: www.eastcoastmountainbiking.co.uk

High Lodge Sporting and Leisure
Haw Wood, Hinton, Darsham IP17 3QT
T: 01986 784347
W: www.highlodge.co.uk

Deben Cruises *(pre-booked)*
Waldringfield Boatyard, The Quay,
Waldringfield IP12 4QZ
T: 01473 736 260
W: www.debencruises.co.uk

Easton Farm Park
off The Street, Easton IP13 0EQ
T: 01728 746475
W: www.eastonfarmpark.co.uk

Flatford Mill *(National Trust)*
Flatford, nr East Bergholt CO7 6UL
T: 01206 298260
W: www.nationaltrust.org.uk/flatford/

Go Ape! Forest Adventure
High Lodge Forest Centre,
Santon Downham nr Brandon IP27 0AF
T: 0333 331 5478
W: www.goape.co.uk/days-out/thetford

RSPB Minsmere Nature Reserve
off Dunwich Road, Westleton IP17 3BY
E: minsmere@rspb.org.uk
W: www.rspb.org.uk

Helmingham Hall Gardens and Tearooms
Helmingham IP14 6EF
T: 01473 890799
W: www.helmingham.com

Jimmy's Farm
Pannington Hall Lane, Wherstead,
nr Ipswich IP9 2AR
T: 01473 604206
W: www.jimmysfarm.com

Southwold Pier
North Parade, Southwold IP18 6BN
T: 01502 722105
W: www.southwoldpier.co.uk

River Cruise Restaurants *(pre-booked)*
PO Box 297, Woodbridge IP12 9ER
T: 01473 736260
W: www.lady-florence.co.uk

Snape Maltings
Bridge Road, Snape IP17 1SR
T: 01728 688303
W: www.snapemaltings.co.uk

Stonham Barns and Suffolk Owl Sanctuary
Pettaugh Road, Stonham Aspal IP14 6AT
T: 01449 711111
W: www.stonham-barns.co.uk

Museum of East Anglian Life
Iliffe Way, Stowmarket IP14 1DL
T: 01449 612229
W: www.eastanglianlife.org.uk

Sutton Hoo *(National Trust)*
Tranmer House, Sutton Hoo,
nr Woodbridge IP12 3DJ
T: 01394 389700
W: www.nationaltrust.org.uk/sutton-hoo

EXPERIENCES AND EDUCATION

Getting close to ingredients, produce and harvest is all part of being a true foodie.

Rose House Butchery
Meat preparation courses
5-7 St. Peter's Street, Ipswich IP1 1XF
T: 01473 213869
W: www.artisanbutcher.co.uk

Upstairs@The Market
Food demos and workshops
Lavenham Village Hall, Church St.,
Lavenham CO10 9QT
E: justine@suffolkmarketevents.co.uk
W: www.suffolkmarketevents.co.uk

Secret Meadows
Rural workshops and therapies
White House Farm Wildlife Site,
Hasketon IP13 6JP
T: 01394 382992
W: www.secretmeadows.co.uk

The Secret Garden
Breadmaking courses
21 Friars St, Sudbury, Suffolk CO10 2AA
T: 01787 372030
W: www.tsg.uk.net

Assington Mill
Rural skills and craft courses
Mill Farm, Bures Road, Assington,
nr Sudbury CO10 5LZ
T: 01787 229955
W: www.assingtonmill.com

Suffolk Dog Day *late July*
Helmingham Hall, Helmingham IP14 6EF
T: 01473 786918
W: www.suffolkdogday.com

Wild For Woods *OTB*
Foraging and bushcraft
2 Tamarind Mews, Eaton, Norwich, Norfolk NR4 6NR
T: 07896 678956
W: www.wildforwoods.co.uk

COOKERY SCHOOLS

If Suffolk Feast has inspired you to do more than pick up a good recipe book, why not join a masterchef and learn hands-on.

Emma Crowhurst at The Cookhouse
Suffolk Food Hall, Wherstead,
nr Ipswich IP9 2AB
T: 07967 212096
W: www. emmacrowhurst.co.uk

Food Hub Cookery School at Kenton Hall
Kenton, nr Stowmarket IP14 6JU
T: 01728 8620627
W: www.kentonhallestate.co.uk

The Cooking Experience *Cookery school*
The Chapel House, 9 High Street,
Hadleigh IP7 5AH
T: 01473 827568
W: www.cookingexperience.co.uk

Suffolk Food Hall *Cookery courses and demos*
Wherstead, nr Ipswich IP9 2AB
T: 01473 786610
W: www.suffolkfoodhall.co.uk

The Gamekeeper's Daughter *OTB*
Game cookery courses
Keepers Cottage, Straight Road,
East Bergholt CO7 6UT
W: www.gamekeepers-daughter.co.uk
T: 01206 298089

EVENT CATERING

Sometimes we just want to relax and leave it all to the professionals. Restaurant-quality food for big parties takes skill.

Bespoke Events *Weddings and parties*
NSSA Chefs Academy, Harrisons Lane,
Halesworth IP19 8PY
T: 01986 802000
W: www.bespoke.events

The Duck Truck *Duck wrap street food*
Woodbridge. Suffolk
T: 07919 160271
W: www.theducktruck.co.uk

The Fish Hut *Seafood street food*
c/o The Bell Inn, Ferry Road,
Walberswick IP18 6TN
T: 01502 723 109
W: www.bellinnwalberswick.co.uk

My Kitchen Your Place
Lavenham, Suffolk
T: 07814682903
W: www.twitter.com/miss_phoebe_c

Whip & Flip Creperie *Pancakes*
Woodbridge
T: 01394 385410

Peter Harrison
T: 07970 913312
W: www.peterharrisonchef.co.uk

The Gamekeeper's Daughter *OTB*
WIld food catering
Keepers Cottage, Straight Road,
East Bergholt CO7 6UT
T: 01206 298089
W: www.gamekeepers-daughter.co.uk

WEDDINGS AND PARTIES

Getting married is one of the most special days, for a truly individual wedding, seek out Suffolk's nuptial professionals.

Jimmy's Farm *Event venue*
Pannington Hall Lane, Wherstead,
nr Ipswich IP9 2AR
T: 01473 604206
W: www.jimmysfarm.com

Vanilla Pâtisserie *Wedding and celebration cakes*
T: 01728 768010
W: www.vanillapatisserie.co.uk

Earsham Hall *Wedding and party venue*
Earsham Hall, Earsham, Bungay NR35 2AN
T: 01986 893423
W: www.earshamhallevents.co.uk

Hengrave Hall
Hengrave, nr Bury St Edmunds IP28 6LZ
T: 01284 768024
W: www.hengravehall.com

Helmingham Hall
Helmingham, IP14 6EF
T: 01473 890799
W: www.helmingham.com

Somerleyton Hall
Somerleyton, nr Lowestoft NR32 5QQ
T: 01502 734907
W: www.somerleytonweddings.co.uk

Kenton Hall
Kenton, nr Stowmarket IP14 6JU
T: 01728 8620627
W: www.kentonhallestate.co.uk

Glemham Hall
Little Glemham, nr Wickham Mkt IP13 0BT
T: 01728 746704
W: www.glemhamhall.co.uk

Bespoke Events *Wedding catering*
NSSA Chefs Academy, Harrisons Lane,
Halesworth IP19 8PY
T: 01986 802000
W: www.bespoke.events

HEALTH SPAS

A proper detox can work wonders for over-indulgence and good living, or just take a break to indulge in a little 'me time'.

Weavers House Spa at The Swan Hotel
High Street, Lavenham CO10 9QA
T: 01787 247477
W: www.theswanatlavenham.co.uk

Clarice House
Bramford, nr Ipswich IP8 4AZ
T: 01473 463262
W: www.claricehouse.co.uk

Clarice House
Horringer Road, Bury St Edmunds IP29 5PH
T: 01284 705550
W: www.claricehouse.co.uk

The Spa at Ickworth Hotel
Ickworth Estate, Horringer,
nr Bury St Edmunds IP29 5QE
T: 01284 735350
W: www.ickworthhotel.co.uk

Aqua Sana at Center Parcs Elveden
Elveden IP27 0YZ
T: 03448 266205
W: www.aquasana.co.uk

The Spa at Bedford Lodge Hotel
Bury Road, Newmarket CB8 7BX
T: 01638 676130
W: www.bedfordlodgehotelspa.co.uk

FESTIVAL CULTURE

Feeding the soul is just as important as feasting. Get a fill enjoying eclectic, local and international music, arts, literature, comedy and all-round entertainment.

FolkEast Festival *late August*
Glemham Hall, Little Glemham,
nr Wickham Market IP13 0BT
W: www.folkeast.co.uk

Latitude Festival *mid July*
Henham Park, Henham, nr Southwold NR34 8AQ
T: 0207 009 3001
W: www.latitudefestival.com

Maui Waui Festival *early September*
Peakhill Farm, Theberton IP16 4TG
T: 01473 786918
W: www.mauiwauievents.co.uk

Places to stay

After a great meal, why not stay the night or find a bolthole for a few days...

The Brudenell Hotel
Aldeburgh
Cosmopolitan chic luxury on the seafront and destination dining overlooking the famous beach.
01728 452071
www.brudenellhotel.co.uk
TA Hotel Collection

Thorpeness Hotel, Golf and Country Club
Relaxing hotel-golf resort in a quirky, beautiful village with 18 hole James Braid course.
01728 452176
www.thorpeness.co.uk
TA Hotel Collection

The Crown At Woodbridge
Boutique inn-hotel in a riverside market town, with contemporary bar and restaurant.
01394 384242
www.thecrownatwoodbridge.co.uk
TA Hotel Collection

Tuddenham Mill
Former watermill, now luxury boutique hotel, restaurant and wedding venue, overlooking the millpond and meadows.
01638 713552
www.tuddenhammill.co.uk

The Swan At Lavenham
Romantic 15th century spa hotel, historic and luxurious, at the heart of this beautiful medieval village.
01787 247477
www.theswanatlavenham.co.uk
TA Hotel Collection

The Westleton Crown
12th century coaching inn-hotel, pub-bar and garden terrace restaurant with stylish modern accommodation.
01728 648777
www.westletoncrown.co.uk

The White Lion Hotel and Brasserie Bleue
Aldeburgh
Comfortable welcoming sea-facing hotel with a continental bar-brasserie.
01728 452720
www.whitelion.co.uk
TA Hotel Collection

The Ship At Dunwich
A short stroll to the beach and its maritime history, traditional pub-with-rooms close to RSPB Minsmere.
01728 648219
www.shipatdunwich.co.uk

The Crown Hotel
Southwold
Informal, relaxing small hotel, wine bar, pub and restaurant at the heart of the High Street and close to the seafront.
01502 722275
www.adnams.co.uk/hotels/the-crown

The Swan Hotel
Southwold
Elegant 17th-century hotel and restaurant on the Market Square, a short walk from the beach.
01502 722186
www.adnams.co.uk/hotels/the-swan

The Angel Hotel
Bury St Edmunds
Chic Georgian boutique hotel and smart restaurant, close to both the Cathedral and Abbey ruins.
01284 714000
www.theangel.co.uk

The Salthouse Harbour Hotel
Ipswich
Indulgent boutique hotel and stylish dining, located on the Ipswich marina waterfront.
01473 226789
www.salthouseharbour.co.uk

The Bell At Sax'
Saxmundham
Victorian coaching inn, revamped into a relaxed modern British restaurant with chic B&B rooms.
01728 602331
www.thebellatsax.co.uk

The Bell Inn
Walberswick
Charming 600 year-old pub-restaurant and rooms close to the harbour and beach, full of historic atmosphere.
01502 723109
www.bellinnwalberswick.co.uk

The Anchor At Walberswick
Stylish 1920s inn and restaurant-with-rooms with spacious garden chalets, a short walk from the sand dunes.
01502 722112
www.anchoratwalberswick.com

The Packhorse Inn
Moulton
Redefining what a pub should be, luxurious contemporary boutique inn-hotel and destination restaurant.
01638 751818
www.thepackhorseinn.com

The Great House
Lavenham
Cosseting small luxury hotel-restaurant with modern French cuisine and centuries of medieval and Georgian charm.
01787 247431
www.greathouse.co.uk

Recipe index

Starters, sides and light bites

Mains

Puddings

Sunset at Denham, West Suffolk: The day closes and a Suffolk night draws in for sheep on the Denham Estate

ACKNOWLEDGEMENTS

Thank you for picking up this book. You are probably a food-lover, you probably enjoy eating out and cooking at home, and like as not you take pleasure in nosing out the best local produce; you might be Suffolk born-and-bred or perhaps you are a visitor to the region. Whatever your reason for opening these pages, this book is for you and we hope you enjoy delving into it.

Inspiration for it has come from family and friends, the people in our lives who have shown us the way to find and enjoy good, local food. The motivation to make it happen has come from years working with the food heroes of Suffolk, those people who fight to put our farming, produce and cooking centre-stage. We have been given determination to see the book in print by the many restaurateurs and chefs, who believed in the project and helped make it happen. It's been an exhilarating process and one we have shared with some wonderfully creative thinkers and doers, many of whom have given their precious time voluntarily.

It has been a true team effort. Specific thanks must go to:

Simon for his sage publishing advice and encouragement, plus occasional devil's advocacy.

Kelly for stepping in with design and proofing support, a warm welcome to the team.

Liz for all her passion for local food ever since those *season* magazine days.

Beryl and Idris for their critical eye and red pen (as well as bringing Glyn up so well!).

Glenn and all the wonderful Leiston Press gang for express printing proofs in such good humour.

Emma (Freud) for so enthusiastically writing such an entertaining foreword; we took a pic of the butcher boys just for you!

Nick at The Bell in 'Wobbly Wick' for hosting our publishing get-togethers.

Jon Tyler at Wild For Woods, the quietest 'eco warrior', for getting us foraging.

We would also like to thank:

Lady Caroline Cranbrook, the directors and organisers of the Aldeburgh Food and Drink Festival for the extraordinary job they do every year in staging one of the UK's best food festivals. This book probably wouldn't have happened if it hadn't been for the way this festival has galvanised interest in food in Suffolk and beyond.

Two inimitable foodie pioneers: the indomitable yet gentle Jason Gathorne-Hardy, whose wonderfully emotive Alde Valley Spring Festival is a holistic wellspring, celebrating the edible and artistic; and similarly, the impassioned intent of David Grimwood, whose Imagined Suffolk Food Village at FolkEast is an inspirational feast for other cultural festivals to aspire to.

The Suffolk Show and the Suffolk Agricultural Association for showcasing all that is so good about this county's farming and food heritage.

Tim and Alex and The Suffolk Coast team for encouraging visitors to enjoy our beautiful landscape, culture and food.

Flavours magazine team for waving the flag for local food, and for their brilliant cookery theatres at the Flavours Festival and the Suffolk Show.

My personal thanks go to Stephen and Rebecca of Bespoke Events for starting the whole idea with that sample chapter 14 years ago in those Earsham Street Café days; and Jonny at The Bell At Sax' for supporting the project so enthusiastically. I dedicate this book to Ambrin, my daughter, who has inherited my love of good Suffolk food; and to the late great Chris Aldred, Suffolk through and through, RIP my friend. *Glyn*

My family – Edwin, Polly, William and Rose – are probably looking forward to not hearing the phrase 'when the book is done' any more. Thank you for your patience and support. Thank you also to our two spaniels on long walks with whom I drafted many an opening paragraph in my mind. They listened with mild interest and didn't mind how many miles it took to get a sentence right. *Tessa*

You all have our huge gratitude. Thank you.